DEVELOPMENT PROSPECTS IN CUBA: AN AGENDA IN THE MAKING

Development Prospects in Cuba: An Agenda in the Making

Edited by
Pedro Monreal

Institute of Latin American Studies
31 Tavistock Square, London WC1H 9HA
http://www.sas.ac.uk/ilas/publicat.htm

This book has been produced with the financial assistance of the European Community. The views expressed herein are those of the authors and can therefore in no way be taken to reflect the official opinion of the European Community.

Institute of Latin American Studies
School of Advanced Study
University of London

British Library Cataloguing-in-Publication Data
A catalogue record for this book is available
from the British Library

ISBN   1 900039 48 6

CONTENTS

ABOUT THE CONTRIBUTORS

Claes Brundenius is Director of Research at the Centre for Development Research (CDR), Copenhagen, Denmark.

Julio Carranza is Associate Professor at the University of Havana, Cuba.

David Dapice is Professor in the Department of Economics, Tufts University and Chief Economist, Vietnam Program, Kennedy School of Government, Harvard, University.

Mauricio de Miranda is Chief of the Economics Department at Pontificia Universidad Javeriana, Cali, Colombia.

Julio Díaz Vázquez is Professor of International Economics at the Centro de Investigaciones de Economía Internacional (CIEI), University of Havana, Cuba.

Anicia García is Senior Researcher at Centro de Estudios de Economía Cubana (CEEC), University of Havana, Cuba.

Francisco León is Senior Researcher at the United Nations Economic Commission for Latin America and the Caribbean (ECLAC), Santiago de Chile.

Hiram Marquetti is Senior Researcher at Centro de Estudios de Economía Cubana (CEEC), University of Havana, Cuba.

Pedro Monreal is Senior Researcher at Centro de Investigaciones de Economía Internacional (CIEI), University of Havana, Cuba.

Lázaro Peña is Senior Researcher at Centro de Investigaciones de Economía Internacional (CIEI), University of Havana, Cuba.

Omar Everleny Pérez is Senior Researcher at Centro de Estudios de Economía Cubana (CEEC), University of Havana, Cuba.

ACKNOWLEDGEMENTS

A collective effort such as this one entails intellectual and organisational contributions from many different sources. In Cuba, Lázaro Peña Castellanos, Julio A. Díaz Vázquez, Alejandro Durán, Oneida Alvarez, Juan Triana, Omar Everleny Pérez, Hiram Marquetti and Anicia García, distinguished economists from the University of Havana; Julio Carranza, now at UNESCO; Luis Gutiérrez Urdaneta; Alejandro Figueras, at the Ministry of Tourism; Rafael Hernández, Director of *Temas* magazine; Aurelio Alonso, from Centro de Investigaciones Psicológicas y Sociológicas (CIPS); Adriano García, from Instituto Nacional de Investigaciones Económicas (INIE), and two sociologists, Mayra Espina, at CIPS in Havana, and Juan Valdés Paz, at Unión Nacional de Artistas y Escritores de Cuba (UNEAC), have shared ideas with us during many extended conversations and controversies, and have commented on previous versions of essays presented in this volume.

In addition, a March 2000 seminar held at the Social Science Research Council and a January 2001 follow-up meeting at the Institute of Latin American Studies at the University of London provided occasions to discuss initial versions of several of the chapters. We benefited greatly from suggestions at those meetings from Victor Bulmer-Thomas, James Dunkerley, Eric Hershberg, Rick Doner, Doug Guthrie, George Lambie, Emily Morris, Maxine Molyneux, Dwight Perkins, Antonio Romero, Barbara Stallings, David Stark and Thomas Vallely. Ishle Park and Mara Goldwyn provided capable administrative support at those meetings.

Translations and editing of English versions of the papers was done efficiently and skilfully by Jo-Marie Burt, Marcial Godoy, Eric Hershberg, Scott Martin and Judy Rein. Financial assistance for these and other aspects of the project was provided by the Christopher Reynolds Foundation, whose Executive Director, Andrea Panaritis, has been crucial to our efforts.

We are most grateful to Eric Hershberg for his decisive role in the edition and publication of this volume.

Pedro Monreal

LIST OF TABLES

LIST OF FIGURES

Racing Once Again to Catch up:
Debating Prospects for Development in Cuba

Pedro Monreal

The last decade of the twentieth century witnessed some of the most significant changes in the economic history of Cuba. Perhaps these shifts were not as extraordinary as those that took place at the conclusion of the eighteenth and in the early nineteenth centuries, when the country transformed itself into a sugar-based economy, but they undoubtedly were comparable to events of other pivotal moments, such as the economic take-off of the early twentieth century or the socialist transformations of the 1960s.

In all of these great moments of change one of the principal dimensions of transformation has concerned the international insertion of the Cuban economy. It could not be otherwise, given the open nature of the island's economy. In each of those instances, as well, the potential role of a leading sector has stood out at the forefront of debates about economic change. Similarly, each of these moments has witnessed a powerful and cohesive political will to promote change as part of an effort to 'modernise' Cuban society.

In the great economic transformations that swept the island from the eighteenth century to the middle of the twentieth century, the implications of each of these dimensions was fairly straightforward: international insertion meant an orientation primarily toward a single large market. The sugar industry was the leader, and the modernising effort invariably took place within a reasonably well-defined paradigm. Yet the 1990s brought unprecedented departures from the typical pattern of great economic transformations in Cuba. Three features of the situation stand out as especially unusual. First, international insertion was no longer directed toward a single large market. Secondly, for the first time since at least the eighteenth century, sugar was not the leading sector of transformation. And thirdly, leaving aside the core objective of maintaining a domestic model of socialist organisation, there was no consensus vision, articulated in an explicit strategy of development, concerning what modernisation of the country actually entailed or how to achieve it in the era of globalisation.

The causes of the change in direction of the first two of these dimensions are easy enough to explain, but contemporary uncertainty about what new paradigm of modernisation might generate consensus in Cuba is a far more complex phenomenon to decipher. One can identify at least three significant background factors as explanations. First, this conceptual uncertainty is not unique to the Cubans, but rather reflects a general problem of social theory in our times. Secondly, though it obviously refers to the objective of development, the very notion of modernisation is ambiguous and, for the most part, conceptually empty, at least as it is commonly used in Cuba. Finally, it is essential to understand that the organised political will in the country was concentrated throughout the 1990s on the objective of survival, a relatively narrow agenda, though a crucial one for the country's future, and this left scant room for reflection concerning transformations taking place along longer time horizons.

Nonetheless, the 1990s was not a period of homogeneous change. During the first half of the decade there prevailed a sort of 'resistance thinking' (*pensamiento de resistencia*) focused on obtaining the adjustments necessary to enable the country to overcome the profound economic crisis that had befallen it. In turn, the second half of the decade was characterised by a logic of 'doing things better' (*pensamiento de perfeccionamiento*) which became more prevalent as actors gained confidence about the durability of the economic recovery process that began in 1995. The latter part of the decade did not see an end to the logic of resistance, but instead superimposed upon it a series of only nascent ideas that, at a minimum, served to reintroduce the question of development into academic and policy debates.

This volume is situated precisely in that context of incipient debate, and has as its fundamental objective the provision of what may well be the first academic text written specifically to assess the development perspectives of Cuba in the new conditions that prevail at the beginning of the twenty-first century. Two clarifications seem in order, however. First, the book does not purport to offer a comprehensive or conclusive account of a topic as broad as Cuba's development. All that can be generated on such a vast question is a contribution to what needs to be an ongoing debate, rather than a definitive treatise on the topic. Thus, the book does not attempt to engage the totality of the problem of development in Cuba, nor does it present a comprehensive strategy for achieving this objective. Rather, it seeks to explore a series of issues that seem to occupy a relevant place in what could best be termed an agenda in the making. Secondly, though to our knowledge there exists no other published academic text that analyses the contemporary Cuban economy from the specific perspective of development studies, we do not mean to imply that there is no other published work of significance on the issue of development in Cuba. Our contention is simply that the topic of development has been taken on as a complement to other themes that represent the analytic core of most studies in the recent literature on Cuban economic affairs.

This book is the result of an intellectual effort by 11 academics who, with one exception, have in recent years dedicated themselves to the study of the development prospects of the Cuban economy. Seven of these authors are professors and researchers at the University of Havana, while three of them are scholars who study the Cuban economy from institutional homes in Latin America or Europe. We are also fortunate to include in this collaborative endeavour a contribution by a North American specialist on development who has analysed the experience of Vietnam, a country that strikes us as a particularly relevant analytic referent for examining the contemporary development challenges of Cuba.

To the extent that the authors have tried to concentrate attention on a single 'big question' concerning the economic transformations sweeping the island, it can be summarised fundamentally in the following terms: 'After recovery, then what?' Stated differently, though in each of the chapters the authors deal with questions of immediate relevance to the Cuban economy and its recent past, emphasis is placed on the implications for long-term prospects for development in the country. This emphasis reflects our conviction that solutions to the challenge of development will require longer time frames of analysis and distinct foci than those which have to this point served as the temporal and conceptual references for most recent studies of the island's economy.

The theme of Cuba's development prospects is examined throughout the ten essays of the book, which are organised in three sections to facilitate reading of the text. The first, entitled 'Components of a New Paradigm', consists of two essays that seek to establish the point of departure and lay out long-term objectives for change. The contribution of Julio Carranza presents a general vision of the nature and extent of transformations achieved by the Cuban economy during the 1990s, while that of Pedro Monreal argues for the need to replace the existing model of import substitution with a new model of development, in which re-industrialisation would be pursued through a substitution of exports. Such a reorientation of the economy would need to occur through insertion into global production chains in which transnational capital occupies a central role, and the role of foreign direct investment is addressed in the chapter by Omar Everleny Pérez, which opens the second section of the volume.

Focusing on 'Elements of Potential Development Strategies in Cuba', the five chapters that constitute the second section share a crucial underlying assumption of the book: however great the departure from the past, economic reconstruction in Cuba should not be thought of as an exercise beginning with some sort of tabula rasa. Following Pérez's analysis of foreign investment and the role that it could play in the development process, the study by Hiram Marquetti and Anicia García provides a critical assessment of the model of industrial growth and the long term perspectives for change that it implies. The following chapter is a contribution by Lázaro Peña Castellanos on the competitiveness of the sugar sector which, though it might appear merely a sectoral study, actually serves to examine a series of general issues concerning the contemporary requirements of the investment process in Cuba, and which sets forth for debate the complex issue of international competitiveness and decision-making relative to the allocation of resources in the national economy.

The second section of the book concludes with two chapters that attempt to analyse issues that can be considered important assets on which Cuba could rely to promote development. In the first instance, Mauricio de Miranda presents a work addressing the relevance of internal markets for the development process. In turn, Claes Brundenius examines the connection that could exist in the Cuban case between industrial upgrading and human capital formation. Undoubtedly, this is an area in which noteworthy successes distinguish Cuba from many other developing countries, although a twofold note of caution is introduced in the sense that, first, having access to a pool of highly qualified labour does not necessarily mean that the labour force always has the relevant skills to cope with rapidly changing requirements in knowledge intensive industries, and second that highly skilled workers who have been 'inactive' for some years — as has been the case in Cuba during the 1990s — might find it difficult to find their 'niches' in a new, but rapidly changing, knowledge-based economy.

The third section of the volume 'International Context and Comparative Perspectives' comprises three chapters, one of which addresses the global context in which Cuban development must take place, and two of which consider potentially useful comparative perspectives. The first piece, written by Francisco León, reviews the international context in which recent economic transformations of Cuba have taken place and which serve as a general point of reference for the development process in the country. This chapter examines first the situation of Cuba vis à vis its immediate geographic environment, particularly in the context of Caribbean integration and relations with the United States, and then examines the real and potential contribution of the European Union (EU) to overcoming the present and future challenges facing the Cuban economy. The chapter concludes by outlining a possible agenda for co-operation between the EU and Cuba for the period between 2001 and 2005.

The first of the comparative chapters, written by Julio Díaz Vázquez, contrasts the experience of economic reforms in China and Vietnam with the changes introduced in Cuba during the 1990s, taking into account developments with regard to the market as an organising axis for possible analytic experiences that could be derived from comparison of these three cases. The second chapter, prepared by David Dapice, is the sole contribution to the book that does not focus explicitly on the problems of Cuba. Rather, it analyses transformations experienced by Vietnam since the 1980s, from the perspective of the challenges that remain to be overcome in that country if it is to achieve development.

These last two chapters seem especially relevant in that they may contribute analytic elements that could be particularly useful for evaluating possibilities of development in a country that, like Cuba, has been characterised for the past 40 years by the dominance of a socialist paradigm as a referent for the design of development strategies. At a moment when analysis of the collapse of socialism in Europe remains a matter of debates that are as passionate as they are inconclusive, the conceptualisation of a socialist path to development in a country such as Cuba — in the so-called post-Soviet era — requires attention to the experiences of economic transformation in a series of Asian countries. After all, to our knowledge there exist today only five countries that continue to define themselves as socialist — China, Vietnam, Cuba, Laos and the Popular Democratic Republic of Korea — and four of them are located in Asia. Thus, more than 99 per cent of human beings who live today in societies that consider themselves to be socialist reside on the continent of Asia. It is thus difficult to make valuable judgements concerning the future of socialism in our times, and regarding the prospects for development that it offers, in the absence an assessment of what has occurred in those countries of Asia.

Even so, researchers seeking to derive lessons from those Asian societies that could be relevant and useful for socialist development in Cuba commonly confront a series of reproaches from their colleagues, purporting to highlight the practical irrelevance of comparative study between Cuba and those countries. The most frequently cited reservations can be divided into two separate categories. The first cite historical and cultural factors, such as differences in the historical trajectories of socialism, the point of departure for contemporary reforms, distinct value systems and institutional disparities, while the second insist on the inconvenience for Cuba of seeking lessons from dramatically different socioeconomic settings. Here the emphasis is on the overwhelmingly rural and low income nature of the relevant Asian economies, as well as differences in demographic factors, resource availability, market scale and so on.

While all of these points are noteworthy and significant, they by no means detract from the utility of comparative study of socialist experiences in Asia and Cuba. On the contrary, introduction of a comparative perspective can be enormously useful to clarifying problems of development in Cuba. This is particularly the case given the fact that, as noted above, this book is intended not as the final statement on Cuba's development prospects but rather as a contribution to an ongoing set of debates about the challenges facing the country and ways to overcome them.

The island's development in a context of increasingly globalised international economy will require new conceptualisations of the problems and opportunities at hand. Contemporary development is, among other things, an intellectual adventure, and one that demands deep and unconstrained debate. In this regard, we hope that the volume presented here will serve to stimulate a much-needed collective reflection on a theme of enormous importance for the future of the country. Nothing less will do, for as we are reminded by the pointed observation offered recently by a well-known Latin American politician, 'the future is no longer what it used to be'.

PART I
COMPONENTS OF A NEW PARADIGM

CHAPTER 1

Export Substitution Reindustrialisation in Cuba: Development Strategies Revisited

Pedro Monreal

Introduction

The 1990s was a decade of multiple economic transitions in Cuba. Some of these changes have been widely reported and studied, such as the transformation of a traditional centrally planned economy into a more decentralised planning system with greater market orientation, or the shift towards external funding sources in which assistance has become a less important component and has ceded space to foreign direct investment, commercial credit and family remittances.

Probably the most noted transformation of the 1990s was the change in the country's export profile. From the analytical perspective of the supply of Cuban products to the international market, the past decade has been the most revolutionary period since sugar became the principal export product at the end of the eighteenth century. That radical change in the country's economic structure had no historical parallel in the following two centuries until the mid-1990s, when the precipitous expansion of international tourism succeeded in displacing sugar as the primary source of foreign currency income.

This process, although significant, has given rise to a number of incorrect interpretations, such as those that ascribe an improved quality to the island's new export structure due to the simple fact that services exports now eclipse commodities. Aside from the general discussion required to clarify that the export of services does not necessarily lead to a better quality of international insertion and development, this chapter proposes to explore, first, to what extent — from the perspective of international development — the change in Cuba's export profile in the 1990s has been a substantial change, and secondly, to present some comments on a possible alternative transformation of the country's export profile, which is identified as export substitution.

The central hypothesis of this chapter can be summed up in the following manner: Cuba's pattern of development in the 1990s maintained significant continuity with the pattern of development of the immediately preceding period (since the mid-1970s) in that it was essentially a process of industrialisation by means of import substitution that was inextricably associated with exports anchored in activities based on the intensive use of natural resources.

A second, complementary hypothesis of the chapter is that this pattern of development and international insertion is not compatible with the country's economic and social development goals over the long term, and that Cuban industrial upgrading necessitates a significant transformation in the paths towards national development, one of the possible courses being the adoption of a reindustrialisation strategy through export substitution.[1]

In recognition of the polemical character of both these hypotheses, an additional clarification will be introduced at the outset. The alternative that is identified as export substitution is not equivalent to the more traditional concept of diversification of exports, the perennial component of all development projects conceived in Cuba in the second half of the twentieth century, and an aspiration of many Cuban thinkers and policy-makers. One of the notions that is introduced in this chapter is precisely that no single type of export diversification leads to development. Diversification would have to be directed toward very specific trajectories, and would be a subordinate component within a more general development strategy that must adequately respond to the challenges facing a small and open economy in the current era of economic globalisation.

The Pattern of Development in Cuba during the 1990s: Adjusting Continuity

From the beginning of the 1990s a change began to occur — very significant in some specific aspects — in the pattern of development that Cuba had been following since the middle of the 1970s. [2] Nevertheless, the transformations of the 1990s did not represent a radical transfiguration of the previous pattern of development, which fundamentally consisted of a structural transformation process rooted in the configuration of an industrial base (which expanded until 1989 and adapted to international conditions during the 1990s). This industrial base was principally oriented toward import substitution, even as complementary industrial capacities were developed for the export of primary and semi-processed goods.

The most visible, but not the only, causes of the change in the pattern of development of the 1990s arose fundamentally from external factors — par-

---

1   In the Spanish original the expression 'avance económico' was used to signify industrial upgrading.

2   In conceptual terms there is an important difference between development strategy and pattern of development, in the sense that the strategy always refers to an ideal representation at the level of policy planners, while the pattern of development consists of a given sequence of events and economic and social results. The distinction is relevant to the extent that a large part of the controversy about strategies turns on what governments are able to do, so that the study of the past (patterns of development) reveals what governments were or were not capable of doing and therefore make possible that this knowledge be assumed as the starting point for the design of new strategies (Dore, 1990).

ticularly the disappearance of the 'socialist bloc' and the increase in hostility of the US government towards Cuba. Apart from its peculiarities, what occurred in Cuba is reflected in well-defined historical models in which the changes in external conditions are a central factor in the transformations in the patterns of development.[3]

In 1975 'the industrialisation of the country' was defined as the central axis of Cuba's development strategy.[4] Fifteen years later the proposals were not completed exactly as initially designed, but the weight of industry within the total economy increased in relative terms, industrial production was diversified and its supportive infrastructure expanded, the commercial network was denser and a management and administrative capacity was created, and the expansion of a skilled industrial labour force was facilitated. The deficiencies and limitations of the process have been extensively discussed by many authors,[5] but what we wish to emphasise here is not so much the situation at the beginning of the 1990s in terms of the culmination of that development strategy, but as a point of departure for possible alternatives that might have existed then and that are currently discernible.

The consequences of the changes in Cuba's pattern of development during the 1990s have been very visible in the composition of the balance of payments and other areas of the economy, for example, the structure of incentives. But, in reality, and despite all the changes that took place, the old agro-industrial structure built in an effort to industrialise through import substitution still predominates in terms of total production and employment, although it is evident that a good part of this traditional structure is not viable under current conditions, nor is it compatible — in its current forms — with Cuba's future development needs.

Through different development strategies since 1959, Cuba has tried to overcome the structural obstacles confronting the economic and social development of a small country with an open economy that is traditionally dependent on the export of raw materials, lacks an abundance of certain essential resources, such as energy, and has an incomplete economic structure.[6] In economic conditions such as those described above, the limited domestic market creates difficulties for an import substitution strategy, while the truncated economic structure requires that exports be the critical variable in industrialisation. Only through exports can the country obtain the resources necessary for investment in industrialisation.

3   Ellison and Gereffi (1990).
4   The Programmatic Platform approved by the First Congress of the Cuban Communist Party, enacted in December 1975, stated that 'the central task for the development and growth of the national economy in the next five years, 1976–80, will be the industrialisation of the country', Cuban Communist Party (1976).
5   ECLAC (2000).
6   Rodríguez (1990).

The heavy weight of the export sector reflects, at root, a narrow economic base and poor diversification of production. Countries such as these historically have developed highly specialised productive structures for the export of basic or semi-processed products that have almost no domestic market. Thus they are countries that are also characterised by a high dependence on imports.

For some time it was assumed in Cuba, and other countries, that the goal of development consisted of advancing toward more diversified and internally integrated economic structures that would produce the double effect of reducing the relative weight of the export sector and imports, at the same time that the export structure became less specialised in raw materials and diversified to include manufactured goods of greater technological complexity.

Nonetheless, the specific case of Cuba is evidently in no way a 'typical' case of a small and poor country that has tried to industrialise fundamentally through an export effort. During the greater part of the period beginning in the 1960s, but especially in the period from the mid-1970s to the end of the 1980s, exports (when valued at international market prices) were not exactly the most important factor in the industrialisation of the country. The existence of a favourable external environment derived from the island's relations with the countries of the old Council of Mutual Economic Assistance (Comecon) allowed Cuba to explore different financing mechanisms to carry out import substitution industrialisation.

Although exports would ultimately have to constitute Cuba's principal source of financing and industrialisation, the maintenance and expansion of the island's cooperation with Comecon made possible indefinite postponement of export diversification and improvement. That alternative to increasing the value added of Cuban exports was abruptly interrupted in the 1990s, at which point it became apparent that Cuba had delayed but not avoided the need to radically transform its export profile.

In this sense, the end of the 'Soviet era' imposed on the Cuba of the 1990s the necessity of achieving a different international insertion in which exports had to acquire an exceptional relevance. Viewed retrospectively, the Cuban economy followed a trajectory over the decade of international reinsertion on the base of three pillars: the intensive use of natural resources to establish its export base (of goods and services), access to external rents (family remittances), and moderate access to foreign credits and investment capital.

This mode of international insertion correlated to a pattern of development in the 1990s that is somewhat different from that which immediately preceded it (1976–89). It differed not in its essential character but in the very mode of insertion, now in the global capitalist market on competitive terms as opposed to the previous guaranteed access and on the terms of the Comecon. Thus, beginning in the 1990s, the country's specific means of connection with the international economy have been different (tourism partial-ly replacing sugar, foreign investment and family remittances attempting to substitute for the compensatory transfers previously originating from Comecon). Yet, the pattern of development of the 1990s maintains signifi-cant continuity with the previous pattern of development in that it has con-tinued to be in essence an import substitution industrialisation process.

It should be clear that from the second half of the 1970s until the end of the 1980s, the explicit emphasis of the development strategy was indus-trialisation — specifically import substitution.[7] The increase in exportable resources was also a stated objective of industrialisation, but as events showed, was secondary to import substitution.

Industrial development for import substitution was the key, but not the sole, element of the pattern of development during that period. Another important component was the increase in exports of raw materials or prod-ucts with a low level of processing (sugar, minerals, fish products, tobacco and citrus). However, this component was subordinated to import substitu-tion industrialisation in that those exports were treated as sources for financ-ing industrial investment and as a basis (via forward linkages) for new indus-trial products for future development in order to substitute for imports (for example, sugar-cane derivatives or metal products).

In addition to import substitution and promotion of exports of raw materials or minimally processed goods, there was a third component to that development model, the promotion of industrial exports, which played a very secondary role and had insubstantial results. In the 1976–80 period 115 new export lines were introduced, but this represented a practically insignificant percentage of the total value of the country's exports.[8]

The pattern of development that went into crisis at the beginning of the 1990s was in essence a model of import substitution industrialisation.[9] It is precisely this central component of the model which becomes unfeasible given the impossibility of continuing to rely on external mechanisms of compensation that made its expansion and even its very operation practi-cable. The second component of the model, raw material exports, was not capable of serving as a source of accumulation for industrialisation in the absence of the preferential prices formerly paid by the socialist countries. In

7   'The principal task of industrialisation is to create the domestic base necessary for the sys-tematic development of productive forces, supply of equipment and materials to industry, agriculture and stockbreeding, increase exportable resources, substitute imports, and produce diverse articles for broad consumption', Cuban Communist Party (1976), p. 77.

8   Pérez (1982).

9   Official Cuban statistics recorded considerable participation of the industrial sector in the national product (Gross National Product) which reached 46 per cent in 1988. The majority of the 22 branches classified as part of the industrial sector were oriented toward production for the domestic market. See CEE (1989).

fact, this component also went into crisis as it could no longer assure its own reproduction, which was exacerbated by the commercial and financial dislocations resulting from the breakdown of 'real existing socialism' in Europe. The third component (industrial exports) was simply marginal to the essential functioning of the pattern of development. It also entered into a profound crisis when it was no longer able to obtain the required external resources.

What is truly remarkable in a retrospective analysis of the 1990s is that the pattern of development that emerged from the crisis represented a basic continuity, rather than a radical transformation of the previous pattern. In other words, in the 1990s import substitution industrialisation was not relinquished as the central component of a long-term vision of the country's development. What did change was the mechanism for connection with the international environment in which that industrialisation had to be conducted in the future. The means, time periods and scale for industrialisation were also reformed.

In the middle of the crisis and the severe restrictions on the balance of payments in the 1990s, import substitution industrialisation could not be carried out as new industrial investment. Maintaining an import substitution industrialisation model meant preserving as much as possible the previously created industrial structure, while introducing necessary adaptations and partially modernising in anticipation of a return to more propitious conditions that would make it possible to reinitiate new investments for this type of industry. The greater priority in terms of investments in some export sectors (tourism, nickel and pharmaceuticals) in the 1990s was not conceived as a substantial change away from import substitution industrialisation; rather, it was understood as the creation of better conditions to continue it in the future.

This implies relatively important adjustments in the other two components of the development model. Exports had to be increased and apparently it was understood that this could only be achieved by two means: first, attempting to incorporate new lines of exports based on intensive use of natural resources; and second, attempting to make a 'leap forward' in one or a few industrial exports, especially in some high technology activities like pharmaceutical products based on biotechnology and medical equipment.

The precipitous development of tourism in the 1990s (at annual rates of close to 20 per cent) indicated that tourism was added in a spectacular manner to the exports profile of the country. Although frequently referred to in such grandiloquent terms as the 'smokestack free industry' or the basis of a purported 'new service economy', tourism is to a large extent based on the intensive utilisation of natural resources.[10]

10   The notable expansion of tourism in Cuba during the 1990s has been accompanied by conjectures concerning supposed advantages afforded by the advance toward a 'tertiarised'

This does not mean that tourism is a sector that should not be developed, quite the contrary. Cuba has undeniable competitive advantages in this sector. Moreover, tourism is currently the only sector of the Cuban economy with the capacity to act as a 'leading sector' for the country's development. The point is only that tourism's take-off in the 1990s has represented an expansion of exports based on the use of natural resources rather than the appearance of a new ingredient in the development model that could be dependent on the country's other assets, such as skilled labour, science or technology. This must also be considered because, in the long run, it is very important for the country's economic structure to be able to move 'up' through technological and organisational improvements, a process in which the sectoral composition of the economy is not a 'neutral' factor.

On the other hand, the venture into industrial exports in the course of the decade was fundamentally in the biotechnology-based pharmaceutical sector, and to a lesser extent in medical equipment. Clearly, industrial exports were not encouraged in a broad spectrum of activities, but in a very selective manner. Nonetheless, the expectations raised in this area in the early 1990s were later considerably reduced.

The industrial structure created before the crisis of the 1990s was operating at very low levels of capacity in the first years of the decade, and therefore experienced a decapitalisation process that was particularly acute in some sectors.[11] The industrial structure was not created to compete internationally (so foreign markets were not a potential outlet for supply) and was highly dependent on imports, which impeded production for the domestic market due to the severe restrictions on the balance of payments.[12]

Nonetheless, part of that industrial structure was favoured by the significant expansion in the 1990s of a process called 'exports within borders' which involved domestic markets operating on the basis of foreign exchange, that is, where demand is not expressed in domestic currency. This demand originated from two sources: the growing number of national, foreign and mixed businesses that operated in foreign currency, mostly in tourism and other export activities, as well as demand from the part of the population that possessed foreign currency, largely from family remittances and also from, in some cases, 'skimming' from tourist activity, and

---

economy. Thus far, these are speculative arguments which have not been established with convincing conceptualisation and which also have not been able adequately to explain what to do with the existing industrial structure, nor how the deindustrialisation of the country will contribute to its development.

11   Cuba's economy contracted from 1990 to 1993, when the Gross National Product fell approximately 35 per cent. In 1994 there was practically zero growth, but at least this indicated the end of the recession. The economy began a relative recovery in 1995.

12   Marquetti (1999).

on occasion the establishment of mechanisms for foreign currency incentives for part of the work force.[13]

The fact that they have been called 'exports within borders' reveals the importance of the availability of foreign currency for the domestic operation of an economy such as Cuba's. The lack of foreign exchange, not the insolvency of other productive assets, is generally the strangulation point of production in the Cuban economy. 'Exports within borders' have allowed some industries originally designed for import substitution to enjoy parity with export sectors in terms of the opportunity for direct access to a resource as critical as foreign currency. Yet, the term 'exports within borders' should not be understood as export promotion since in reality it has been a mechanism for facilitating import substitution in the new context. Hypothetically, domestic currency markets could serve as a 'springboard' for the generation of real exports, but this possibility has hardly materialised in the recent experience of Cuban industry.

The domestic demand for foreign currency has created new productive links and has reconfigured some that already existed. 'Exports within borders' have favoured the creation of commercial networks, in some cases very dense ones, that have facilitated the (still insufficient) reactivation of part of the country's import substitution.[14]

Two lessons can be drawn from the 'exports within borders' experience of the 1990s. First, industries that are still relatively inefficient have managed to reactivate and even partially modernise, especially since they sell in markets that do not require the efficiency levels demanded by participation in the global market.[15] Under these conditions, it is not likely that strong export incentives will develop, and therefore the realisation of the potential in the 'springboard' mechanism for exports faces great difficulties. The second lesson is that 'exports within borders' have served as an important mechanism for social and political stability in the 1990s by providing higher levels of employment, due to a minor relative efficiency, over that made possible by an alternative model predominated by real exports.

In sum, the change in the Cuban pattern of development in the 1990s was concentrated in the mechanisms of international insertion and not in its essential component; in other words, in its core attribute as an import substitution industrialisation process. In the judgement of this author, the continuation of the current development model is an obstacle for the process of industrial upgrading of the country.

---

13   Beginning in 1993, dual monetary circulation was established in Cuba, with the consequent creation of a dual market economy. Some markets operate in the national currency (Cuban peso) and others operate in foreign currencies (mostly the US dollar).

14   Marquetti (1999).

15   It is true that as a rule, businesses that generate 'exports within borders' have been restructured and are currently less inefficient than before, but even so they are generally less efficient than would be required if they had to operate under conditions of international competition.

The Export Profile of the 1990s: Reliance on Resource-Based Exports

To evaluate the importance of natural resources in Cuban exports during the 1990s and assess perspectives on possible changes in the country's export profile, it is useful to adopt an export classification that is different from the typologies generally used for Cuba's export sector.

Probably the most common classification that has been used is separating Cuban exports into 'traditional' and 'non-traditional', although recently other more complex classifications have been employed that attempt to incorporate key dimensions of international competition like market participation and sector contribution, establishing four groups of exports, 'rising stars', 'fading stars', 'lost opportunities', and 'retrogressions'.[16]

Without debating the particular merits of these export classification systems, the concern here is to adopt an alternative typology that is especially useful in analysing the economic performance and possible trajectories of development of countries which, like Cuba, are highly dependent on exports based on the intensive utilisation of natural resources.

To this end it is useful first to consider some previous studies, particularly on Asian cases (Malaysia and Thailand), in which exports based on natural resources have played an important role in economic growth and structural transformation.[17]

Traditionally, the classification of exports was limited to two categories: raw materials and manufactured goods. This typology considered sections 0 to 5 in the Standard International Trade Classification (SITC) to be raw materials, and 6 to 8 to be manufactured goods, although at times division 68 of the SITC (non-iron metals) was included in the group of raw materials. Nonetheless, interest in analysing the relationship between the intensity of the utilisation of different economic assets and the patterns of international trade led to more complex classification systems. Recent efforts have been made to establish differences among products that are usually classified as raw materials, particularly separating the unprocessed and processed goods which are derived from the intensive use of natural resources.[18]

The fundamental reason for this differentiation is that so-called 'semi-manufactured' goods can represent an important first step in countries that count on natural resources and that try to modify their export profiles in ascendant directions. The semi-manufactured export allows countries to exploit natural advantages at the same time that technological learning that is vital to development can be acquired.

---

16   ECLAC (2000).
17   Reinhardt (2000).
18   *Ibid.*

This chapter uses a classification system for exports that contains five categories.[19]

Table 1.1: Classification of Exports of Goods

Category	Abbreviation	Characteristics
Primary Product Exports	PRIM	Unprocessed raw material (excluding minerals). Intensive in natural resources and unskilled labour.
Mineral Exports	MIN	Non-iron ores. Intensive in natural resources and capital.
Semi-manufactured Goods Exports	SEMI	Simple process manufactured goods. Intensive in natural resources but with greater value added than non-processed raw materials.
Manufactured Goods Exports	MFR	Relatively low value of natural resources.
Other Goods Exports	OTHER	Art objects and other goods.

As indicated above, the SEMI category is very important for the analysis of structural transformations and growth in underdeveloped countries. It involves exports of goods that have been located between raw materials and manufactured goods. Included are goods that in other studies have been classified as raw material exports (lumber, wood pulp, canned fish, and processed fruits and vegetables among others). The SEMI category also includes products that other studies have considered to be manufactured goods (plywood, paper, fertiliser and petroleum by-products, among others). In the case of Cuba's current exports of goods there are four predominant products: sugar, minerals, tobacco and fish products. As a group, these four products represented 82.6 per cent of total exports in 1999.[20] None of these products is classified as manufactured goods (MFR) while the semi-manufac-

---

19   *Ibid.*
20   Oficina Nacional de Estadísticas (2000a).

tured goods (SEMI) — like tobacco — are a relatively small percentage within the 'four big ones'. The two primary Cuban exports at the beginning of the twenty-first century are a raw material export (sugar) and a mineral (nickel); in other words, activities that are located far down the export scale, if viewed from the perspective of technological complexity, value added and potential for technological learning.[21]

The situation is no different when the spectrum of exports is expanded beyond the 'four big ones' (sugar, nickel, tobacco and fish products). There are only five other Cuban products that are classified as 'principal' exports, that is, those products whose share of total exports is 1.5 per cent or greater. These five are iron and steel products, pharmaceuticals, fruits and vegetables, coffee and cement. In other words, three manufactured goods (pharmaceuticals, cement and iron/steel), one raw material (coffee), and one category, fruits and vegetables, that represent a combination of PRIM (fresh products) and SEMI (canned).[22]

Among these five products, some, such as coffee and fruits, are 'traditional', while among the 'non-traditionals' some are new exports derived from an industrialisation process originally oriented toward import substitution (steel and cement), and others, such as medicines (MFR) and canned fruits and vegetables (SEMI), are the result of industrial activities that are biased explicitly for export.

As demonstrated in Table 2, with very few exceptions, the contribution of the country's industrial base to the export of manufactured and even semi-manufactured goods is relatively insignificant.

In addition to an export profile excessively dependent on low level processing of natural resources, another important characteristic of Cuban exports during the 1990s was its relative lack of dynamism and the 'stagnation' of the supply structure in its failure to progress toward greater export activities with greater value added and technological complexity.

21   An opportunity for industrial upgrading exists in the case of nickel, in that a Cuban company has entered into a joint venture with a Canadian company that allows the Cuban company to place itself for the first time in all phases of the chain of value added to the product. Although up to now part of the Cuban company's upgrading has taken place outside Cuba, the technological and organisational learning facilitated by the agreement have placed the Cuban company in a very good position to implement upgrading within Cuba.

22   In 1998, the value of fresh fruit and vegetable exports was $19.1 million, of which exports of fruit preserves and canned goods was $15.8 million (Oficina Nacional de Estadísticas, 1999).

Table 1.2: Cuba — Principal Exports (a), 1998

Export	Category	SITC Code	Value in Millions US$	% of Total Exports (b)
Sugars, sugar and honey preparations	PRIM	06	605,494	39.30
Mineral ores	MIN	28	351,926	22.85
Tobacco and tobacco products	SEMI	12	219245	14.20
Fish, shellfish and fish preparations	PRIM	03	102,786	6.67
Iron and steel	MFR	67	45,985	2.98
Medical and pharmaceutical products	MFR	54	39,075	2.53
Vegetables and fruits	PRIM/SEMI	05	35,201	2.28
Coffee, tea and cacao, and preparations	PRIM	07	31,378	2.00
Cement	MFR	66	27,053	1.75
Subtotal 'four big exports'			1,279,451	83.10
Subtotal principal exports			1,458,143	94.7
Subtotal PRIM and MIN (c)			1,091,584	70.9
Subtotal SEMI and PRIM/SEMI (c)			254,446	16.5
Subtotal MFR (c)			112,113	7.3
Total Exports of Goods			**1,539,533**	**100.0**

Source: Oficina Nacional de Estadísticas, *Anuario Estadístico de Cuba* (Havana, 1999).

(a) Principal exports: exports with 1.5% or greater share of the total.

(b) Totals may not be exact as percentages have been rounded.

(c) Subtotals for export categories included in this table only.

Table 1.3: Cuba — Evolution of Exports (1990–99)

Exports	Category	1990		1995		1999	
		Value	% of total	Value	% of total	Value	% of total
1 Sugar	PRIM	4,337.5	80.0	714.3	47.9	462.5	31.7
2 Mining	MIN	398.2	7.4	331.1	22.2	396.3	27.2
3 Tobacco	SEMI	114.4	2.1	102.1	6.8	202.6	13.9
4 Fishing	PRIM	101.9	1.9	122.8	8.2	97.0	6.7
5 Agricultural products	PRIM	183.9	3.4	44.8	3.0	44.0	3.1
6 Others	(various)	279.0	5.2	176.5	11.8	253.9	17.4
Subtotal (1-5)		5,135.9	94.8	1,315.1	88.2	1,202.4	82.6
Subtotal PRIM and MIM		5,021.5	92.7	1,213.1	81.3	999.8	68.7
Total exports		**5,414.9**	**100.0**	**1,491.6**	**100.0**	**1,456.1**	**100.0**

Source: Oficina Nacional de Estadísticas, *Cuba en cifras* (1998 and 1999), Havana.

In terms of dynamism, during the 1990s Cuba experienced a sharp contraction in production for export, principally due to the significant fall in sugar exports caused by the decline in physical production as well as the decline in prices. With the exception of greater dynamism in tobacco exports and the increase in the available supply of minerals for export (despite lower prices at the beginning of the decade) the rest of the country's principal exports performed poorly. The reduction in the supply for export — especially of sugar — explains the superficial character of the variations in the percentages of the export structure. At first blush this suggests a more balanced structure in which the relative proportion of the category 'others' is multiplied more than three times.

The figures should not be a source of confusion. If sugar as a percentage of total exports was reduced so considerably, it is because there was an acute production crisis in the sector and not because other export activities grew (with the exception of tobacco). Even more important is the fact that during the decade the composition of the supply for export did not improve in any significant way, if this is measured according to the typology adopted in this chapter. The export of primary products (PRIM) and minerals (MIN) have maintained a relatively excessive percentage. Among the four principal export groups only one semi-manufacture, tobacco, has grown in a significant manner, but this is one of Cuba's oldest economic activities and it is not exactly a case of increased exports of semi-manufactured goods based on the recent incorporation of value added to goods that until recently were primary products or mineral exports.

As indicated above, there are some cases of manufactured and semi-manufactured exports that clearly show a movement 'upwards' on the export scale, but the slight relative weight of this export supply has not changed the nature of the export profile of goods dominated by primary products (PRIM) and minerals (MIN).

At this point it is appropriate to raise the issue of services exports and the role of these in the possible qualitative transformation of the export profile, especially with respect to whether this has facilitated new means of international insertion based not on natural resources but on other factors like the skilled labour force or scientific and technological innovation.

Service exports — principally in the form of income from tourism — have doubtless been the most significant of the transformations in Cuba's export supply in the 1990s. So much so, that although only representing a minimal fraction of exports at the beginning of the decade, at its end the balance of payments income from non-factor services (tourism, transportation and others, like communications) was almost double the total exports of merchandise from the country.

Table 1.4: Cuba — Exports of Goods and Services, 1990 and 1999

	1990		1999	
	Value	% of total	Value	% of total
Goods exports (a)	5,414.9	95.7	1,456.1	36.05
Services exports (b)	243.4	4.3	2,582.4	63.95
Exports of goods and services	5,658.3	100.0	4,038.5	100.0

Source: Oficina Nacional de Estadísticas, *Cuba en cifras* (1998 and 1999), Havana.

(a) Exports of goods.
(b) Services exports are not always reflected in the Cuban balance of payments. The 1990 figure includes only income from tourism (which in that year represented a substantial part of services income), while the 1999 figure reflects information from the balance of payments, which includes all services exports (Banco Central de Cuba, 2000).

Nonetheless, there is no solid evidence to support the assumption that this transformation is in itself an indisputable indication of industrial upgrading. Although the information necessary for a detailed analysis of this question is not available, the published data are sufficient to put in proper perspective the significance for Cuba during the 1990s of the notable increase in income for services.

Table 1.5: Cuba — Income from Services in the Balance of Payments, 1999–2001

	1999		2000 (a)		2001 (a)	
	Value	% of total	Value	% of total	Value	% of total
Income from Transportation	542.8	21.0	420.2	16.8	428.6	15.8
Income from Tourism	1741.1	67.4	1813.0	72.6	2014.4	74.1
Income – Remaining Services	298.5	15.6	262.5	10.6	275.6	10.1
Total – Income from Services	2582.4	100.0	2495.7	100.0	2718.6	100.0
Memo: Goods Exports	1465.5	–	1882.0		2070.0	–

Source: Banco Central de Cuba (2000).
(a) Estimates

A country's balance of payment statistics generally group services income into three large categories: transportation, travel and other services. The category 'transportation' includes the movement of passengers and cargo (by air and sea), the category 'travel' refers to international tourism, and the category 'other services' encompasses a wide spectrum of activities: finance, insurance, real estate, communications, renting and leasing equipment and professional services (consulting, engineering, accounting and specialised services, etc.), among others.

Analysis of the international accounts clearly shows that income from services occupies an important role in the balance of payments of underdeveloped countries, such that the increase in these (with respect to merchandise exports) is not in itself a reliable indicator of advancement toward qualitatively superior modalities of international insertion. The significant correlation between services income and the level of development is found not in the level of income, but in its composition. Underdeveloped countries do not show relative strength in the so-called services to production, particularly in the sub-group of professional services. In reality, income from tourism is generally the only source that has an important role in the international accounts of underdeveloped countries.[23]

This does not imply that tourism causes or perpetuates underdevelopment; rather, it is the simple empirical observation that tourism is not incompatible with underdevelopment and does not lead necessarily to moving beyond it.

In Cuba's case tourism occupies a disproportionate place within the total income from services, and even a part of the income from airline transportation depends on tourist activity. The extraordinary growth in tourist activity in Cuba during the 1990s brought definite economic benefits: rapid access to a growing source of foreign currency income from international markets that are much less protected than product markets, relatively rapid recovery of investments, reactivation of other sectors of the economy through productive links, the establishment of an important sector whose growth dynamic is 'exogenous', i.e., that is not limited to the general rate of economic growth, relatively increased employment generation given the intensity of the use of the workforce for this activity, and relatively less energy consumption.

Without a doubt, the expansion of tourism has made a positive contribution to the economy, but its accelerated growth has not necessarily meant structural change leading to an international insertion based on the use of assets other than natural resources. Even after the transformations of the 1990s, natural resources continue to be the key economic asset defining Cuba's export profile. Thus, tourism, like sugar, mining and fishing, is highly dependent on natural resources.

Nonetheless, as a result of the expansion of tourism and other services, the country's export structure adopted a relatively more 'advanced' profile at the end of the 1990s than that existing at the beginning of the decade. Based on the growth of the SEMI type of exports that make use of natural resources to add value, the country's economic structure could gradually improve with respect to the possibility of advancing towards a more intensive use of other assets such as skilled labour, technological innovation and the application of science.

The international tourism that predominates in Cuba, so-called 'sun and beach' tourism, is an activity that requires intensive use of natural resources. Nonetheless, given its complexity, tourism is able to incorporate value added to natural resources to a greater degree than primary product (PRIM) and mineral (MIN) exports. In effect, tourism is not just a service; it is also a complex process that involves productive activity, including manufacturing. Some of the facets in the chain of value of tourism, such as lodging and food service, are characterised by intensive use of labour and natural resources, and to a lesser extent, capital, while other activities, such as air transport, are capital intensive, or intensive in specialised knowledge, such as tour operators and travel agencies.

---

23   Hockman and Karsenty (1992).

Applying the five category typology used in this chapter (PRIM, MIN, SEMI, MFR and OTHERS), the tourism generally conducted in Cuba ('sun and beach' tourism) could fit in the semi-manufactured goods category (SEMI), and will be identified here as 'equivalent to semi-manufactured goods' (SEMI–EQ).[24]

To simplify the analysis, the other two large categories of income from services (transportation and other services) in Cuba are equivalent to the manufacturing category, and can be labelled (MFR–EQ).

Table 1.6: Cuba — Exports of Goods and Services, 1990 and 1999 (Selected Categories)

	1990		1999	
	Value	% of total	Value	% of total
Sugar PRIM	4337.5	76.7	462.5	11.5
Mining MIN	398.2	7.0	396.3	9.8
Tourism (a) SEMI–EQ	243.4	4.3	1741.1	43.1
Tobacco SEMI	114.4	2.0	202.6	5.0
Fishing PRIM	101.9	1.8	97.0	2.4
Income – transportation (a) MFR–EQ	–		542.8	13.4
Income – remaining services (a) MFR–EQ	–	–	298.5	7.4
Total Exports of Goods and Services	5658.3	100.0	4038.5	100.0
Subtotal PRIM and MIN (b)	4837.6	85.5	955.8	23.7
Subtotal SEMI and SEMI– EQ	357.8.	6.3	1943.7	48.1

Source: Banco Central de Cuba, *Proyección de la balanza de pagos de Cuba 1999–2001* (Havana, 2000).

(a) Because of the lack of detailed public information on income from services in 1990, only tourism has been included for that year, based on data from the Oficina Nacional de Estadísticas (1999). There is detailed information on income from services for 1999. (Banco Nacional de Cuba, 2000).

(b) The subtotals only include the entries on this table.

24   Other types of tourism such as 'cultural' tourism, 'medical' tourism or 'convention' tourism could be compared with the export of manufactured goods given the role of specialised knowledge and the greater capital intensity involved.

The fact that tourism generates the greatest income of Cuba's exports does not reflect that dependence on natural resources has been overcome as the key factor in the country's international insertion, but it has modified the export profile in the proper, if still insufficient, direction.

From the perspective of the export typology applied here, the change in Cuba's export profile in the 1990s was based largely on the use of natural resources for the development of an activity — tourism — that could be classified with semi-manufactured goods. Tourism was the most important factor in the movement of the structure of exports of goods and services toward a new profile dominated by the categories SEMI and SEMI–EQ. This is clearly more advanced than the profile composed only of goods, which is predominantly PRIM and SEMI.

Thus, Cuba's trajectory differs from that of other countries in which the relative weight of manufacturing in exports increases through the use of resources that are relatively 'universal' and abundant, such as unskilled labour, in which international competitiveness is less stable and not very profitable. In Cuba's case, changes in the export profile have not led to giving manufacturing adequate weight. This continues to be a weakness in the export profile of the country, but at least a moderate advance of the export profile has occurred (toward the SEMI type) which is based on natural resources (climate, beaches) or scarce factors (geographic location), where despite the existing competition, Cuba's competitive margin is relatively greater and more sustainable.

Nevertheless, clearly the development of an open economy like Cuba's requires a much more radical modification in its export profile, in which manufactured goods or service activities that are comparable to manufacturing (in terms of added value, application of knowledge and complexity) should occupy a growing portion of total exports.

With the current export profile — independent from the changes brought by tourism — the Cuban economy's international competitiveness depends on the possibility of maintaining low costs. Thus, it is not based on more dynamic and potentially more advantageous factors like skilled labour and the application of technological progress, factors which Cuba also possesses and which are not currently used in an intensive manner for Cuba's international insertion.

During the 1990s the export profile of the country advanced toward an intermediate situation, something which should be clearly understood as the correct direction but not the final trajectory of changes that are necessary. The principal challenge that Cuba faces in this area is that any subsequent significant change ('upward') of the export structure does not appear to be compatible with the current pattern of development.

Export Substitution: Discontinuing the Adjustment

In the context of a globalised economy, should Cuba rely on a development strategy based on intensive use of natural resources and reindustrialisation fundamentally oriented toward the domestic market, or is the more appropriate strategy intensive utilisation of a skilled workforce with high learning capacity directed toward export oriented reindustrialisation? Which option is the most promising in terms of the country's development? This is in essence the fundamental dilemma currently facing the formulation of Cuba's policies for international insertion.

In the 1990s Cuba used (with partial success) the first of the above mentioned means to 'adjust' its economy to the new international context. Nevertheless, the type of adjustment adopted in the previous pattern of development does not appear to be the most appropriate mechanism to promote national development in the future.

Cuba's development requires (among other factors) the reindustrialisation of its economy. Nevertheless, this should not be conceived as reconstructing the industrial structure to be fundamentally directed at reactivation and diversification of production for the domestic market. Given the current conditions of the international economy, creation of the domestic base necessary for the systematic development of the country's productive forces should result from a process of export oriented reindustrialisation, although the development of local clusters (associated with exports) definitely should be a factor that leads to 'deepening' the process and developing domestic markets.

In the short and medium term Cuba should aspire to become a new location for the manufacture of global products and the supply of services to producers in categories of modes of insertion that, in the long run, create the conditions for the nation's industry to move 'up' in technological and organisational learning curves.

Cuba needs a reindustrialisation based on export substitution, i.e., the adoption of a pattern of development in which 'technologically intensive' exports replace product and service exports based on the intensive exploitation of natural resources that currently make up the bulk of the country's total exports.

This would represent a radical change in the pattern of development in place until now in that it would displace import substitution industrialisation as a central element. It would mean a qualitative change in emphasis from the pattern of development of the 1990s since export oriented reindustrialisation would cease to be a secondary component superimposed over the core of the pattern of development (import substitution) in order to become the essential element of a new pattern. An additional fundamental difference presented by the export substitution pattern of development is that not only would industrial exports occupy a growing part of total exports, but a broad spectrum of activities would be produced. No credit is claimed for the conceptual innovation of 'export substitution' which is central to this argument. But it is here introduced, as far as possible, for the first time into the study of the Cuban case.[25]

This concept is not the same as 'diversification of exports,' at least in the way that the latter is usually employed in Cuba. Many believe that Cuba's path to development must pass through the growth of exports, but not in any way. It is not solely a question of increasing traditional exports and 'diversifying' the universe of exports through the expansion of the group of exportable sectors including manufacturing and services.

An effective diversification should not be understood simply as an indiscriminate aggregation of new exportable sectors, but an (absolute and relative) expansion of exports based on technological factors and intensive use of the skilled workforce. The critical aspect of diversification should be the extent to which these new exports become a growing part (to the point of becoming the majority) of total exports. In other words, there should be substitution of some exports for others in the country's export structure. According to the export classification adopted in this chapter, successful export substitution entails an increase in the relative weight of the categories SEMI and MFR in the country's total exports.

Export substitution can be considered the equivalent of export diversification only when the latter develops in the direction described above. To summarise, export substitution is export diversification when the diversification follows a rising trajectory of technological learning.

There is not the space here to develop a more detailed exposition of this alternative, but it should be clear that a reindustrialisation strategy through export substitution starts from the assumption that structural limitations are not to be accepted, but overcome. The transformations that this would require entail an economic reform of a type that elsewhere I have called 'fundamental',[26] but it is also necessary to make use of the opportunities that could be offered by foreign investment and global production networks to achieve technological learning.

---

25   The concept has been used here as it was introduced in the studies on development by René Villareal (See Villareal, 1990, p. 310). In the most recent discussions on Cuba, the concept has been broached, without its complete adoption, by the researchers of the Sección de Industria del Instituto Nacional de Investigaciones Económicas (INIE) (Adriano García, Hugo Pons, José Somoza and Víctor Cruz). See the 1999 article cited in the bibliography by these authors.

26   Carranza, Gutiérrez and Monreal (1995).

Conclusions

Cuba's economic transformation in the 1990s cannot be considered the solution to the formidable challenge of substantially modifying the current productive structure of the economy in order to achieve development. Despite the changes, the reconstruction of the Cuban economy is an incipient process with a high level of indeterminacy. To put it simply, it is a challenge awaiting resolution.

The central argument here is simple: the most appropriate development strategy for Cuba under current conditions consists of abandoning the current process of adjusting the pattern of development based on import substitution and replacing it with a reindustrialisation process with export substitution that advances the country in terms of technological and organisational learning.

CHAPTER 2

The Cuban Economy during the 1990s: A Brief Assessment of a Critical Decade

Julio Carranza Valdés

Introduction

The last decade of the twentieth century was complex and difficult for the Cuban economy. If two concepts can express the essence of those ten years, they are 'crisis' and 'change'.

The great challenge has been, and is, to understand the profound character of the crisis and imagine and articulate the necessary changes to overcome it strategically and recover the viability of the Cuban economy in an international context that is difficult in the extreme and to a large extent hostile.

It could be said that this situation, in this era, is not exclusive to Cuba, since the vast majority of the so-called periphery has also experienced critical processes in the same context of international difficulties. Nevertheless, there are sufficient reasons to affirm that the case of Cuba is distinct. Cuba is a country with a socialist economy which was integrated for decades into the structures of the old Council of Mutual Economic Assistance (Comecon) and allied with the Soviet Union. This arrangement conferred important economic advantages and created an appreciable level of certainty in the medium term.

The relationship with Comecon also served as effective compensation for the pressure of the US government blockade of the island in effect since the 1960s. It should also be noted that Cuba's endowment of natural resources is relatively meagre and that the island has an underdeveloped economic structure.

Thus, the changes in the world system at the end of the 1980s had a much greater impact on Cuba than on most other countries. Yet, although obviously the fall of the European socialist bloc is the factor that triggered the economic crisis, its causes can not be reduced only to this event, nor are they solely external in origin.

There were strong tensions in the Cuban economy beginning in the second half of the 1980s that reflected the limits of the extensive growth model in effect and the vulnerability of its external sector. Nonetheless, until 1989 compensating factors were maintained until the fall of the socialist bloc. This new situation heightened the effects of the North American blockade, and the limitations of the economic model became more acute.

For years, resources received from the socialist camp allowed Cuba to maintain a high level of investment and growing social expenditure. From 1976 to 1985 the national product grew at an average annual rate greater than 5.3 per cent. The extensive nature of economic growth was the principal characteristic of the Cuban economy in the 15 years preceding the deep crisis at the beginning of the 1990s.[1] This extensive growth took place with poor efficiency and a high level of external compensation.

There have been diverse consequences of the crisis that can be measured by a variety of indicators, as has been examined in previous studies. For the purposes of this chapter, I shall refer to those indicators that are directly related to the challenges that faced Cuba at the beginning of the 1990s and their evolution in recent years. The purpose is to evaluate existing conditions in order to take on current problems, and in particular, the logic of a new development strategy.

It is possible to enumerate the problems that the crisis posed to the economy as follows: a) sharp drop in the national product and investment; b) strong contraction of foreign trade and corresponding imbalances in the balance of payments; c) serious macroeconomic disequilibrium; d) reinforcement of low levels of efficiency; e) a decrease in the standard of living of the population; and f) disarticulation of the existing accumulation model and the strategy of economic development.

According to these dimensions of the crisis it was required to achieve four major important goals: a) macroeconomic adjustment; b) structural adjustment of the economic system; c) recovery of growth; d) redefinition of the economic development strategy in the new international context. Of course, each of these dimensions is intimately related to the rest, and the advance of one depends to a large extent on the advance of the others.

Changes were taking place throughout the decade and they were increasing, mainly from the spring of 1993, when the objective was not only to achieve an equitable distribution of the crisis' social costs and reinsert Cuba in the international economic circuits, but also to carry out transformations in the domestic economic organisation system in order to recover growth, starting from higher levels of efficiency.

A decade on, the evolution of these four major goals, along with their situation and perspective at the moment, can be analysed.

1   In fact, there was also extensive growth prior to this period, and it currently continues to be the growth pattern of the Cuban economy, but the period beginning in 1975 is particularly relevant for two significant reasons. First, it coincides with the implementation of the only economic model of the revolutionary period that was prepared a priori in an integrated manner. And second, during part of that period there was a notable, if not spectacular, growth in the national economy, followed by a second phase, prior to the crisis of the 1990s, that involved economic stagnation. Thus, the 1975–89 period has defining moments (growth and stagnation) that in the context of an extraordinary growth model facilitate the analysis of the factors of economic reproduction.

Macroeconomic Adjustment

From the beginning of the most acute phase of the crisis, in 1990, the Cuban government tried to confront it with a policy that favoured an equitable distribution of the difficulties and scarcities imposed by the economic decline. In this effort, in addition to preserving the most important social gains (health, education and social security), measures were implemented that averted massive unemployment and increases in official prices.

Additionally, in 1990 all available products and services were rationed so that prices did not increase due to falling supply, and the limited supply was distributed equally among the population at subsidised prices accessible to all social groups.

Many of the enterprises affected by the inability to guarantee materials or difficulties of another kind were not closed in order to avoid the growth of unemployment. They continued to function with subsidies.

This policy, despite achieving a relatively equitable sharing of the costs of the crisis among the whole population (which was critical for sustaining consensus under such difficult conditions), generated a notable increase in liquidity, as a result of growing demand (salaries, social security, subsidies, etc.) facing a sustained depression in supply (strong contraction of production and imports). At the end of 1993 accumulated liquidity reached approximately 11,044 million pesos,[2] the equivalent of more than thirteen months of the average salary.

In this same period a large budget deficit was created. The principal traditional sources of income to the national budget (earnings from businesses, sales tax, etc.) were very affected. In May of 1994, 69 per cent of the country's enterprises were operating with losses and up to that time, taxed products had limited circulation.[3] Nevertheless, until 1993, in order to maintain its social objectives the state continued to increase its budget expenditures, especially business subsidies, until it accumulated a deficit of 5,050 million pesos in 1993,[4] which represented a 90 per cent increase in that same indicator for 1989.

In this context of financial disequilibrium, the lack of supply in the state network led to the rapid growth of the informal market, in its legal or tolerated versions as well as illegal manifestations. By mid-1993 the value of the informal market had grown more than seven times from its 1989 level. The sources that fed this market were diverse, from the resale of rationed articles to the misappropriation and embezzlement of resources. The sustained

---

2   Rodríguez (1994).
3   Beginning in June 1994, the production and marketing of cigarettes was stabilised. The increase in cigarette prices was the central feature of a group of measures for monetary contraction adopted by the Cuban government.
4   Rodríguez (1994).

depression of supply in the state network forced the majority of the population to turn to the informal market to complete the basket of basic goods, especially food. This market was inflationary until the first half of 1994.

The disequilibrium caused the depreciation of the national currency, and at the end of 1993 it reached its lowest level (US$1 for 120 Cuban pesos). For this reason, salaries lost their function as a stimulus mechanism for sustaining the intensity and productivity of work. Salaries were much greater than required to purchase goods available in the rationed market and insufficient to cover the increase in prices in the informal market. Thus, part of the population was forced to enter the informal sector, not only as consumers, but as sellers, in order to obtain the income necessary to continue consuming in that same market. This created a growing speculative spiral until the end of 1994. This phenomenon aggravated the situation of separation from work for a growing number of workers, which tended to go from temporary separation to permanent, given the strong contracting effect on the link to the formal labour market under acute conditions of monetary disequilibrium.

The growing tendency to financial disequilibrium in the national economy imposed changes on the country's economic policy to restore domestic financial balances.

In June 1994, after a broad national debate, a series of measures to increase the capture of circulating currency was implemented: increased prices on non-essential consumer goods, elimination of some free services, and a new tax policy and reduction of subsidies.

This programme produced a relative reduction in liquidity, especially in the first year. Nevertheless, in December 2000, 79 months after it began, the effects of excessive liquidity were still evident despite the relative improvement, considering the relative decline in circulating currency and the growth in production with its corresponding increase in supply. This caused the national currency to appreciate from 120 pesos to the dollar in 1994 to 22 pesos to the dollar in 2001.

An estimated 10,350 million pesos were in the hands of the population at around this time (December 2000). Despite the official view that the situation is in equilibrium, there is still a disjuncture between the average salary (249 pesos in 2000) and the prices of products in the state as well as non-state open markets, with the exception of the market for rationed goods. This is especially important in the case of the agricultural markets. The financial recovery measures put in place in 1994 to reduce the money supply had decreasing effectiveness after the first year and a half of implementation. There has been a significant tendency toward concentration of currency holdings. Eighty-four per cent of the money deposited in savings accounts belongs to only 13 per cent of account holders.

The relatively high price levels in the agricultural market and its relative rigidity after six years of financial and monetary adjustment is not explained by lack of supply alone. One of the central causes of this phenomenon is the persistence of an excess and concentrated money supply (including bank deposits) that creates significant inflation pressure.

The lack of correspondence between prices and salaries creates rigidities in the structure of individual consumption,[5] limits the possibilities of re-establishing work as the fundamental source of income, and creates a series of complex problems in the national economy, including: a) distortions in agricultural production due to the profit differential between the regulated and unregulated sectors; b) relative stagnation in the economic activity of some of the legalised market that is not agricultural; c) the disincentive to farmers and some co-operatives that already have a high level of savings in the national currency without corresponding supply; and d) the heavy transfer of monetary resources from the city to the country.

The most relevant result in the field of domestic finances has been the reduction of the budget deficit (it was 30 per cent of the GDP in 1993 and 2.5 per cent of the GDP in 1999), due to a more restrictive financial policy, taxes and reduction of enterprises' subsidies. However, one should be careful about this last point: in the absence of improvement in the entrepreneurial reform, the reduction of these subsidies has generated an increase of debts among the enterprises. It is important to note the effort that has been made to maintain social expenditure, which has enabled social services to continue even in the most critical times.

The removal of cash from circulation has involved a double process: the total amount of currency has been reduced, and its greatest relative concentration is in passive currency, or bank deposits, which contains an implicit threat of becoming cash and unleashing greater inflationary pressures in the event of new market opportunities that would trigger this pent-up demand.[6]

---

5   A large part of the urban population has to use the majority of their salary in the free market as a necessary complement to the quota of foodstuffs and other essential products that can be obtained at subsidised prices in the regulated market. See *Granma*, 23 December 1998; *Juventud Rebelde*, 3 April 1998.

6   In my view, passive currency is an economic problem that should not be minimised in Cuba's case for several reasons. First, because it largely explains the inflationary pressures that determine price levels in the free markets that have no rational relationship to the average earnings of workers. After an initial period of reduction, these prices have stayed at very high levels in relation to the average salary. The fact that there are supply limitations in these markets is not in itself the explanation for high prices. Second, there are not firm barriers between active and passive currency. In fact, variations in bank accounts have reflected a growing source of active currency. Third, the high level of concentration of accumulated liquidity is a significant barrier to the necessary broadening of market segments of non-state economic activity. In that context, it would be highly questionable from a socialist perspective to open new spaces in the private sector, particularly in terms of legitimacy and equality of opportunity. On this last point, it is clearly necessary to integrate the demonetisation process with other components of a larger programme of economic transformation.

The demonetisation programme seems to have reached its limits: the empirical evidence suggests that the levels of active currency in the hands of the majority of the population are now greatly reduced. This implies that this sector of the population can no longer serve as the principal 'source' of extraction in the context of a currency reduction programme based primarily on price increases on consumer products. Thus, even if part of the problem has improved (relative reduction of liquidity), adequate levels of equilibrium and reduction of the concentration of money have yet to be achieved.[7]

As stated above, despite some advances, demonetisation continues to be an unrealised goal in the reordering of the Cuban economy. Achieving this is a necessary condition for the integrated advancement of the restructuring project.[8]

Finally, in addition to the present concern about the real pressure of excess liquidity, including bank deposits, is the central question of its impact on the subsequent course of restructuring. Decentralisation and greater diversification of the forms of ownership and organisation of production and services is, in our opinion, the inevitable path in the immediate future to raise the level of efficiency in the state sector and take positive action on the employment problem.

At the same time, it is necessary to take into consideration the monetary duality problem. In the spring of 1993 the holding and circulation of hard currency for the Cuban people were legalised, which meant a recognition of the situation that in fact had been imposed by the crisis, when the fall of the consumption levels was combined with the highest opening to international tourism, the growth of family remittances in the hands of one part of the population, as well as the increase of the foreign investment.

This measure, which was absolutely necessary, taking into account the prevailing conditions in that moment, favoured an important increase in family remittances, while it also contributed to a reduction in the balance of payments deficit. However, the dollar circulation confirmed the duality that has characterised the Cuban economy during the period of crisis: it is the coexistence of two sectors which operate with different currencies and under different conditions. The consequences range from serious alteration in the incentive system to distortion of internal prices, as well as in the calculation of costs and therefore in the fundamental economic decisions.

The double monetary circulation constitutes one of the pending problems that needs a solution. Economic integration under a unique national

---

7   The problem posed by this situation for the restructuring of a socialist economy is different than that dictated by a capitalist paradigm. For the latter, the concentration of income is not a negative effect; rather, it is viewed as a legitimate and desirable source of capital accumulation.

8   The best option in 1994 would have been a programme of rapid demonetisation. (Carranza, Gutiérrez and Monreal, 1996)

currency is a structural necessity, however this goal is only possible with greater macroeconomic balances. The deadlines and the ways to get them have been debated during the 1990s and surely they will be debated in the coming years.

Structural Adjustment of the Economy

Analysis of the national economy during the 1975–89 period reveals two important conceptual aspects: first, the pattern of extensive growth sowed the seeds of its own exhaustion, and second, the replacement of this pattern with intensive growth must be an indispensable condition for the future development of the Cuban economy.

The important advances in the economic and social spheres during that period should not be underestimated, but it is important to understand their limitations, and in particular to consider that that development occurred in concrete international circumstances with very specific characteristics, the repetition of which is very improbable under current conditions. The fact that that context is not repeatable should be a determinative argument for motivating the search for a different growth model. Nevertheless, this argument in itself is insufficient.

Several studies on the extensive growth of the Cuban economy in the 1970s and 1980s demonstrated its limitations.[9] First, it was incapable of being self-sustaining, or put another way, the presence of external sources of compensation was an indispensable condition of the model's operation. Thus, a mutual reinforcement developed between the two conditions that over the long term would have perverse characteristics: the economy, despite its inefficiency, could grow extensively thanks to the sustained transfer of resources from outside sources, and at the same time, that transfer, by guaranteeing the extensive pattern, served as a strong disincentive for the move toward an efficient and intensive model.

As for the dependence on foreign transfers, the truly pernicious element of the pattern of extensive growth in Cuba was not that it was associated with the need for investments that characterises all development processes. In the case of an economy like Cuba's, the creation of the material and human bases for development requires an investment process that in terms of quantity and pace need greater resources than can be generated domestically and which for a time must grow more rapidly than the economy as a whole. Thus, extensive growth underpinned by foreign transfers for a period of time is not a priori undesirable. Cuba's problem during this period was not the increase

9   Many assessments of the period were produced as documents for restricted use, particularly those prepared by researchers at the Instituto Nacional de Investigaciones Económicas (INIE).

in formation and utilisation of productive resources at more accelerated rates than economic growth, but that resources were used inefficiently.

The appropriate solution in the second half of the 1980s was the adoption of economic policies that were oriented toward intensive development, a view that was widely shared at the time. Even in conditions in which it was possible to maintain a relatively comfortable level of financial imbalance, it was not possible satisfactorily to adjust the extensive model. An efficiency leap that could only be conceived in the context of an intensive model was required.

Various factors impeded moving beyond the extensive model in the 1980s — inefficiencies in investment policy, problems with the economic management system, difficulties in making the newly created capacities function, falling international prices and weather problems. The changes introduced in the second half of that decade, in the context of the so-called rectification of errors and negative tendencies, did not address this situation.

Low levels of efficiency necessitated great resources not only for accumulation but also for its ongoing operation. At the end of 1987 the indicator for effective material expenditure had fallen to the level of the early 1980s.[10] Furthermore, the investment process not only failed to engender the necessary transformation in the country's export structure, it also did not sufficiently modify the poorly integrated national economy, which therefore continued to be highly vulnerable to imports. Intersectoral relationships continued to be very weak. A low level of integration among principal sectors together with high energy consumption, a very important issue, created the need for a high level of imports of intermediate goods necessary to the functioning of the installed productive capacity.[11]

Thus, the national economy had strong structural barriers to self-sustaining growth in addition to the relative scarcity of natural resources. The lack of a sector producing durable goods, which are vital to capital accumulation, causes a heightened vulnerability to imports. Since intersectoral ties are inadequate, the economy is also vulnerable to imports of intermediate goods, which are necessary for accumulation as well as the ongoing functioning of the economy. As was evident in the 1990s, contraction in imports of intermediate goods is a powerful mechanism of disconnection in the national economy.

Finally, the import structure in the 1980s, and even more so in the 1990s, showed that the vulnerability of growth was multiplied by external factors. In 1989, consumer goods, especially food, made up 10.4 per cent of imports; in 1998 that percentage reached 21.7 per cent.[12] The fact that

10 Unanue and Martínez Carrera (1989). The indicator for effectiveness of material expenditure used by these authors was the 'material density of the Gross Social Product (GSP)', calculated as the quotient of the consumption of productive material and the GSP, both in real 1981 terms.

11 Torras and Ilizástegui (1988).

12 CEPAL (2000).

necessary goods such as foodstuffs were a growing proportion of decreasing total imports, accentuating import dependency, inevitably means that any 'adjustment' in terms of imports had to be produced by the means of production (intermediate goods and especially capital goods) which directly affect the very capacity of the reproduction of the economy.

With the point of departure for recovery being a low level of imports with a rigid structure (heavily weighted towards food and fuel) the prospects for economic growth are not significant, and much less so once recovery from existing capacity is exhausted. This type of rigidity serves as an 'anchor' burdening economic recovery.

It could be said that the crisis of accumulation in the Cuban economy that began in the 1980s and continued to the present encompassed two stages in the extensive accumulation model. The first, which has been widely discussed, corresponds to the period that begins in the mid-1970s and extends to the end of the 1980s. The acute period of economic contraction in the first half of the 1990s (1990–93) and the current economic reactivation have been against a background of a second point in the extensive accumulation model, with poor efficiency and flawed, like the previous stage, but with the difference of a low level of external compensation.

Overcoming the accumulation crisis would only be possible with the switch to an intensive accumulation model, which would have greater economic efficiency. This is only possible in the context of a fundamental restructuring of the Cuban economy.

The need to establish high levels of efficiency is widely shared. The most polemical issue is how to achieve this and in what stages. This is an essential component for any economic restructuring within the logic of a viable and socialist development strategy.

As noted above, this problem became acute during the crisis, but it had appeared strongly in the previous period when important external resources were still available. As the historic experience of different countries demonstrates, movement to an intensive model is necessary for the development even in the presence of abundant natural resources, and especially when natural resources are scarce.

The changes in the Cuban economy, especially since the summer of 1993, have substantially altered the profile of the economy: greater business autonomy, relative diversification of forms of ownership — independent farm and worker co-operatives, opening of new spaces in the domestic market — mostly for agricultural products and crafts, opening to foreign investment, banking reform, free exchange of currency for domestic operations, reduction in subsidies, new incentives for the workforce, change in concepts of planning and, more recently, the business reform that is underway. Without losing its fundamental characteristics as a socialist economy, the rigidities in the old concept of the centrally planned economy have been substituted for a more flexible dynamic.

The impact of these measures in the reactivation of several sectors of the economy together with the availability of new sources of foreign exchange, such as tourism, new joint ventures, foreign investment and family remittances, explain the relative recovery of the economy since 1994. Nevertheless, in 2001 growth in the Cuban economy was still far from being intensive. The completion of the economic reform and its greater coherence is a necessary condition to achieve that leap.

The most dynamic element in the current situation is the business reform in progress, called 'business improvement', which should grant a high level of autonomy and generate a stronger market dynamic in the context of the incentive system, without jeopardising the predominance of social property but practising it in a different way. Nonetheless, its development is still in the initial stages and implementation is slow. In December 2000, of the approximately 3,000 enterprises in the country, only 50 were operating under the new form of management, while another 1,300 were at some stage in the process.[13] One issue that has been insufficiently explained by the economic authorities is the subsequent course that the business reform will take. It will obviously generate a redundant labour force as a consequence of the inevitable adjustments that businesses will have to make as they adopt the new model. The challenge is how to create new sources of employment.[14] As the most developed countries show, the service sector is today very dynamic, and it generates a growing proportion of employment. In the Cuban condition this sector could also have a very important place. However, it must not be ignored that a great part of this sector corresponds to budgetary activities, and if they surpass determined limits they will cause greater macroeconomic imbalances with the well-known consequences.

Recovery of Growth

The return to economic growth during the 1994–2000 period in a very difficult context is a very important achievement, but it is still insufficient strategically to overcome the crisis. Growth in those seven years reached 85 per cent of the GDP in 1989, meaning that the country still has not recovered from the loss suffered in the four years of acute contraction (1990–93). Utilisation of existing industrial capacity is still below 1989 levels, and new investment has not played a more significant role in the reactivation, which indicates that the factor that will allow growth to be sustainable over the long term has at present a minor presence in the process. Furthermore, economic growth has not ameliorated, and in many cases has increased, dise-

---

13   Lage (2001).
14   Carranza Valdés, Gutiérrez Urdaneta and Monreal González (1995) considers the answer to this problem, although clearly the policy implemented up to the moment is different.

quilibrium in the balance of payments, which is a drag on growth. The low probability of finding sufficient external compensation reinforces the need for an efficiency leap and greater mobilisation of domestic savings.

In addition to the objective factors that largely explain the depth and complexity of the crisis it is necessary to have a rigorous debate on the alternatives that could reduce its impact and accelerate a solution within the logic of an economic development strategy that is both socialist and viable.

The evidence indicates that the embargo is hardly going to be lifted in a short period of time. The difficult conditions that the current globalisation imposes on the world economic system are not going to be modified either, and the future American Free Trade Association (AFTA) — from which Cuba was excluded because of strong US pressure — shows clearly that the international condition in which the Cuban economy will have to operate will be extremely challenging. This context confirms that the step towards a more efficient economy, of intensive growth, is an urgent necessity.

The search for greater efficiency and significant increase in exports have been traditional, but unreached, goals of the country's economic policy. Nonetheless, unlike previous periods, the possible contribution of those factors to growth is substantially more important.[15] It is widely recognised that the Cuban economy cannot grow as it did before 1990 on the basis of an extensive low efficiency accumulation model compensated by diverse mechanisms of international collaboration with the socialist camp, particularly the USSR.

Thus, the most important question is not the conceptualisation of the recent economic recovery as a succession of phases susceptible to articulation, but the examination of factors that could achieve sustainable satisfactory levels of economic growth under current conditions. Questions such as what should be the rate of accumulation, in which sectors should there be investment and to what ends and how to achieve greater levels of efficiency, are open to diverse answers, which will affect not only the short term, but imply different trajectories for growth, economic structure and development over the long term.[16]

The Cuban economy managed to halt the strong decline in GDP from 1990 to 1993 and maintain growth for seven consecutive years. Although production has yet to reach the levels of the end of the 1980s, and to overcome the strong disequilibria in the balance of payment, which in many cases have become worse, the situation has certainly improved notably and more favourable conditions exist to continue the changes that will lead to overcoming the crisis strategically and definitively. As is explained above, the low prob-

15   The Economic Resolution of the Fifth Congress of the Cuban Communist Party states: 'Efficiency is the central objective of economic policy since it is one of the greatest potential assets of the country', *Granma*, 7 November 1997.
16   Monreal and Carranza (2000).

ability of finding sufficient external compensation reinforces the necessity of an efficiency leap and greater mobilisation of domestic savings.

Redefining Development Strategy

Import substitution industrialisation has been the focal point of the development strategies defined in Cuba during the revolutionary period. The changes that can be identified, at least until 1990 (when the crisis imposed a very short-term vision), refer to the specific ways that this could be achieved.

In 1975 the focal point of Cuba's development strategy was defined as 'industrialisation'.[17] Fifteen years later the country had not exactly fulfilled the plans as they were initially drawn up, but industry did have a relatively greater weight within total production, industrial production had diversified and broadened its infrastructure support, the business network had been extended and made more dense, management capacity was created and the skilled industrial workforce had expanded.

The 1990s saw the beginning of a period of tolerance towards measures for sharing the costs of the crisis as equitably as possible to protect the principles established in the revolution. Additionally, decentralisation was introduced and central planning virtually disappeared. As a logical consequence of the emergencies imposed by the crisis, it is more difficult to identify the components of a strategy for economic development in those years. There was an effort to restore sugar production, which had deteriorated in the previous years, and there was sustained growth in tourism, which has been the most dynamic sector in the last ten years with over 15 per cent annual growth. Nickel and oil production also increased due to heavy foreign investment. The communications infrastructure improved and the biotechnology sector remained steady, but did not penetrate international markets. A significant factor during this period has been family remittances, which in 2000 were estimated at around $1,000 million.[18] This financial flow allowed the reactivation of important sectors of the economy, such as light industry, stimulated by increased demand in the domestic currency markets.

Despite these notable changes, it cannot be said that there is an explicitly defined new economic development strategy that is different from import substitution industrialisation, even though it has been complemented with certain non-traditional exports that give it a greater export orientation.

17   The Programmatic Platform approved by the First Congress of the Cuban Communist Party in December 1975 stated that 'the central task of the plans for national development and economic growth for the next five year period, 1976–80, will be the industrialisation of the country' (Cuban Communist Party, 1976).

18   For an extensive analysis of the impact of family remittances on the Cuban economy, see Monreal (1999).

At the beginning of this decade, when the capacity of the country to manage and restore the economy in an extremely difficult situation had been demonstrated, a greater challenge was posed: articulating an economic development strategy that is both socialist and viable in the difficult and hostile context of globalisation, where the possibilities for third world countries are very limited.

Cuba enjoys certain advantages that allow it to consider development, even in those difficult conditions. Of course, it is not a linear process and not predetermined; it is plagued with challenges and will depend essentially on what is actually done. Greater improvement in efficiency is a necessary condition that should be complemented by a strategy supported by the principal resource that distinguishes Cuba as an exceptional country in the third world: the skill level and good potential for technological learning of its workforce and general population — the result of four decades of the Revolution's policy. This is Cuba's principal asset for development.[19]

Nonetheless, the country's export structure continues to be essentially made up of primary products typical of underdeveloped countries (sugar, nickel, tobacco, fish and tourism), which indicates that the nation's principal resource is still not being used intensively. The options for future development, given the current international context, depend on the success of resolving this contradiction in a reasonable period. Advances in sectors such as biotechnology, computers, medical equipment, etc., and a dynamic science and technical system in the country are important steps in that direction.

This is not to say that traditional sectors of the Cuban economy should not recover and continue to occupy an important place, as well as sectors with more recent growth and dynamism, such as tourism. But the focal point of the development strategy should be constituted by sectors that intensively use the skilled workforce in processes of increasing technical complexity, for which it is necessary to redefine the insertion in the global economy and modify the export structure of the country.

Development is a complex multidimensional process. Without forgetting any of its essential dimensions, such as social justice, sectoral and social equilibria, sustainability, culture, etc., here the emphasis is on development as positioning a substantial part of the workforce in ascendant trajectories of technological learning, an issue which is vital to the design of Cuba's current development strategy.[20] First, this dimension leads to a substantial connection between the country's chance for advancement and the dynamic of the global economy, even though it is faced with transnational hegemony.

19   There is a forthcoming study on Cuba's development options in the context of globalisation by the author with Dr Pedro Monreal, Professor at the Centro de Investigaciones de la Economía Internacional of the University of Havana. This section is based on the results of that study.

20   Monreal and Carranza (2000).

Second, it is clear that in a globalised world, those societies that are not capable of constantly raising their educational and scientific/technical standards and achieving innovation are penalised. Third, it relies on the role of the workforce, particularly the skilled workforce, which is Cuba's great asset, as previously noted. And finally, placing the skilled workforce in sectors with high value added will permit increased individual and collective incentives, thus attenuating, and ultimately resolving, the existing contradiction between remuneration and expectations based on qualifications.

The development process in a context of globalisation like the current one is essentially a dispute over shares of the material and technological bases of contemporary production that greatly exceeds the simple vision of the country's 'adaptive' insertion into the international economy. At least two initial conditions are indispensable to this process: the quality of the available human resources and a state that is capable of leading and carrying out the promotion of development. It is in precisely these two areas that the Cuban Revolution has made a decisive contribution that should be decisive for the design of new development strategies in the face of the formidable challenge presented by globalisation.

For an open economy like Cuba's, a transformation of its economic structure that is focused on development is a process that occurs within a set of restrictions that cannot be ignored.[21] The first restriction is that the new structure must guarantee the country's insertion into the international economy. Cuba has no viable alternatives outside 'export oriented strategies', which will always be problematic, although not impossible, while the country is subject to the US economic blockade, and even beyond that.

The second restriction is that the most dynamic sectors in the international economy are organised in global production chains under transnational hegemony, and development opportunities for a nation like Cuba are increasingly defined by the frameworks and evolution of these chains.[22] The preceding does not mean that the nation-state has lost relevance in the field of development. In fact, the opposite is true; the nation-state can and does act as one of the principal 'localising' forces of global production. Nonetheless, what is important here, is that the advancement of a country in ascendant trajectories of technological learning is more a function of its progress in the context of international production chains than the self-centred promotion of 'national industries'.

The third important restriction in Cuba's case is that economic restructuring must be part of a broader process that transcends the partial reform of the traditional mechanisms of central planning.[23] The likelihood of successful reorientation of the economic structure is minimal without relatively

21   Carranza (1997).
22   Monreal (2000).
23   Carranza, Gutiérrez, Monreal (1996).

significant transformations of the basic economic institutions and ownership consistent with socialist principles.

Finally, another very important restriction is that the identification, selection and development of the sectors and activities that will constitute the new economic structure should be understood as aspects of a complex process that will be determined largely by social and political considerations. No transformation of the economic structure would be sustainable over the long term if it takes place at the cost of the welfare, expectations, identity and culture of the population.

Cuba's 'forced march' international reinsertion in the 1990s has been a key factor in the economic survival of the Cuban people, in the preservation of important social gains and in the continuation of the political system established by the Revolution in 1959. Nevertheless, the partial change in the economic structure during this period and the foreseeable dynamic in the current patterns of accumulation have not been transformed, nor does it appear that they will alter the economic structure to the degree required for advancement towards development in the current international context.

In sum, during the critical period of the last decade of the twentieth century, the Cuban economy achieved a great deal considering that the difficult conditions caused more than one analyst to doubt its ability to survive. Growth recovered in 1994 and has been sustained for seven years, the country's international insertion has been substantially modified, the domestic economy is more dynamic and has greater macroeconomic equilibrium, new production and service sectors have been consolidated and the government has gained greater experience in managing economic policy in the new international conditions and under strong external pressures, especially the North American blockade.

Notable improvements have been achieved in all the areas that the crisis demanded responses, but in no case have the tensions and risks been definitively overcome. Macroeconomic adjustment is still insufficient and continues to generate economic and social tensions. Restructuring the economy's system of organisation needs to be completed and levels of efficiency need to be raised so that a model of intensive growth can be articulated. Growth has recovered but it still has not regained the losses accumulated in the first several years of the crisis, and balance of payments deficits persist. Finally, a new economic development strategy that would take advantage of Cuba's notable strengths in the context of the global economy has still not been explicitly defined.

Thus, the first decade of the twenty-first century is again a challenging period for the Cuban economy, a challenge that requires creativity. The capacity demonstrated in overcoming the difficulties of the last decade of the twentieth century augurs well for the attainment of the goals that have yet to be achieved.

PART 2
ELEMENTS OF POTENTIAL
DEVELOPMENT STRATEGIES IN CUBA

CHAPTER 3

Foreign Direct Investment in Cuba: Recent Experience and Prospects

Omar Everleny Pérez Villanueva

Introduction

An important part of the Cuban government's response to the crisis of the 1990s focused on opening the country to foreign resources in order to capture foreign exchange, which had reached minimal levels, in the shortest time possible. This economic opening was critical for reactivating the economy and confronting the reality of the global economy and Cuba's insertion in it.

The most important aspects of the economic opening on the international plane were the promotion of and opening to investments of foreign capital, trade restructuring and the accelerated development of international tourism.

By mid-1993 it had become evident that fundamental changes in consumption, international relations and the socioeconomic structure of the country were necessary. At this point Cuba initiated a process of complex and experimental economic transformations and restructuring involving the implementation of numerous economic policies. Nonetheless, because of the contradictory nature of these transformations, and given the peculiarities of the Cuban situation, there has been an effort to maintain social stability and political control above all else. The economic changes have not been linear, and therefore have followed a trajectory of phases or stages of greater or lesser transformational dynamism.[1]

The problems associated with foreign financing of the Cuban economy have become a priority issue given the impossibility of generating domestic savings sufficient for growth and development. The great dilemma was that financing was needed for growth, yet it was possible to get financing without achieving growth. Thus, it was absolutely necessary to maintain the recovery initiated in 1994 with foreign resources allocated to those areas of rapid recovery that were technologically advanced, such as mining, tourism, communications and products for tourism.

Foreign financing has traditionally been considered an important complement to domestic savings to increase investment and to stimulate sustained economic growth, but the island's restrictions on obtaining capital are well known, and its exports are not well diversified.

---

1 Romero (1996).

Growth, Financing and Technology

Developing countries generally have abundant sources of talent, productive capacity and natural resources, among other resources. Transforming these resources into effective instruments for development requires constant increase in its potential economic utility through investments: investments in specialised knowledge and human resources, and investments in physical capacity for production (this is the case of Cuba and other countries that invested heavily in human resources). This requires that the resources that are acquired be fully channelled through effective distribution.[2]

The investments necessary to transform those resources into agents of development must be centred on industrial upgrading, or technological improvement of existing industries or of the industries that are created. The volume of capital available for this purpose will be one of the principal long-term determining factors for growth and economic development.

Clearly the principal source of financing for development is domestic savings. Nevertheless, during the launch period, and even during consolidation, additional resources in the form of capital, technology or markets are always necessary, whether through bilateral or multilateral mechanisms. Gaining access to those resources is the short and medium term challenge facing the Cuban economy.

Efficient use of resources in production, avoiding unnecessary impacts on consumption, the generation of savings in foreign exchange that amply covers international obligations and the maintenance of stable financial flows in rational conditions are essential requirements to ensure that foreign financing does not create more lasting problems than solutions.

Foreign financing in the form of development assistance has been very limited in the Cuban case, producing few results. Soft credit, which is necessary for some goals, has not been available to Cuba for many years, both for political and economic reasons.

For a country that aspires to get beyond its underdevelopment, foreign credit or loans should enable the mobilisation of material and technical resources to promote new production that generates domestic savings, acquires technologies and raises the level of exports necessary to pay for financing. Beginning in 1991 most of the loans Cuba has received have been short-term export credits with high interest rates. Some countries, including Mexico, Argentina, Italy, Germany, France, Chile and Spain, have offered guarantees to businesses that trade with Cuba, making it possible to maintain commercial ties with those countries.

Contracts with suppliers are established under conditions that could also be described as tense; credit with favourable conditions is scarce. And as for

2   UNCTAD (1987).

foreign aid, donations and scientific-technical collaboration have experienced little increase.

The interaction of all these financing sources has allowed the country to obtain resources to attenuate the difficulties and implement reform, but these are insufficient, costly and offer few opportunities for growth until some problems are solved, especially the accumulated foreign debt and the servicing of that debt.

The easiest means for Cuba to obtain financial resources, and consequently, the technology capable of improving industrial competitiveness, has been direct investment. Foreign Direct Investment (FDI) has played a significant role in financing development in many countries, especially in Asia, where results are encouraging, and in some Latin American countries. But it is not sufficient for the recipient country to improve its foreign investment policy for FDI to play a more important role in financing development; a national effort to resuscitate growth and financial viability must be undertaken.

Given an international context that is unfavourable to Cuba, including the strengthening of the US economic blockade, it is necessary to obtain greater amounts and higher quality sources of foreign financing. In addition, a systematic focus for the country's insertion in the global economy that prioritises activities to stimulate domestic savings must be established.

Economic restructuring in Cuba has been gradual since the island does not have much room for manoeuvre, nor can large or complicated risks be taken. The current international economic isolation imposes additional limitations on the feasible rate of national reconstruction. For example, a lot could be gained through the easing of tensions between Cuba and the United States, which could at least bring about the attenuation of the blockade imposed on the country. The need for stable sources of external financing has led to promoting and liberalising the foreign investment regime.

It is important to note that technology transfer can be accomplished through foreign investment, and thus, foreign investment can be classified in two categories: Passive and Active effects (see Appendix 1).

The active effects are very relevant for Cuba in the future, given the existing scientific potential, since engineering programmes or contracts can be undertaken with centres for research and development, and producers of capital goods. Additionally, adaptation and improvement of local technology can occur, along with other programmes that include training in foreign countries.[3]

In the Cuban case, demonstration effects (passive) have been the most common outcome of foreign investment, with good results. New technology has been introduced and has been effectively deployed, leading to an improvement in productive indicators.

---

3   Dahlman (1988)

Global trends have caused developing countries to open up more and liberalise foreign investment to a greater extent, given that access to high technology can only be obtained if greater control is given to the foreign investor who has the technology. However, it has become increasingly necessary to invest simultaneously in developing technology domestically.

Karl Dahlman, a World Bank economist, posits that countries aspiring to overcome underdevelopment should elaborate a strategy that increases technological growth and the role of foreign investment in that growth. He proposes three components that must be included in this strategy:

1.   Be able to take advantage of and use foreign technology, much as Japan, South Korea and Taiwan were adept at attracting different forms of foreign technology.

2.   In any industrial sector there is a very large dispersion of productivity. Therefore, efforts must be made to increase productivity through the diffusion and extension of the technology obtained.

3.   The role of research centres should not be merely to 'reinvent the wheel', but to truly provide assistance to the industrial sector in order to create, diffuse and adapt technologies.

To attract foreign investment in such a way that it contributes to the economic development of the country, one cannot wait for it to come, it must be promoted by identifying the type of industry that is desirable and researching and administering information on what type of technology exists and who possesses it. Cuba's challenge is to acquire the most modern technologies through FDI and incorporate it with the active effect described by Dahlman.

Foreign Direct Investment in Cuba

In the 1990s Cuba began a process of reinsertion in the international market for which the island has few apparent advantages after more than 30 years of virtual absence. An important aspect of this economic opening is the economic associations with foreign capital, or joint ventures.

The decapitalisation that began in 1990 had a powerful effect on industry, which was an important impetus for reaching out to FDI. The entire productive infrastructure was subjected to strong pressures: deterioration of basic resources, insufficient maintenance and overloads generated by use in excess of technical capacity. Thus, the lack of raw materials and the need for industrial reconversion created by reinsertion into increasingly monopolised and demanding markets brought pressure for perfecting business practices and therefore the search for technologies. In the experience of Cuba in the 1990s this was possible through associations with foreign capital.

The process of opening to foreign capital has been oriented to the solution of problems specific to the Cuban economic growth process, including: diversification of exports in quality and quantity, acquisition of raw materials, need for fresh capital, insertion into new markets, acquisition of advanced technologies and introduction to modern practices of economic management.

The potentially dynamic effect of foreign capital is especially pronounced for small and medium-sized enterprises in Cuba. These units need to be promoted along with development of the infrastructures necessary to boost levels of competitiveness.

Viewed prospectively, FDI flows depend on the depth of economic reform, the sustainability of recovery and measures to reduce the effects of the North American trade policies of extraterritoriality, in particular the Helms-Burton Law, which was adopted by the United States in 1996 in an effort to strengthen the economic blockade of the island. Some recent contributions to investment theory that consider uncertainty and the irreversibility of decisions provide a relevant analytical framework to explain the cautious behaviour of some foreign investors in Cuba, despite improvements in the economy and other factors that should stimulate that investment.[4] Despite the caution of investors towards Cuba, the number of joint ventures has been increasing. Considering that the most powerful country in the world is attempting to impede the flow of FDI to Cuba, which affects the so-called country risk,[5] the amount of foreign investment has much greater significance for Cuba than emerges from a simple qualitative comparison with investment flows to other countries in the region.

At first glance, the growth sustained since 1990 seems to confirm that there is a favourable pattern of investment in the domestic sphere since the positive elements have a stronger balance than the adversities. For example, between 1988 and 2000 more than 530 international economic associations (joint ventures) were formed in Cuba, with 392 associations remaining active at the end of 2000. The following graph shows the evolution of operating firms by year of incorporation. Notably, the number of firms dissolved for various reasons, including the termination of the contracted period, is less than 20 per cent of the businesses incorporated.

If a correlation is established between the indicator for gross fixed capital formation at current prices between 1991 and 1999, US$21.4 billion,[6] and government figures for FDI in Cuba during that period, US$1.577 billion, the resulting indicator is seven per cent. This is comparable to average

4   Vera and Molina (1999).
5   Most of the agencies or publications specialising in country risk have always placed Cuba among the most risky countries for investment for several reasons, including macroeconomic indicators, especially trade deficits, debt, the US blockade, etc.
6   ONE (1998) and BCC (1999).

world figures, although in Cuba's case these sums are still far from meeting the needs of the national economy.

Figure 3.1: Active and Dissolved Joint Ventures by Year of Incorporation

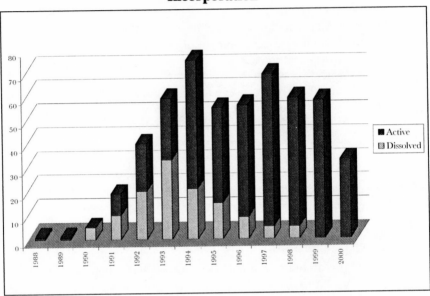

Source: Statistics from the Ministry of Foreign Investment and Collaboration. February 2001.

As far as the qualitative and quantitative effects are concerned foreign investments have impacted on the work of some sectors, principally in tourism, mining, fuel, agriculture, communications, industry and services.

It is important to recognise that after a decade of foreign capital in Cuba (in the post-1959 period), it has undergone a maturation process with positive results. For example, foreign investment increased from 1998 to 1999 in the following:

Total Sales	26 per cent
Exports	25 per cent
Direct Income	27 per cent

Figure 3.2: Indicators of Foreign Investment in Cuba, 1992–2000

Total Sales

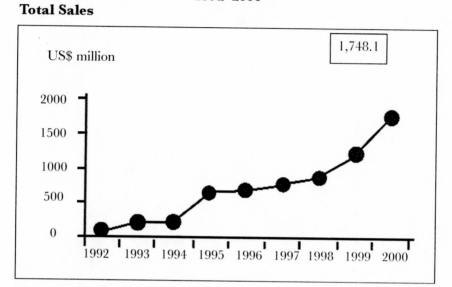

Direct Income

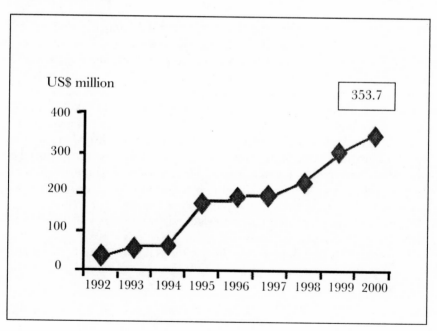

Total Sales

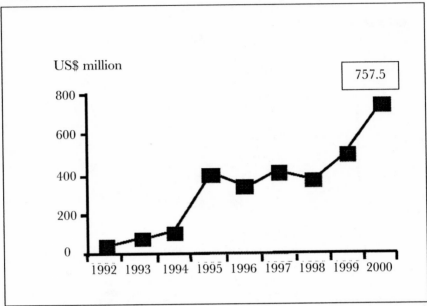

US$ million

757.5

Beginning in 1998, economic associations directed at new activities emerged, including public services. For example, in 1999 the company ENERGAS (Cuban-Canadian) was formed to produce electricity using the gas accompanying the oil wells in the zone north of Havana. At the same time, the first business totally financed by foreign capital (from Panama) was created to construct and operate an electric generating plant on the Isla de la Juventud. Financial institutions were formed with Cuban banks, such as the joint venture between Banco Popular de Ahorro and Caja Madrid de España.

In 1999 58 international economic associations were created. The most representative associations include the one by Habanos, S.A. with the European entity Altadis for marketing Cuban tobacco, and the creation of the firm Aguas del Oeste for managing water service for some municipalities on Havana's west side. In the paper industry, three associations were created with Canadian firms to renovate existing factories in Cárdenas, Santa Cruz del Norte and Jatibonico.

In terms of the number of mixed firms formed, the greatest percentage is linked to the industrial sector, followed by tourism and to a lesser extent in services.

Figure 3.3: Associations with Foreign Capital by Activity in 2000

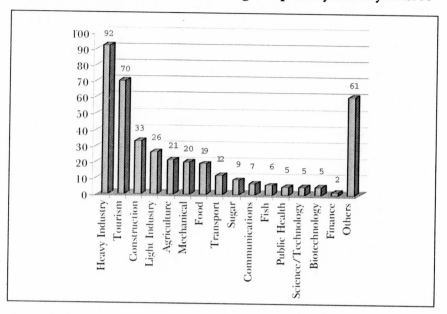

Source: Statistics from the Ministry of Foreign Investment and Collaboration (February 2001).

Additionally, there are tangible and intangible benefits; externalities are produced from the joint ventures that are difficult to quantify, such as management capacity obtained by Cuban administrators.

The data on employment generation shows it is not significant, since this type of business generally comes with greater automation and more efficient systems of organisation. Job growth has not been dynamic, although the new jobs are in relatively high-income areas. In 1995 there were already 13,800 workers employed in the mixed firms and by 1999 the number had increased to 19,800 workers, less than 0.5 per cent of the total employed in the country. In 2000, the average wage of workers in these businesses was about 243 pesos, yet their average income, which included other benefits, was 334 pesos, way above the national average. The fact that compared to workers in other countries in similar positions, Cubans receive a lower wage and fewer economic benefits should not be minimised, although the state guarantees those workers other social benefits, such as free universal health care and education. Thus, in the strict sense, the real income of those workers is greater than the figures for nominal income suggest.

If the efficiency of the mixed firms is analysed from a sample of those located in Havana, where most such firms are concentrated, spending on wages in pesos in commercial production in 2000 was 5.80 cents, signifi-

cantly lower than the 19.08 cents spent by state enterprises and also less
than the 13.27 cents of the Cuban commercial enterprises (state firms that
operate in a more decentralised and flexible framework than conventional
state enterprises).

Although FDI originates from more than 40 countries, it is fundamentally concentrated in the following countries:

Figure 3.4: Associations with Foreign Capital by Country of Origin in 2000

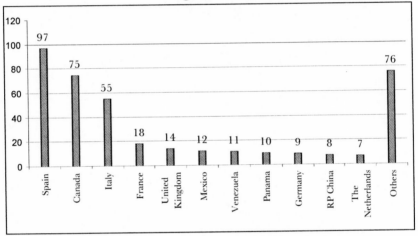

Source: Ministry of Foreign Investment and Collaboration (February 2001).

Foreign Direct Investment in Selected Industries

The analysis of FDI in certain Cuban industries, especially those with significant outcomes, such as tourism, beverages and alcohol, communications
and others, clearly indicates that industrial upgrading has taken place in
Cuban enterprises, and some global production networks have included
Cuban companies.

Tourism

Beginning in the 1990s the tourist industry introduced new operational modes
through diverse forms of association with foreign capital that led to a restructuring of that sector, creating the chains Gran Caribe, Horizontes and Isla
Azul together with the corporations CUBANACAN and GAVIOTA. These
organisations group together different types of hotels, restaurants and other
specialised deals.

The dynamism of the Cuban tourist sector has attracted FDI with the
number of visitors increasing at average rates of 18 per cent between 1990

and 1999, increases in gross income exceeding 30 per cent annually and room construction rising by 13 per cent annually.

Application of the theory of Oligopolistic Rivalry and its analysis of prevention leads to the conclusion that many foreign firms that today show interest in the Cuban market do so predicting that in the future more powerful businesses will establish themselves, including those from the United States, or that Cuba will have access to the North American tourist market.

In 1990 Cuba received 327,000 tourists[7] with 12,900 rooms available for international tourism, most of which required renovation. Management capacity was scarce in the tourist centres because this activity had not been prioritised for many years. A key element in the long-term tourist programmes that were initiated at the beginning of the 1990s was the transfer of management skills through hotel administration contracts and the creation of mixed enterprises in hotels and the hotel industry.

In 1999, the number of joint ventures for hotel construction reached seven, which led to 19 foreign hotel chains operating in the country. Some of these hotels are considered among the best at the international level, such as the Sol-Meliá chain, which after acquiring the TRYP chain has become the tenth largest hotel chain in the world. Other important companies from Italy, Canada and Germany have initiated operations in Cuba, and have thus included the country in their international circuits. Thus, at the close of 2000 there were 3,679 hotel rooms in mixed firms and more than 6,000 were constructed with foreign partners. There were 50 hotels under foreign administration, which amount to 15,870 rooms, or 50 per cent of the hotel rooms for international tourism operating under hotel management contracts.[8]

Foreign capital in tourist enterprises is greater than US$1,000 million, with more than 100 associations with foreign capital involved in tourism, of which more than 30 were classified as hotels.

Agreements in tourism include restrictions. For example, foreign direct investment in Havana, Varadero and Cayo Largo is generally conditioned on the international partner's investment in other areas of the country. This is done to avoid overloading the effects of FDI in certain areas.

Tourism is itself a large importer. Thus, Cuba should increase national production of some goods and develop hotel-related infrastructure even

---

7   ONE (1998).

8   The rooms that are managed by administration contracts are not FDI, although the UNCTAD methodology considers them to be FDI. UNCTAD, *World Investment Report* (1997), in its appendix of definitions states, 'Foreign direct investors may also obtain an effective voice in the management of another business entity through means other than acquiring an equity stake. These are non-equity forms of FDI, and they include, inter alia, subcontracting, management contracts, turnkey agreements, franchising licensing and product sharing. Data on transnational corporate activity through these forms are usually not separately identified in balance of payments statistics,' p. 296.

more, particularly in areas such as construction of theme parks, golf courses and marinas. Cuba is already becoming part of the Caribbean tourist cir-
cuit, so its investment programme in the coming years should be directed at
activities that will interest international hotel chains.

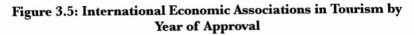

**Figure 3.5: International Economic Associations in Tourism by
Year of Approval**

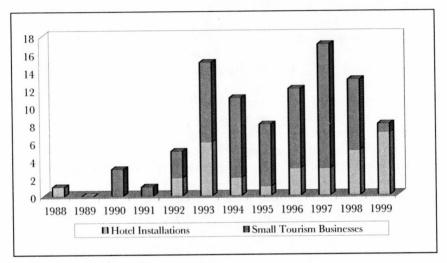

If Cuba does not change its productive structure to meet the needs of
tourism in the medium term, it will have to import US$3 billion annually to
do so. So that this does not happen there is already an effort to generate
national supplies using national and foreign financing to renovate existing
installations and create new productive and service capacities. In order to
reduce imports of inputs for tourism, competitive companies are needed
that meet international standards, and this is where FDI is necessary.

In sum, tourism has been acting as the engine for the Cuban economy
and it is likely that it will continue to do so. It is thus vital that plans for
expansion of the tourist sector include (as already has begun) policies that
incorporate FDI not only in tourist activities but also in the rest of the areas
that form an integral part of the development of Cuban tourism.

Mining

Cuba has important multi-metal mineral ore deposits. The country is especially rich in nickel and cobalt reserves, which are among the largest in the
world. In 1999 a record level of nickel production was achieved with 66,503

tons, and of these almost 50 per cent were obtained in the joint venture Moa Nickel.

Within the productive sphere, there is a concentration of projects under implementation and in contract in solid mining for the short and medium term, with varying degrees of foreign interest. There are more than 50 agreements with foreign companies to develop geological or exploration projects in a territory of some 40,000 square kilometres, with 37 prospective areas.

Work is being conducted in the evaluation, prospecting and exploitation of deposits of copper, gold, silver, chromium, magnesium, lead, zinc and nickel. Bilateral accords between foreign companies and the Cuban enterprise Geominera SA are based on risk contracts. They also include marketing of the minerals, with the exception of nickel, which due to the volume of reserves has an independent structure.[9]

There are three types of mining contracts:

1. Contracts in which foreign companies assume the risk of prospecting.

2. Exploration contracts, in which risk is shared between the Cuban and foreign parties.

3. Joint ventures in mining exploration.

The most promising contracts are those with Holmer Gold Mines, whose explorations have discovered gold, lead, copper and zinc in Pinar del Río; Caribgold Resources from Canada, which has discovered gold in Camague; and the Miramar Mining Company, which is operating a gold mine on the Isla de la Juventud. These contracts entail significant technological advances, which has enabled the exploration and extraction of minerals that were inaccessible with the previously existing technology.

The Case of Nickel

Beginning in 1992, sulphur from the Cuban Ni+Co was sent to the Sherrit company refinery in Canada, and in 1994 three joint ventures were created between the Unión del Níquel from Cuba and the Canadian company Sherrit International: Moa Nickel, S.A., which includes the mining operations and nickel processing in the plant 'Pedro Soto Alba' in Moa, Cuba, The Cobalt Refinery Co., Inc., that encompasses the installations in Port Saskatchewan, in Alberta, Canada for refining the mineral, and the International Cobalt Co., Inc., based in the Bahamas, for marketing activities.

9   Geominera SA has agreements with the following companies: Republic Goldfields, Minamerica, Metal Mining Corporation, Miramar Mining, Heath & Sherwood International Inc., Mining Italian Spa, Macdonald Mines Exploration Ltd., Rhodes Mining NL, Carigold, Holmer Gold Mines Ltd., Bolivar Goldfields Ltd., Scintrex, Joutel Resources Ltd., Ninanfrica SA, among others.

As a result of the agreements, the Canadian company became the owner of half the Cuban enterprise and its deposits, while the Cuban company acquired half the ownership of the Canadian refinery and of the third largest joint venture in the world marketing nickel and cobalt products.[10]

This joint venture has introduced technological improvements, leading to lowered production costs and increased volumes of production reaching levels of plant design capacity. The company has the following well-defined objectives:

(a) Raise quality and costs to international levels.

(b) Increase the recovery of nickel and cobalt contained in the mineral to international levels.

(c) Cost reduction through improved energy efficiency in the plant.

The results from this plant as well as the modernisation of the other two plants in Cuba and the renovation of all mining equipment, such as trucks and conveyer belts, have been impressive. Cuba accounted for ten per cent of the global production of cobalt in 1999 and has become the sixth largest producer of nickel. With sales to more than 30 countries, new production records have been achieved.

Petroleum and Gas

The association with foreign capital in this area has produced heartening results with the introduction of the most modern technologies available internationally. There are 20 risk contracts for the prospecting and exploitation of petroleum signed with important companies from Canada, France, the United Kingdom, Sweden and Brazil, among others.

Foreign companies have introduced top level technologies that have enabled increased production in crude oil and associated gas and its more efficient use, including the following:

1. Horizontal and multi-pipe perforation, which reduces perforation points by four or five times and raises production levels to five or six times above traditional levels.

2. Improvements in the ROTAFLEX pumping system, thus increasing the productivity per well by two or three times.

3. Use of the associated gas in generating electricity and domestic consumption, eliminating pollution and recovering sulphur.

10   Figueras (1998).

4. Construction of gas and oil pipelines, reducing transportation costs and increasing security.

5. Construction of plants for the treatment of crude oil capable of reducing the percentage of water and salts and eliminating sulphur, which saves time and energy.

These cutting-edge technologies have increased the production of petroleum and gas; for example, the production of crude oil increased by a factor of six between 1991 and 2000, as indicated in the following graphs.

Figure 3.6: Production of Crude Oil

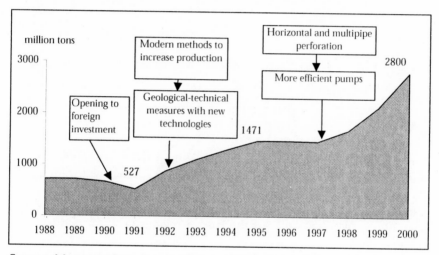

Source: Ministry of Basic Industry, *Report on Business Opportunities* (Havana, October).

These levels of production have impacted import substitution in the year 2000 by more than US$410 million through the use of national oil and gas in electricity production, cement, nickel and domestic gas, among others.

**Figure 3.7: Increase in the Use of Accompanying Gas
Eliminating Pollution**

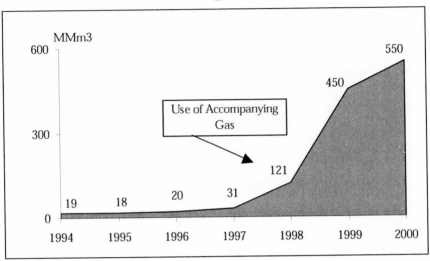

The joint venture between a Cuban firm and the Canadian company
Sherrit, ENERGAS, with levels of investment of around US$150 million,
has constructed a 210 megawatt plant with significant environmental
impact. Through the use of the natural gas associated with petroleum
extraction, which had polluted the coastal regions north of Havana and
Matanzas, it was possible to recover 20,000 tons of sulphur and 12,000 tons
of pressurised liquid gas that went into the atmosphere, while producing
electricity. In 2001, a US$120 million investment in a new 150 megawatt
expansion of the plant will be completed with the installation of two combined gas and cycle turbines.

The exploration of a new marine zone in the west, called an Exclusive
Economic Zone, is divided into 59 blocks encompassing an area of more
than 112,000 square kilometres for risk exploration with foreign companies.
This exploration could increase the large volumes currently obtained,
which together with new technologies will increase oil production by 4.75
million tons and gas production by 1.385 billion cubic metres in 2005.[11]

Telecommunications

One of the most important FDI agreements in Cuba was the creation in
1994 of ETECSA, a joint venture between the Cuban telephone company

11 MINBAS (2000).

and the Mexican company CITEL. That venture involved more than US$1,500 million with a 55-year concession and US$740 million in the first seven years for modernisation of the enterprise. Cuba controls 51 per cent of the shares.

This agreement was very sui generis in that it covered all of Cuban communications and created organisational structures that were very centralised, as opposed to the territorial organisation that predominated in the 1970s and 1980s. Already by 1995 the company was billing close to US$145 million, with a net of US$108 million, although international mergers in the industry have had the effect of reducing income from these services.

In 1995 CITEL, which originally owned a 49 per cent share of the company, sold 25 per cent of its shares to STET International, an Italian firm. In 1997 STET bought additional shares that had been owned by CITEL. With that transaction the Italian company became the majority foreign shareholder. In 1997 the Sherritt Corporation of Canada acquired part of the communications firm CUBACEL, and Sherritt has discussed the purchase of shares with ETECSA.

FDI in this area has had a very positive effect. The ETECSA joint venture put an end to the serious deterioration of telephone service in the country, constructed very modern digital plants, installed microwaves in several parts of the country, introduced up to date technology such as fibre optics in the local networks, and modernised the vehicle fleet. Most importantly, the improvement in service has been palpable to the users, since for the first time in 30 years new services have been offered to the general population. It is expected that within the next few years there will be 20 telephones for every 100 inhabitants.

One of the technological advantages of this type of business with internationally recognised European firms is that service quality has improved significantly. Currently available services are superior to those obtained from obsolete plants.

Food and Beverage Industry

One of the industries with the most extensive involvement of foreign capital is the Ministry of the Food Products Industry (MINAL), which at the close of 2000 oversaw 16 joint ventures.

In 1996 the Corporación Alimentaria S.A. (Coralsa) was established with the objective of developing associations with foreign capital to find markets, technology and financing for the development of the rest of the MINAL industries, with the exception of the production of alcoholic beverages. The corporation also seeks to strengthen the income potential of the resulting associations. Currently there are 16 joint ventures and 12 associations for co-operative production. (See Appendix 2.)

The 16 joint ventures in MINAL produce six per cent of the industry's total production, but they are a very valuable asset in terms of participation in the domestic market in foreign currency and exports. Significantly, not only have sales from joint ventures increased, technological improvements in production quality and in packaging and product presentation have been introduced as well.

Noteworthy companies include the firm Havana Club International, made up of a partnership between Havana Rum & Liquors and the prestigious French firm Pernod Ricard, which is co-owner of 50 per cent of the second most important rum in the world, Havana Club. This company's sales have increased from 250,000 cases in 1994 to 1,250,000 cases in 1999. Current investment in the business will enable the company to reach five million cases within ten years.[12]

Figure 3.8: Sales of Joint Ventures in MINAL (millions of US $)

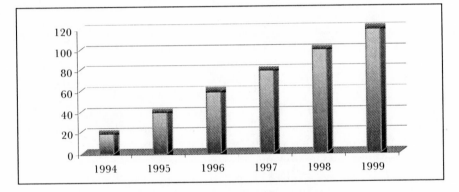

Source: Cámara de Comercio, *Cuba. Foreign Trade*, no. 3 (2000).

In the meat industry there is Industrias Cárnicas Hispano-Cubanas (Bravo, S.A.), a joint venture between the Cuban company Coralsa and Provalca of Valencia, Spain. This company has the advantages of the experience and know-how of the Spanish meat industry, adapted to Cuban conditions. It is a leading firm in terms of return on investment in the foodstuff sector and is expanding to the Caribbean and Central American markets. The company introduced cutting edge technology, which led to growth in production by 30 per cent in 1999.

Los Portales, S.A. is a partnership of Coralsa and the Swiss group Nestlé that produces and markets the biggest selling soft drinks and mineral waters in the country. The company owns several mineral water bottling plants. It

12 Cámara de Comercio (2000).

introduced the use of plastic (polyethylene terephalate) containers for soft drinks and introduced new lines of canned beverages. Annual sales are increasing greatly and improved quality has led to expansion into markets in the Caribbean and MERCOSUR. The capital contribution of foreign partners is around US$80 million, which together with the Cuban contribution makes a total investment of US$118 million.[13]

Companies relying on sales in the domestic foreign currency market have retooled their relationships with the national agricultural sector by entering agreements for high quality raw materials in exchange for advances of inputs and financing to the producers at mutually advantageous rates.

The integration of agro-industrial relationships into more dynamic, direct and less bureaucratic forms is an issue that should be more fully developed in the future, along with consideration of the new forms of production that have emerged in the agricultural sector.

This type of joint venture has on balance been positive for Cuba, in that Cuban products have reached markets and Cuban companies have benefited from the experience of the rigours of competition. Thus, it is desirable to expand these possibilities in the near future.

Nevertheless, it is necessary to eliminate the current division in the markets generated by monetary duality (markets in national currency and foreign currency) and apply measures to reduce dollarisation that favour greater relationships among producers. This is one of the most important problems inherent in the attraction of foreign investment flows.

Conclusions

- The problems associated with external financing have become a first order task given the impossibility of generating sufficient levels of domestic savings for the growth and development of the Cuban economy. But the acquisition of this financing should have an even greater link to access to foreign high technology.
- The strategy that the government should pursue to obtain foreign financing in the amount and of the quality required cannot be delinked from the strategy to generate domestic savings. To the contrary, these should be complementary goals in the process of insertion in the world economy.
- The investments necessary for transforming these resources into agents of development also require financing, and the volume that is available for this objective will be in the long run one of the principal determinative factors for growth and macroeconomic stability.
- The experience of recent years shows the importance of economic policies that maintain a stable investment flow to recipient countries.

13 González (1998).

However, in order to attract significant levels of capital, sound macro-economic policies are not sufficient; deep internal reforms in economic and financial relationships are also necessary.

- Even if and when the strategy and tactics for using foreign capital are well defined, this process will not achieve all the results possible if a series of fundamental transformations are not undertaken. Necessary reforms include increased levels of decentralisation, especially with respect to firm autonomy (managerial improvement should lead to enterprise autonomy); promotion of the role of small and medium businesses; elimination of the current market division arising from monetary duality; and implementation of an appropriate exchange rate for the Cuban peso.

- From a prospective view, foreign financial flows depend on the depth and direction of reform, the sustainability of recovery and the coherence and intelligence that are deployed to reduce the effects of the US extraterritorial practice of the blockade policy, especially the Helms-Burton Law.

- The growing level of speculation in international financial activity exacerbates the exclusion of underdeveloped economies in that the level of risk and exposure in capital transactions increases, especially in the short term. Thus, Cuba should continue the process of opening to foreign investment, and improving the rules that are established for it, so that it can be obtained without transgressing the limits that jeopardise control of the nation's fundamental riches.

- Finally, the experience of the analysed sectors leads to the conclusion that the foreign investment process in Cuba has been successful at acquiring technologies and management capacities, and has achieved industrial upgrading in those areas where it has a strong presence. This success should be a guide for improving the development of other sectors or areas for greater dynamism in world trade so that Cuba can insert itself in the world economy as it is evolving in the new century.

Appendix 1

Forms of Technology Transfer through Foreign Direct Investment

1 – PASSIVE EFFECTS
A. Experiences acquired by nationals and transmitted through turnover.
B. Demonstration effect. This is greater when the investment is in a new industry for the recipient country.
C. Contact with suppliers of raw materials and components.
D. Contact with distributors.
2 – ACTIVE EFFECTS
A. Training programmes in the country and abroad.
B. Technical assistance programmes for suppliers of raw materials and components.
C. Technical assistance programmes and training for distributors and repair service providers.
D. Contracts with FDI institutes, machine and equipment producers, and engineering firms for services and technological equipment.
E. Adaptation and technological improvement used in the country although not directly linked to FDI.
F. Research and development efforts in the country. For foreign companies that engage in FDI, almost all their research and development takes place in the country of origin.

Source: Dahlman (1988)

Appendix 2

Associations with Foreign Capital in the Food and Beverage Industry

Companies	Producer	Production and Marketing	Marketing	Objective
Bravo S.A		X		Meats
Campo Florido S.A.		X		Meat byproducts
Tasajo Uruguay S.A.	X			Meats
Carnes del Mercosur S.A.			X	Meats
Bucanero S.A.	X			Beer
Biotek S.A.		X		Soy research
Río Zaza Ingelco	X			Dairy
CORALAC S.A.		X		Dairy
CORACAN		X		Instant foods
Francesa del Pan	X			Bread
Haricari S.A.			X	Milling
Procesadora de Soya S.A.	X			Soy Products
Stella S.A.			X	Sweets
Meztler S.A.		X		Sweets
Cubagua S.A.	X			Soft drinks and waters
Vinos Fantinel		X		Wines
Los Portales S.A.		X		Soft drinks and waters
Papas & Co	X			Snacks

Source: Dirección de Planificación. MINAL (1999).

CHAPTER 4

Cuba's Model of Industrial Growth: Current Problems and Perspectives

Hiram Marquetti Nodarse and Anicia García Capote

The crisis of the 1990s had a negative impact on the Cuban manufacturing industry, paralysing the industrialisation process that had developed over the preceding decades. A model of industrial development based on a leading role for the traditional export sector was undermined significantly. In this context, efforts were made to preserve the industrial fabric that had resulted from the industrialisation process while at the same time evaluating alternative options for a new model of industrial development. The objective was to promote the international reinsertion of the Cuban economy while avoiding an externally-induced collapse of the local productive system. Given the significance of industrial manufacturing to domestic production, this sector would play a crucial role in the economic transformations during the 1990s, a decade during which Cuban industry responded with partial success to the challenge of improving the international economic insertion of the island.

Because of the favourable impact of reforms applied during the 1990s, macroeconomic stabilisation was accompanied by a relatively stable performance of the industrial sector. This was due primarily to the ability of industry to respond to the growth of effective demand stimulated by several specific factors, such as the opening to foreign direct investment, the increased flexibility of mechanisms of management of foreign trade, and the sustained growth of tourism and the internal market operating in hard currency. Indeed, the evolution of these sources of demand has helped to maintain the overall dynamic of economic recovery and to foster new sources of accumulation, which have made possible a gradual restoration of the material and financial bases of economic growth.

The potential impact of this shifting structure of demand is all the more significant to the extent that it tends to become a basic support for a 'new model' of industrial growth. Thus, the past decade has witnessed a gradual adaptation of productive capacities to real demand as enterprises tend to concentrate their efforts in those productive areas that have real potential for generating profits. In this sense, the tendency toward modifying traditional productive and managerial profiles has gathered momentum across a variety of industrial sectors.

Significantly, this new model of industrial development does not fully replace the previous model. On the contrary, it seeks to take maximum

advantage of its potential and to promote its gradual restructuring with minimal destruction of existing productive forces. Here, the advances of the industrial sector attest to the wisdom of the overall and sectoral measures applied
by the government in the aforementioned period, particularly those aimed at
enterprise organisation and management. Nevertheless, there remain numerous uncertainties, at least at a general level, that will demand future responses.
Among these, the absence of an explicit competitiveness policy or an effective
regulatory framework for enterprise competition are especially noteworthy:
these gaps account both for a tendency toward the emergence of monopolistic structures in the economy and for the lack of appropriate correspondence
between regulatory and revenue-raising functions of state institutions. In practice, these shortcomings have prevented a more intensive deployment of
reserves of efficiency that exist latently in the Cuban economy.

This chapter presents a general characterisation of the new model of
industrial development and analyses the principal restrictions that it con-
fronts, both with regard to technology and in terms of the new demands that
accompany Cuba's quest for reinsertion into the international economy.

Crisis and Adjustment in the Industrial Sector

The changes that took place in the external context of the island at the close
of the 1980s provoked a noteworthy decline in the industrial sector and
even brought about a crisis in the model of industrialisation that the country had developed after its incorporation into the international socialist division of labour. In response to this situation, there occurred a reassessment
of priorities for industrial development.[1]

The abrupt rupture of economic relations with the former socialist countries implied an important challenge for the preservation of Cuban industry
as a key link in national economic development, since achievements of the
sector were increasingly based on financial facilities provided by those countries. To this was added, at a structural level, the fact that the industrial capabilities that Cuba had developed were built upon a technological base that
was notably backward by world standards, with high consumption levels of
energy, fuel and raw materials, inflexible production arrangements and low
levels of internal integration, co-operation and complementarity. This situation obliged the country to consider urgently how the potential of the industrial sector could be achieved in the external reinsertion of the island, thus
avoiding the 'international collapse' of the Cuban economy.[2]

---

1   Some observers consider these steps to be the beginning of a new stage of industrial devel-
     opment in the country (Pons, 1997).
2   Marquetti (1995).

Table 4.1: Decline of Production in Selected Branches of Industry in 1993

	1989=100%
Industrial Sector	41.7%
Energy Infrastructure	72.5%
Export Branches (sugar, nickel, fishing, etc.)	63.2%
Food Consumption Goods	47.2%
Non-Food Consumption Goods	18.2%
Intermediate Goods	35.1%
Capital Goods	24.5%

Source: Author's elaboration based on CEE (1991); García (1996); and relevant ministry reports.

The evolution of the crisis also caused a significant decline in indicators of plant efficiency, which led to a significant increase in the flow of subsidies to different branches of industry. Among the most heavily subsidised were iron metallurgy, apparel, textile, food processing, leather and footwear, as subsidies aimed at enterprise support increased by rates of 12.1 per cent, 30.5 per cent, 25.9 per cent and 11.1 per cent, respectively, between 1989 and 1993.[3]

In this context, the policy criteria applied by the government in the industrial sector reflected the process of adjustment underway in the economy. Corresponding with this logic, those branches of industry capable of generating hard currency, and those that directly or indirectly met basic needs of the population, were given priority. Simultaneously, there began an evaluation of each branch of industry, with the goal of facilitating its participation in the process of external opening.[4] These aspects became the minimal bases for the subsequent design of more specific policies — encompassing organisational and technological change, employment promotion and financing, and criteria for determining wages, investment and development priorities — that in one manner or another were implemented subsequently by the various productive ministries.

One result of the process was the beginning of a search for a 'new model' of industrial development, in which several factors would be combined. In addition to maximum utilisation of advances achieved during the previous industrialisation process, the new model sought to pursue all opportunities to export, to substitute current industrial imports of all kinds,

3   Instituto de Investigaciones Financieras (1995).
4   This refers primarily to foreign direct investment and changes introduced in the management of external trade.

and to increase savings reserves and efficiency.[5] In practice, the articulation of these elements entailed a complex process, not only because it emerged during a context of crisis, but also because: i) the diversification of the productive and industrial fabric that had been achieved with industrialisation was not oriented in real terms to increase the supply of national exports;[6] ii) the industrial development that had been achieved in the past aimed to create a material and productive infrastructure necessary in light of the geographic distance separating Cuba from its principal trade partners, and this had implied a structure in which many characteristics were typical of settings characterised by *inward-oriented* industrialisation.[7]

Alongside these conditions was the fact that in the prevailing circumstances of the 1990s it would prove difficult to preserve the leadership of traditional branches of industry in the context of the new model of development. This was due, among other factors, to transformations of international price structures and their tendency to reward the exploitation of economies of scale, which would pose serious difficulties in a context of major financial restrictions and low rates of accumulation.[8] Despite the objective limitations constraining the development of traditional branches of industry, efforts began to alter their position in the relevant value chains and thus to create conditions that would encourage promotion of *mature production complexes*.[9]

The factors discussed above, along with difficulties facing the country in its attempt to gain access to international markets and the weakness that characterised its productive linkages with other branches of industry, explain why sectors reliant on development of scientific and technical progress — pharmaceutical industry, biotechnology and electronics — were not prepared to lead the process of industrial restructuring and to constitute the core of the new model.[10] Thus, whereas the industrial development pattern model since 1976 was based on the pre-eminence of policies and factors linked to indus-

---

5   The process of industrialisation made possible a significant diversification of the productive structure of the country, a substantial increase in participation of capital goods producing branches in the overall structure of industry, a relative equalisation of levels of industrial development across regions of the country, and achieved partial self-sufficiency in an important array of inputs and productive chains, while encouraging emergence of new activities linked to scientific and technical progress.

6   Marquetti (1998b).

7   The internal market was the beneficiary of more than 70 per cent of the total increase in industrial production between 1976 and 1990.

8   García Hernández (1996). The traditional sector (i.e. sugar, mining) and energy infrastructure absorbed 73 per cent of industrial investment effected between 1976–89, representing by the end of the period two thirds of all assets in the industrial sector.

9   Ramos (1998).

10   Today, most of the impact of these branches is concentrated in import substitution, in maquila assembly activities, international marketing and generation of minimal income through exports (Marquetti, 1999b).

try, conditions reigning after 1990 meant that while industry would remain a strategic priority, its dynamics of transformation and growth would reflect collateral effects of developments in other sectors, such as tourism. The transition from one model to another was determined as well by the need to promote activities that would permit a faster return on investments while at the same time contributing, through hard currency generation, to lowering the balance of payments deficit. Finally, the transition that is underway is not aimed at reducing the weight of the industrial sector. Rather, the changes to date, and the industrial shifts associated with them, seek to enable the manufacturing industry to preserve its leadership with regard to employment, its capacity for generating spillover effects, and its overall economic impact.

Key Factors in the New Pattern of Industrial Growth

The recessive impact of the fiscal adjustment measures adopted during the mid-1990s were virtually cancelled out by the response of Cuban industry to the growth of a new sector of *effective demand* which results from the opening to foreign investment, greater flexibility in managing foreign trade, and the sustained growth of tourism and the hard currency market. At the same time, the evolution of this demand contributed, inertially, to preserving the overall tendency toward economic recovery. In various branches, it actually has contributed to the development of sources of accumulation that are not derived from the central budget.[11] The role of this potential demand is becoming the basic support for the new model of industrial growth.

Figure 4.1: The New Pattern of Industrial Growth

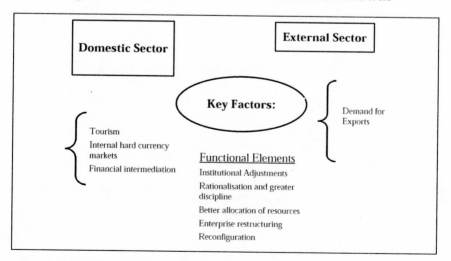

---

11   Marquetti and García (1999).

The principal particularity of the elements underlying this pattern is that they combine the capacity to demand and to supply resources. At the same time, they entail a greater level of support for the service sector, especially in areas that were developed inadequately during the period prior to the crisis, such as business management support services, banking and financial services.

Our analysis has considered the impact of these aspects on the following directions of change: the effect on sectoral leadership potential; the impact on inter-sectoral relations and on linkages between macro, micro and meso levels; the extent of technological transformation; and the probable tendencies toward structural change in the economy. In turn, in keeping with this logic of transformation, there has been success taking advantage of greater intensity of existing reserves of entrepreneurial scale, at the same time that there has been an improvement in the mechanisms for assigning and control of resources. Overall, these aspects have contributed to the positive performance of manufacturing since 1994. It is worth noting as well that the impact of industry on this outcome is even greater when one considers that the fall in industrial production was higher than that of GDP more generally between 1989 and 1993.[12] Nevertheless, since that date, the average annual growth of industry has doubled that of GDP, reaching rates that surpassed six per cent, while that of GDP was below five per cent, as evidenced in Figure 4.2.

Figure 4.2: Trends of GDP and Manufacturing Industry (1990=1.0)

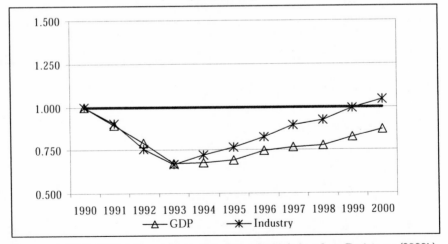

Sources: ONE (2000a); Banco Central de Cuba (2000a); José Luis Rodríguez (2000b), 23 December.

---

12   The reduction of GDP in 1993 compared to 1989 was 34.8 per cent and the decline in industrial production exceeded 37 per cent.

Analysis of trends concerning key elements suggestive of the potential effective demand — international markets, tourism and internal hard currency markets — indicates that exportable production of the Cuban manufacturing industry grew by more than 20 per cent between 1994 and 1998, while the segment of industry destined to tourism and the hard currency market came to satisfy more than 40 per cent of demand. An overall view of these results can be seen in Table 4.2, which groups exports and production directed to satisfying demand of tourism and internal hard currency markets, according to origin as classified by the ministries responsible for the relevant enterprises.

These data show that the greatest potential for growth is concentrated in the internal market, a finding that is consistent with the model of industrial development adopted during the 1960s. In addition, one can see that national industry has potential that remains less than fully satisfied. This situation favours the import substitution process, which in turn contributes to reducing financial outflows in hard currency.

After 1997 production for export exhibited unstable performance, due among other reasons to the negative impact of the international financial crisis which caused erratic prices in the country's principal export products.[13] Nevertheless, production geared toward tourism nearly doubled. A medium term projection suggests that production that meets the requirements of the internal market should acquire the potential to export, though the process is of course complicated. In general, the effect of a takeoff in this segment of effective demand on the evolution of the Cuban economy would remain insufficient to reduce levels of external dependence faced by the island. Still, it would make it possible to maintain a relatively stable dynamic of growth, in which industry would continue to play an essential role. The following section analyses in order of importance the areas that would tend to favour the articulation of a new model of industrial growth.

a) Tourism

Tourism constitutes the leading sector in the new model that is emerging, not only because of its capacity for generating foreign exchange and employment, but also because it is the only sector that has the potential to play this role. The singular status of tourism is due to several factors, including i) there is potential demand that is insufficiently met; ii) it takes place on a relatively large scale and there are strong inter-sectoral linkages that make possible diffusion of sectoral growth to the remainder of the economy; and iii) its rate of growth is susceptible to exogenous forces, that is, it is relatively independent of the overall rate of growth of the economy.[14] Taking advantage of these factors has made

13   Marquetti (1998b, 2000b).
14   Monreal (1999a).

Table 4.2: Trends of Exports and Production Directed to Tourism and Hard Currency

Organ	1996			1997			Total		Percentage Of Commercial Production					
									Exports		Stores		Tourism	
	Exports	Stores	Tourism	Exports	Stores	Tourism	1996	1997	1996	1997	1996	1997	1996	1997
SIME	40.9	9.4	22.9	76.7	21.0	28.8	73.2	126.5	6.0	9.5	1.4	2.6	3.4	3.6
MINBAS	417.1	4.3	0.9	414.9	4.3	2.5	422.3	421.7	20.7	19.5	0.2	0.2	0	0.1
MINIL	4.2	59.7	18.5	17.1	82.0	20.8	82.4	119.9	1.0	4.0	14.1	19.1	4.4	4.8
MIP	126.1	1.8	10.4	126.3	1.9	11.9	138.3	140.1	26.4	26.5	0.4	0.4	2.2	2.5
MINAL	(1)11.2	29.2	48.8	12.5	51.2	60.9	89.2	124.6	1.1	1.1	2.8	4.7	4.7	5.6
MIMC (*)	19.7	-----	-----	33.3	0	7.7	-----	41.0	6.7	10.1	-----	0	-----	2.3
TOTAL	619.2	104.4	101.5	680.8	160.4	132.6	825.1	973.8	12.6	12.9	2.1	3.0	2.1	2.5

SIME: Ministry of Steel and Mechanical Industries (e.g. steel products, machinery and other metal-mechanical products).

MINBAS: Ministry of Basic Industry (e.g. minerals and energy).

MINIL: Ministry of Light Industry (e.g. textiles, shoes, furniture, hygienic and toiletry products).

MIP: Ministry of Fishing Industries (e.g. fresh and frozen fish and shellfish).

MINAL: Ministry of Food Industry.

MIMC: Ministry of the Construction Materials Industry.

* not including sales to tourism and stores of the Ministry of Construction Materials Industries in 1996.

(1) Includes only beverages.

Sources: Annual reports of the relevant ministries; National Statistical Organisation; Sales of national production directed to hard currency stores and tourism in 1997; Directorate of Economic Statistics (Havana, 26 January 1998), pp. 5–6.

tourism the sector of greatest impact on the Cuban economy during the 1990s. At the same time, tourism has contributed to increasing the weight of the service sector in the economy and encouraged closer integration of several branches of the national economy.

The priority assigned to tourist development must be understood in terms of the search for an alternative to the excessive dependence on the sugar industry, and as one of the steps intended to gradually vary the model of external insertion and of comparative advantage of the island. The growing importance of the leisure industry is expressed in several indicators, but perhaps the most illustrative is the fact that this sector contributed more than ten per cent of the accumulated growth of the economy during the second half of the 1990s, as noted in the following figure.

Figure 4.3: Evolution of Tourism and GDP, 1990–99

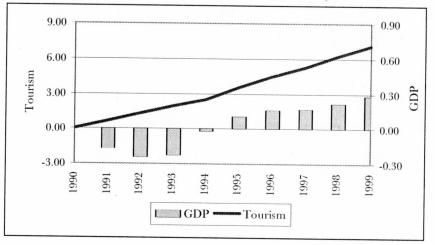

The growing contribution of tourism to the accumulated growth of the economy was based on sustained expansion of the leisure industry during the 1990s. Here, it is worth noting the presence of tourism as a percentage of GDP, which rose from 1.2 in 1990 to more than eight per cent in 1999. Similarly, its contribution to exports of goods and services rose from 5.8 per cent to 30.3 per cent from 1990 to 1999, while induced income in other branches advanced from $54 million to more than $800 million during that same period, with substantial increases attributable to air transport, which grew more than threefold after 1989. To this one can add that progress in the tourism sector has occurred despite the absence of preferential price formulae, practically without tariff protection and in full keeping with demands of the international market.

Table 4.3: Cuba: Basic Indicators of Tourism 1990–99

Items	UM	1990	1991	1992	1993	1994	1995	1996	1997	1998	1999
1 Gross Domestic Product (GDP) (*)	MMD	19644.8	16,248.1	14,904.6	15,094.5	19,200.8	21,737.1	22,814.7	22,951.8	23,900.8	25,503.6
2.– Total Revenue	MD	327.4	378.0	549.5	720.0	850.0	1,100.0	1,333.1	1,515.0	1,759.3	1,901.0
3.– Revenues of Enterprises in the Sector	MD	189.0	276.1	366.8	467.0	492.5	566.6	703.4	860.3	901.9	1100.5
4.– Induced Revenues	MD	54.0	126.0	182.7	253.0	357.5	533.4	676.6	670.0	857.4	800.5
5.– Exports of Goods and Services	MMD	5,605.0	3,270.0	2,309.0	3,858.7	4,210.8	4,393.0	5,474.2	5,622.0	5,162.9	6,278.2
6.– Total Merchandise Imports	MMD	7,416.5	4,233.8	2,314.9	2,008.2	2,016.8	2,882.5	3,569.0	3,987.3	4,181.2	4,676.5
Total tourism revenues as a ratio of GDP 2/1	%	1.7	2.3	3.7	4.8	4.4	5.1	5.8	6.6	7.4	7.5
Total Tourism revenues as a ratio of Exports of Goods and Services (2/5)	%	5.8	11.6	23.8	18.7	20.2	25.04	24.4	26.9	34.1	30.3
Import Coefficient (%)	%	2.4	7.04	16.2	26.8	31.7	26.7	36.4	38.9	45.2	48.9

* in current prices
Assuming the official peso-dollar exchange rate of one to one.
Author calculations based on ONE (2000a); BCC (2000).

Another important consideration is that resources targeted to the tourism sector have been recovered with relative speed. Thus, from 1980 to 1989, investments of more than $62 million were assigned, while income grew progressively from $43.6 million to $195.9 million from 1981–89. During the 1990s tourism received direct and indirect investments amounting to more than $3.5 billion, and the ratio of income to investment implied a highly favourable net result for the economy of $2.94 per dollar invested, with income during the period reaching $10.43 billion.

One of the most significant results of tourism development is the increased participation of domestic production in providing supplies for the sector. This process should not be understood simply in terms of the delivery of merchandise and inputs, for it has contributed to technological transformations and to the achievement of higher levels of competitiveness in productive activities, as well as more intensive employment for sectors in so-called soft technology, that is, in those areas concerned with design, presentation, packaging and branding. In 1990, national production satisfied only 18 per cent of demand for inputs in the tourism sector, whereas by the end of 2000 that number has reached 61 per cent. The following figure presents the evolution of local industrial inputs for the tourism industry since 1990.

Figure 4.4: National Production for Tourism

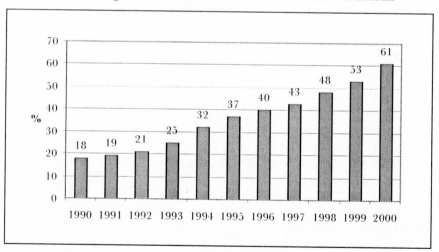

The increased presence of national production in supply chains for the tourism industry is related as well to the provision of financial resources to support such production. In this respect, the Tourism Financing Agency (Financiera de Turismo, FINATUR) guaranteed direct financing for national industry to the tune of more than $430 million between 1992 and 1998.

Development of this financing mechanism means that the final consumer is the ultimate supplier of much of the working capital.

Table 4.4: Financing Awarded by FINATUR 1992–98 (in millions of dollars)

Ministries	1992	1993	1994	1995	1996	1997	1998	Total
MINIL	4.3	8.7	9.9	16.0	16.5	17.8	21.1	94.3
MINBAS	1.8	2.6	2.2	1.4	1.9	3.1	6.1	19.1
SIME	0.8	1.5	0.8	1.1	1.8	2.3	3.4	11.7
MINAL	6.8	14.4	12.4	9.9	17.2	19.6	28.7	109.0
MINAGRI	9.1	19.2	26.6	28.4	54.5	36.4	35.4	189.6
MITRANS	—	1.2	2.8	0.6	0.1	—	—	4.7
OTHERS	—	—	0.2	0.7	1.9	2.8	3.2	8.8
Total	**22.8**	**47.6**	**54.9**	**58.1**	**73.9**	**82.0**	**97.9**	**437.2**

MINIL: Ministry of Light Industry (e.g. textiles, shoes, furniture, hygienic and toiletry products).
MINBAS: Ministry of Basic Industry (e.g. minerals and energy).
SIME: Ministry of Steel and Mechanical Industries (steel, machinery and related products).
MINAL: Ministry of the Food Industry.
MINAGRI: Ministry of Agriculture.
MITRANS: Ministry of Transportation.
Source: CEPAL (2000).

A novel aspect of local supplier relations with tourism is that production that fails to meet standards demanded by the sector can be rejected, even when financial guarantees may have been extended. In this way, application of standards more demanding than those faced in the past opens opportunities to effect a transition from a system of inadequate import substitution to an alternative framework, which would tend toward diversification of export capacities over time.

Despite progress that has been achieved in terms of participation by domestic producers in supplying the tourism industry, it is important to continue working on several interrelated aspects to advance in future. First, quality standards must be guaranteed. Second, mechanisms must be enhanced for improving post-production and marketing services. Third, product certification to meet international quality standards must be introduced gradually. Finally, it is expected that tourism will continue to lead the process of economic recovery in Cuba, as the requirements of industry continue to increase in both quantitative and qualitative terms. That process will require further investments to enhance prospects for modernisation and technological updating of a variety of industrial activities, so that they will be prepared to meet the challenges of international competitiveness.

b) Internal Hard Currency Markets

The universal opening to dollar-based economic activities has contributed to stabilising economic performance in Cuba while at the same time helping to achieve fiscal adjustment by avoiding expansion of inflationary pressure. Similarly, reliance on hard currency measures has provided an instrument that reflects price signals necessary to assign resources, while facilitating adaptation toward production of tradeable goods and services in world market conditions. At the same time, dollar-based transactions have enabled the government to introduce greater discipline in the management of various financial variables.[15]

The gradual extension of different modalities of self-financing, elaboration of budgets with expenses and revenues, and new emphases on planning, have been based on hard currency calculations. This situation has also led to a gradual adjustment of productive capacities of firms to reflect real demand, independent of general demand. In addition, firms have tended to concentrate solely in those productive activities that have real potential for commercial profitability.

Over the short term, the internal hard currency market has exerted a positive influence on recent trends in industry, but full achievement of its potential will require broader extension of criteria applied to the supply of goods for the tourist sector. Above all, there is a need to establish mechanisms to stimulate those institutions that manage to articulate commercialisation strategies that are viable both domestically and internationally, and to set up more realistic frameworks for ensuring competition and for evaluating the quality of products generated for competitive markets. Indeed, one of the problems that remains unresolved is that production destined for the internal market shares the same characteristics as that oriented toward export.[16] Despite these limitations, the dollarisation process, which has unfolded in tandem with the widening of national economic space operating in hard currency, has become essential for the process of economic recovery beginning in the mid-1990s, as can be seen in Figure 4.5.[17]

---

15   González (1999).
16   Marquetti (1998a).
17   Implementation of some sort of neutral policy concerning exports is needed in order to ensure that production oriented to external markets is not less profitable than that oriented to meet domestic demand.

Another important consideration is that the need to raise income levels of this segment of the market has been satisfied through the incorporation of local production without regard to quality performance. In practice, the outcome amounts to a mechanism for protection of domestic industry, which undermines efforts to raise competitiveness of domestic production. This situation applies equally to production geared to supplying the population and to inter-firm transactions. In this regard, it is necessary to highlight the degree to which the Cuban economic system was organised in the past, privileging producers and stimulating monopolistic practices in various ways, and thus avoiding diffusion of a culture that promoted quality, among producers and consumers alike. To this can be added the enduring disjuncture between behaviours of productive actors and conditions that prevail in international markets, as well as the limited role of the internal market as a complement to efforts to achieve competitiveness.[18]

Figure 4.5: Relationship of Trends in the Growth of GDP to Sales in Hard Currency Stores

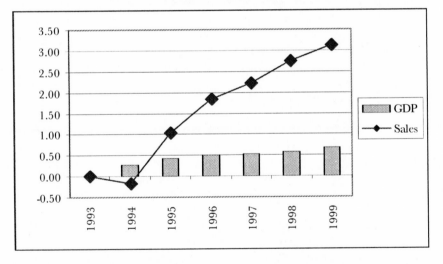

Similarly, the Cuban enterprise system was not designed to achieve competitiveness through efforts of its own or to function effectively in conditions of uncertainty and systematic risk. Rather, it was designed to work with stable inputs, a circumstance which shaped its evolution and its tendency to operate within strictly limited parameters. In turn, the use of imported products as a reference point for local production is often inappropriate. Here it is worth recalling that the principal function assigned to the market,

18 Marquetti (1998a).

basically retail distribution, is to generate revenues, which leads to a situation in which high volumes of trade take place in products where the price-quality relationship often fails to reflect international norms. A parallel situation is also produced frequently in inter-firm supply relationships.[19] It is doubtful, as a result, whether this production can achieve the status of 'exports within borders' (*exportaciones en fronteras*). To these concerns one can add that the priority assigned to the presence of national production in this segment of industry means that the branch ministries assign absolute priority to this goal, in detriment of the need to increase exportable supplies, which over the long term actually merit the priority.

Figure 4.6: Percentage of Domestic Production in Hard Currency Retail Sales

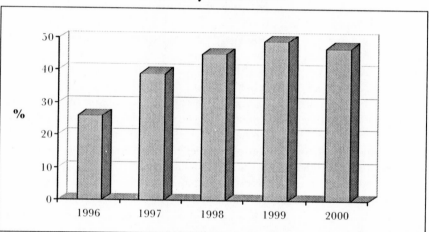

A gradual overcoming of these difficulties should contribute to raising quality demands on those seeking access to the domestic market. In future, consolidation of this favourable trend could become an important national asset, as products traded at home would achieve conditions needed to become exportable.

c) Foreign Direct Investment (FDI)

The process of decapitalisation that buffeted various industrial sectors was one of the decisive factors in motivating the search for foreign direct invest-

---

19 These situations reflect the impediments to accessing sources of finance, which obligate firms to acquire domestically produced goods that may not fully satisfy their needs.

ment (FDI). In turn, shortages of raw materials and the need to effect a technological restructuring in various industries required the reconfiguration of firm activities and a search for new technologies. Opening to foreign investment also became one of the principal axes of the essential process of restructuring experienced by the external sector as a result of the disintegration of the European socialist bloc. To this can be added the updating and creation of an appropriate legal framework for enterprise development, as well as the study of all available options for linking the Cuban economy with the regional and international context.

In policy terms, there was a rapid shift from a climate that discouraged and impeded investment to one in which aggressive efforts were made to foster relationships with foreign capital. This transition was determined both by the very sharpness of the crisis and by the positive results achieved in those branches of industry which at an early stage managed to develop effective linkages to foreign investors.

According to government sources, the level of commitments secured by the end of 1999 surpassed $4.3 billion, and more than eight per cent of gross capital formation between 1990 and 1998 consisted of foreign direct investment. In general, foreign investment has made it possible to close productive cycles, to re-establish operations in plants where capacity was being utilised inadequately and to gain access to new markets — including the consolidation of specific niches — and to diffuse new techniques of firm management. To this can be added the incorporation of another potential source of demand that local production needs to satisfy at high quality levels.

The opening to foreign direct investment has also contributed to the formation of a different organisational culture, while making it possible to raise productivity and competitiveness in various branches of industry. In some instances, this has even entailed the introduction of significant technological transformations. In this regard, it is worth mentioning advances in oil exploration and drilling which, as a result of agreements with foreign capital, have made possible noteworthy increases over production levels of 1989 and encouraged maximum utilisation of natural gas for electricity generation.

The levels of growth achieved in both segments over the past decade have been significant, to the point where they have substantially increased the weight of the energy sector in the national economy. Domestic crude and natural gas production supplied more than half of Cuba's demand for electricity generation in 2000, compared with 30 per cent the previous year. This increase compensated for 61 per cent of the effect of the increase in hydrocarbon prices during 2000.[20] The issue goes beyond promotion of a greater role for domestic energy producers in electricity generation, as initial steps have been taken as well toward introducing more efficient and environmentally sustainable technologies.

20 Rodríguez (2000b).

While foreign investment is making possible a gradual resolution of strategic issues through an increase in local production, similar processes are evident in such branches of industry as metal mining, and in the production of lubricants, cleaning and personal hygiene materials, nickel, mineral water, and citric juices and concentrates. In all of these cases, enhanced insertion into productive chains has been achieved alongside growth in production volumes, improvement in quality indicators and completion of production cycles.

As for the sectoral distribution of foreign investment, at the end of 1999 more than a third of joint ventures with foreign investors were concentrated in industry, with the Ministries of Basic Industry, Light Industry and Foodstuffs accounting for more than 70 per cent of these investments. Taken as a whole, foreign investment will continue to occupy a significant place in supplying the resources required by Cuban manufacturing industry to back up the anticipated growth of tourism and the mining potential in the country.

d) Demand of the Export Sector

Demand in this sector has played a decisive role in the growth of Cuban industry. The process of industrialisation in previous decades had generated significant levels of productive integration, particularly in sugar. Yet as a consequence of financial constraints unleashed by the crisis of the 1990s, intersectoral relations suffered seriously. Under the combined effect of the collapse of the socialist bloc and the expansion of other activities, the relative importance of the sugar sector declined, to the point where its contribution to the national hard currency balances is currently 38 per cent, whereas in 1990 it accounted for more than 95 per cent.

The 1990s witnessed a trend toward greater flexibility and adaptation of Cuban foreign trade to the new international circumstances confronting the island. These changes have made possible a growth in exports of specific goods, such as tobacco and rum, and facilitated progress in diversifying the supply of exportable goods in a variety of industrial branches operating under the auspices of several different ministries. The relative growth of exports has also been related to the adjustment of quality control mechanisms and development of strategies directed to international markets, in some instances including more intensive use of marketing and pursuit of alliances with foreign capital

Despite noteworthy advances to date, full realisation of the country's productive potential remains far from being achieved, and much more work is needed to improve results, especially with regard to the development of new market niches and the consolidation of a more diversified supply of exportable goods characterised by higher levels of competitiveness. To accomplish these objectives will require continuous efforts to transform

Cuba's position along the 'value chains' of traditional export products, in pursuit of a situation in which products of greater value-added take on greater importance in Cuban exports.[21]

Figure 4.7: Possible Trajectory of the Structure of Cuban Exports

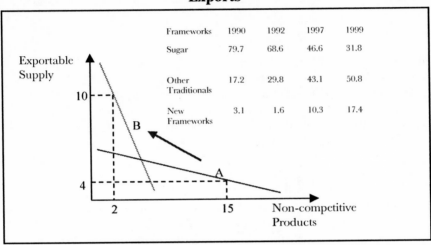

Frameworks	1990	1992	1997	1999
Sugar	79.7	68.6	46.6	31.8
Other Traditionals	17.2	29.8	43.1	50.8
New Frameworks	3.1	1.6	10.3	17.4

e) Evolution of Financial and Banking Services

The process of restructuring experienced by the national banking system, and with it the diversification of financial institutions, has tended to overcome gradually one of the historic weaknesses of the Cuban economy. In addition, it is helping to make funds channelled by these institutions an important source of resource allocation to industry and other sectors of the economy. Parallel to this process has been a steady recovery in the quality of loans in the national banking system, a trend which reflects both the logic of the dollarisation process and the policy of restricting investment to hard currency.

The criteria used to allocate these resources internally resemble very closely the conditions that Cuba must meet for securing financing in international markets. Thus, the typical situation is one of short-term credits at high interest rates. The principal purpose of applying these stringent criteria is to encourage improved utilisation of existing resources and to imbue among firms a culture of work in which *powerful financial restrictions* are taken as a constant.

21 Marquetti (2000b).

Table 4.5: Cuba: Gross Financing Provided by the Financial System, by Productive Sector, 1997–99 (in millions of dollars)

	1997		1998		1999	
	Value	Structure	Value	Structure	Value	Structure
Total	779.1	100.0	1,005.4	100.0	1,522.7	100.0
Industry	387.2	49.7	544.1	54.1	745.8	49.0
Commerce	285.9	36.7	214.2	21.3	121.8	8.0
Transportation	49.1	6.3	82.5	8.2	137.0	9.0
Agro-Fisheries	30.4	3.9	49.3	4.9	91.4	6.0
Construction	12.5	1.6	21.1	2.1	45.7	3.0
Tourism	3.1	0.4	23.1	2.3	106.6	6.0
Culture	1.6	0.2	2.0	0.2	—	—
Other	9.3	1.2	69.4	6.9	274.1	18.0

Sources: BCC (1999); BCC (2000).

f) Current State of the Import Substitution Process

Import substitution is an integral part of the new model of industrial growth, for it is consistent with the development of those activities that have the greatest potential hauling effect within that model. Import substitution is also congruent with the financial restrictions that the country faces and the need to maximise possibilities for broadening the range of national exports. In addition, import substitution constitutes a mechanism that contributes to better use of the scientific potential of the country.

An important aspect of the import substitution strategy is that industrial policy has taken on more precise and selective characteristics, in marked contrast with the situation that prevailed in the past. Continued import substitution should encourage margins of self-sufficiency along progressively more complex levels of productive chains, while facilitating as well the encouragement or restructuring of productive capabilities that promise a greater degree of economic autonomy for Cuba. Maintenance of import substitution as an essential aspect of industrial promotion in Cuba has promoted the revival of integrated development programmes for the country.[22]

22 Rodríguez (2000a).

Table 4.6: Determinants of Growth in Industrial Production 1989–99

Industrial Branch	Internal Market	Exports	Import Substitution	Total (%)
Electrical Energy	100.0	0.0	0.0	100.0
Fuel	274.0	19.4	-193.5	100.0
Mining and Iron Metals	98.7	-8.1	9.3	100.0
Mining and non-Iron Metals	-26.5	108.7	17.8	100.0
Non-electronic Machinery Construction	-148.5	-1.7	250.3	100.0
Electro-technical and Electronics	-17.6	-11.1	128.7	100.0
Metal Products	327.0	0.6	-227.6	100.0
Chemicals	-8.0	17.0	90.9	100.0
Paper and Cellulose	93.8	3.7	2.6	100.0
Forestry and Wood Processing	173.3	3.3	-76.6	100.0
Construction Materials	111.3	-8.4	-2.9	100.0
Textiles	90.9	1.0	8.1	100.0
Apparel	62.3	5.3	32.4	100.0
Leather and Shoes	64.8	-0.3	35.5	100.0
Sugar	17.1	82.9	0.0	100.0
Foodstuffs	156.6	-6.0	-50.6	100.0
Fishing	52.0	24.6	23.4	100.0
Beverages and Tobacco	-82.6	238.0	-55.4	100.0
Other Industrial Activities	60.3	-1.8	41.5	100.0
Total Industry	**-401.0**	**-39.4**	**540.4**	**100.0**

Source: Authors' calculations based on ONE (1998a); CEPAL (2000); BCC (2000a).

In analysing the determinants of Cuban industrial development between 1990–99, the internal market, and by extension import substitution, continues to be the most important factor. Of greatest significance is the production of the capital goods industry, particularly the production of non-electrical, electro-technical and electronics machinery. A recent study focused on the performance of this sector noted, for example, that SIME had achieved productive growth in production in almost all of its enterprises through import substitution, responding effectively to demands of the sugar, tourism, transport, agriculture and fishing industries. The table above illustrates this finding with data spanning the decade of 1989–99.

In a similar manner, it is worth noting that, on average, the domestic contribution of different industries to satisfying consumer demand represented more than 60 per cent from 1975–89, and that it had actually expanded to 70 per cent by 1996.[23]

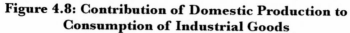

Figure 4.8: Contribution of Domestic Production to Consumption of Industrial Goods

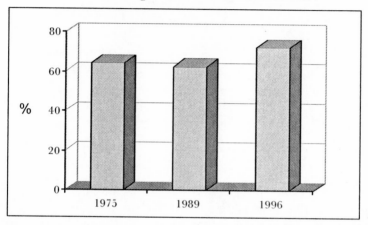

Source: Authors' calculation based on CEE (1991); Fernández de Bulnes (1994).

Finally, it is worth noting that import substitution constitutes a strategic option for Cuba: the country must restrict the objective tendency toward growth of imports, which is accentuated in the new model given the difficulties that industry faces in seeking to satisfy potential domestic demand.

g) Restructuring of the Entrepreneurial Order

The development of the crisis implied wider margins of autonomy and decentralisation for firm managers, at the same time that it led to the need to introduce new methods for strengthening linkages within the domestic economy, and made necessary the use of an essentially indirect regulatory system based on allocations of hard currency. The principal goal of promoting greater leadership for the firm sector is related to gaining greater use of the reserves of efficiency that it possesses. At the same time, measures are being implemented in an effort to increase quality of firm management, thus mitigating the negative effects associated with the limits of material and financial resources. This relation is illustrated in Figure 4.9. While progress to date is certainly laudable, it remains insufficient to satisfy the long-term requirements for transforming the enterprise sector.

23   Marquetti and Garcia (1999).

Figure 4.9: Growth Trend

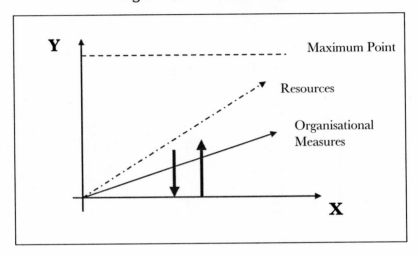

The changes that took place during the 1990s have attracted unprecedented attention to the potential of management factors to influence prospects for national development, for these shifts imply a departure from historic conceptions of the firm and imply the formation of a new enterprise culture. Nonetheless, the particular way in which economic reforms have developed in Cuba, together with the difficulties that obstruct a more effective mode of reinsertion into the international economy, constrain possibilities for taking fuller advantage of this potential asset.

Principal Limitations of the Industrial Growth Model

The evolution of the new development model for Cuban manufacturing faces one of its principal constraints in the performance of the sugar industry, which despite the decline it suffered during the 1990s retains significant weight on overall trends in the economy. Other structural problems generated by industrialisation impact negatively on the new model, including new demands placed on the island by the process of international reinsertion and difficulties derived from the complex situation posed by external finances.

Figure 4.10: The New Model of Industrial Growth (cont.)

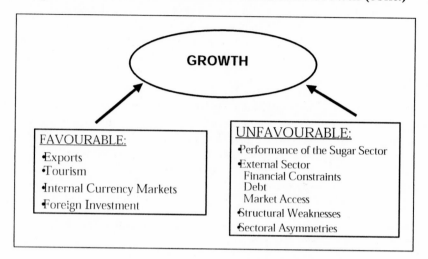

a) Problems of the Sugar Industry: An Important Constraint on Performance of the New Model

The sugar industry has long constituted the principal sector of the Cuban economy, hence its decisive role in the dynamic of social and economic reproduction, as well as the country's historic pattern of insertion into the international economy. The crisis has had profoundly negative consequences for the sector. Initially, the greatest impact was the reduction of external sales, which led to a substantial decline in levels of competitiveness. Later, the considerable decline in availability of fuel, fertiliser and herbicides affected notably the productive performance of agro-industry as a whole, with successive declines of 4.5 per cent, 5.2 per cent, 44.2 per cent, 47 per cent and 57.2 per cent from 1991 to 1995.

The negative consequences for volumes of sugar production were even greater, for a number of reasons: the increased cost of financing during this period; the absence of a comprehensive strategy for the sector that took into account the realities imposed by the crisis; the relative lack of attention paid to agricultural activity in general; and the persistence of an overall logic for agro-industry that reflected pre-crisis circumstances and thus privileged material production. In this context there was a decline in investment in the sugar industry, which directly affected maintenance of facilities, support industries and portions of the rail transport system essential to the sugar sector. At the same time there was a notable process of decapitalisation in all activities relating to the Ministry of Sugar Production. In turn, successive reductions in sugar production contributed not only to a decline in export revenues attributable to the sector but also to the loss of a significant flow of external finance which has yet to be replaced by other sectors of the economy.[24]

Nevertheless, despite the decline of production levels in the industry, sugar retains an important presence in the sphere of economic reproduction, and it remains the sector with greatest potential for leadership, given its extensive linkages to other productive sectors. Thus, the unstable performance of the sugar industry has exerted a powerful influence on the pace and contours of recovery throughout the economy as a whole.

Cuban economic performance from 1996–98 confirms this assessment. The highest rate of economic growth and of sugar production during this period was achieved in 1996, whereas the ensuing years witnessed repeated declines which affected manufacturing and the overall economy.[25] The following figure illustrates this trend.

Figure 4.11: Trends in Sugar Production and GDP, 1989–98

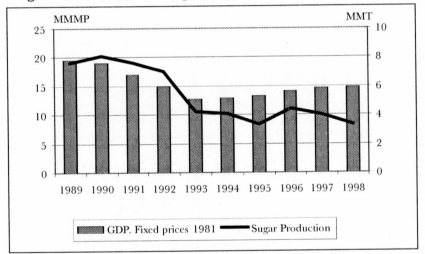

The continuation of a traditional approach of 'material balance' to the management of the sugar industry meant that this sector lagged considerably behind the overall economy in implementing a series of organisational and institutional changes that had developed elsewhere in the economy, in keeping with the process of economic reform. Both macro and meso-economic

24   The average income for sugar exports went from 4.1 billion pesos between 1986 and 1990 to 1.12 billion between 1991 and 1996, representing a decline of 72.7 per cent.

25   According to estimates of the Ministry of Economy and Planning, had anticipated levels of sugar production been achieved during these years, the overall growth of the economy would have been nearly double the rate that was attained.

factors are crucial to explaining this situation: sugar-related agro-industry involves 72 municipalities distributed across the national territory, and the sector directly provides employment to more than half a million workers.

Indeed, as Lázaro Peña Castellanos argues elsewhere in this volume, the strategy of industrial restructuring of the sugar sector encompasses a broad array of changes, including a profound alteration in the relationship between agriculture and industry, adjustment of the system of firms to new conditions facing the country, updating of systems for managing trade and finance, improved utilisation of human resources, substantial growth in levels of efficiency, a gradual reorientation of productive capacities, development of new managerial and enterprise capacities and the creation of conditions to take maximum advantage of existing and potential infrastructure for producing by-products of sugar-cane.

The principal elements of the process of agro-industrial restructuring include: reducing personnel in the relevant ministry and provincial delegations by 50 per cent, reconfiguring the enterprise system through creation of seven corporate groups, reorganisation of research and planning institutions, transformation of agro-industrial complexes into 1,017 business units, creation of conditions for introducing ISO quality standards and supporting diversification within the sugar industry. In addition, the current plan is to produce more than five million tons of raw sugar, while diversifying the supply of different types of sugars (vitamin enriched, organic, amorphous, liquid, etc.), and broadening computerised management of production facilities and increasing the capacity for electricity generation.

Restructuring along these lines should promote recovery of agro-industry, and on foundations different from those of the past, in that these results are to be achieved through maximum utilisation of the potential of the sector. Results of the 2000 sugar campaign may be considered an initial return on the investment in reform, as the harvest was the most successful of the past 15 years, with reduced levels of subsidisation, and in the context of a strategy designed to promote the gradual recovery of various by-products.

b) Financial Constraints

The favourable trend achieved by the manufacturing industry since 1994 has occurred despite an adverse context characterised by growing financial constraints, on the one hand, and increased cost of financing, on the other. The circumstance is best understood in terms of a 'vicious circle': in order to maintain the momentum of recovery the economy requires resources beyond those that can be generated internally, yet when they are available at all, these resources are being provided at an increasingly high price and with progressively shorter periods for repayment. The situation is such that the cost of amortising loans often exceeds the capacity of the productive system to generate the necessary resources during such short periods of time.[26]

This vicious circle has its external expression in the principal bottleneck facing the Cuban economy today, namely, the systematic increase in the external deficit. The dimensions of this problem go beyond the balance of payments deficit, for a simple evaluation of current accounts does not capture the full extent of the situation.[27] The size of the deficit compels the Cuban economy to operate amidst profound tensions, and to seek to adjust economic performance to the effective financial coverage available to the country. At the same time, it implies adoption of a model of growth that seeks only gradual change. In other words, under present circumstances, levels of growth are being constrained in order to reflect the financial constraints under which the country must operate, lest serious instabilities be encountered.

Yet despite the undeniable financial difficulties confronting Cuba, there has still not been an optimal utilisation of resources available to firms and other productive entities, and the costs of obtaining a dollar of exports — whether in domestic or hard currency — remain excessively high. In recent years, because of the priority assigned to financial questions, firms have been restricted with regard to the use of hard currency. Nevertheless, results have been disappointing, since the measurement of economic management is by gross revenues and these as a whole have increased, this leads to insufficient attention being paid to obtaining improved results. These conditions have also impacted on the possible debt carrying capacity of the country.

For these reasons, a decision has been made to award greater importance to evaluations of the real level of growth in net revenues, with the objective of making hard currency function as a restrictive factor for firms, since today there has been a substantial decline in its impact. Indeed, according to some specialists, the current system of assigning hard currency resources responds more to a logic of functioning in material balance conditions than to the use of financial categories.

Another abnormality resulting from financial constraints is the gradual decapitalisation of firms due to the demand that they meet financial obligations incurred at higher levels. This situation militates against the normal operation of collections and payments in the national economy, at the same time that it obligates more than a few firms to become indebted beyond their capacity. In general, tensions around external financing issues provoke a situation in which the singularity of the present process of economic revitalisation in Cuba is the coexistence of clear tendencies toward recovery

---

26   Marquetti (1997b).

27   An illustration is that the current account deficit remained at around two per cent of GDP throughout the period between 1992 and 1999, which remains lower than the standard of three per cent that is customarily applied to developing countries with characteristics akin to those of Cuba.

alongside a continuing environment of crisis. Finally, several factors continue to impede articulation of the new model of development, including restricted access to markets, the lack of equal treatment assigned to production for domestic and export markets, the historic problems of integration in national industry, as well as the limited achievements with regard to technological and productive restructuring.

Conclusions

The new model of industrial development in Cuba is distinguished by the absence of an active and explicit industrial policy. Rather, the trends toward transformation and growth of manufacturing industry have been related to collateral and induced effects of the development of other, non-industrial sectors or activities.

The transition from one model to another has not been designed to reduce the weight of the industrial sector. On the contrary, the changes that have been induced and the re-industrialising effects that have been achieved through pursuit of new activities aim to promote continued leadership of industry in providing employment and propelling the remainder of the economy.

CHAPTER 5

The Sugar-Cane Complex:
Problems of Competitiveness and Uncertainty in a Crucial Sector

Lázaro Peña Castellanos

Introduction

The prospects for the recovery of the Cuban sugar industry are a controversial topic and the source of widespread debate both inside and outside the country. For Cuba, sugar exports continue to be the largest source of external revenue and the sugar industry remains the most influential sector within the country's economy. Sugar continues to predominate in the economy despite the production decreases that began in the early 1990s and the growing priority ascribed to other sectors of the economy during the past decade.

Notwithstanding its importance, however, the Cuban sugar agro-industry has been lagging due to both technological obsolescence and to low agricultural and industrial yields. Making this sector competitive would require high levels of resource reallocation and investment, and many both inside and outside Cuba doubt the economic rationality of such a move. This is, in fact, a highly controversial topic which requires in-depth analyses that must account for multiple factors. Among the issues that require consideration are the competitive potential of Cuban agro-industry as well as the uncertainties of the evolution of the global sugar market in the medium and the long term.

Outside Cuba, the opinions and interests with regards to the reactivation of the Cuban sugar agro-industry are also mixed and contradictory. For its competitors, the recuperation of the sugar industry on the island, which was once the primary exporter of sugar-cane, is seen as another serious problem at a time of price instability and over-saturated markets. The opposite is true for potential foreign investors given that the investment needs in this sector as well as its potential competitiveness create interesting prospects for profitable business.

A third dimension that also generates controversy among specialists and policy-makers is the role and the significance of this sector within the framework of the growth and development model of the Cuban economy. In this context, the subject of debate becomes the multiple problems stemming from the temporal transformations of the Cuban economy (technological, productive, financial, commercial, social, etc.,) as well as the changes in sectoral priorities, particularly with respect to investment policies.

This chapter will approach each of the dimensions outlined above from the perspective of the industry's recent history and from the uncertainties surrounding its evolution, both in terms of technology and competitiveness.

The Sugar Agro-industry and the Cuban Economy

During the 1980s, the production of the sugar agro-industry represented between nine and 12 per cent of the Global Social Product (GSP) in terms of value, accounting for between 12 and 15 per cent of all investment, and employing more than 11 per cent of the country's civilian labour force.[1] During the 1990s, this sector lost ground within the broader intersectoral scheme of the national economy, but remained a principal activity nonetheless. In 1990, for example, the production of goods and services in the sugar industry represented approximately seven per cent of Gross Domestic Product (GDP) at constant prices (20,350 million pesos). During the second half of the decade (1996–98), however, this figure dropped to a level between five and six per cent of GDP (16,245 million pesos).

With respect to employment, a comparison of the data for the past two decades does not reveal a significant variation. Today, as in the past, the Cuban sugar industry directly employs approximately 460,000 people and indirectly some 1.5 million, accounting for close to 50 per cent of the country's total available labour force.[2]

Within the sugar industry it has been in the arenas of investment and net capital formation where relative indicators have been unfavourable. With respect to the availability of resources, this sector has fallen behind in relation to other economic activities such as tourism, the nickel industry, the oil industry, light manufacturing and fishing.[3] The sugar industry has also suffered the negative effects of decapitalisation due to its inability to restore — even to baseline technological levels — the productive capabilities of its deteriorating plant and equipment.

An analysis of the factors that might justify such a policy extends beyond the scope and objectives of this chapter. Yet, as far as internal resources are concerned, these factors are linked to a strategy of concentrating scarce resources in economic areas that can turn revenue levels around within a relatively short period of time and that require relatively low levels of expenditure, or in other areas that can produce non-traditional exports or substitute imports.

The opening of the sugar industry to direct foreign investment, moreover, has in practice only been a partial one, concentrated primarily in the production of sugar-cane derivatives (a lesser activity when compared to the

1   CEE (1989).
2   ECLAC (2000).
3   Lage (1998).

production of raw sugar). This has obviously had negative effects on quantity of resources available for implementing the kinds of changes that would make the sector more competitive. The causes which have determined this restricted investment strategy in the sugar industry appear to be political and social, given the effects that a structural transformation would eventually have on the levels of employment. Nevertheless, it should be noted that none of the activities in this sector are formally excluded by Law No. 77, which is the legislation that regulates the activity of foreign capital in the country. This means that changes in current policy are possible under the existing laws.

By the end of the 1990s the industrial segment of the sugar industry accounted for approximately 32 per cent of all the machinery and productive equipment of Cuban industry, for more than 35 per cent of all its energy equipment and machinery, and for more than 65 per cent of all the commercial ground transportation existing in the country.[4]

The agricultural segment of the sugar industry possesses almost 50 per cent of the country's cultivated land and a significant proportion of all the agricultural machinery that exists on the island (more than 35,000 tractors, 300,000 standard ploughs, 3,000 deep-bottom ploughs (*subsoladoras*), some 8,000 cultivating machines, 4,000 harvesters, etc.), which in most cases surpasses 50 per cent of the total number of machines existing in the country.[5]

During the 1980s the sugar industry was undoubtedly the country's principal source of foreign income, with levels in excess of 70 per cent of the total. Today, this situation has changed. Tourism currently accounts for 53 per cent of the income generated from the commercialisation of goods and services as reflected in the country's overall balance of payments, while sugar presently accounts for only 19 per cent of the total. Nevertheless, sugar continues to be the most important export commodity — capturing 34 per cent of the total export income — and is the country's principal domestic source of net foreign currency.[6]

Sugar, moreover, acts as the guarantor of the Cuban economy insofar as it is the principal product that is required and accepted as collateral to cover short and medium terms loans made to the country within international capital markets, and its availability or scarcity strongly influences the country risk evaluations of the economy.[7]

In summary, the sugar agro-industry continues to be Cuba's most important economic activity, above and beyond particular disagreements of greater or lesser importance regarding the possible changes in the model of growth and development of the Cuban economy.

4   Peña and Alvarez (1997).
5   ECLAC (2000).
6   *Ibid.*
7   EIU (2000a).

Sugar in the Highly Competitive Sweeteners Market: Perspectives for the Coming Decade

Many elements come in to play in the global competitive arena of the market for sugar and other sweeteners, but most specialists agree that in the medium term, sugar will continue to be the principal sweetener on the market.

The following table shows the total demand for sweeteners in the world market in 1995 and a forecast for the first decade of the millennium.

Table 5.1: Total Demand for Sweeteners in Millions of Metric Tons (MMT) and in Per Cent

	1995		2010	
Total	144.00	100%	203.00	100%
Sugar	112.32	78%	146.16	72%
Natural Sweetener	17.28	12%	30.45	15%
Artificial Sweetener	14.40	10%	26.39	13%

Source: LMC International, Ltd. (1997).

There are diverse arguments that support these forecasts. In our opinion, the most important are the following:

- The foreseeable evolution of demand for sweeteners in relation to the rate of population growth.

- The expected competitiveness of different sweeteners in direct consumption as well as industrial markets.

- The foreseeable effects on the sugar market and on the commercialisation of sugar of the government policies, regional trade agreements and international accords currently in place.

- The effects of the tendency towards the consumption of natural products on the sugar market.

- The foreseeable trends in the behaviour of the global economy and its income levels.

Sugar is a traditional sweetening additive that is relatively inexpensive to produce and that is present in the diet of the population in most regions of the world. For many low-income nations, sugar provides a highly important and relative low-cost caloric and nutritional base — one not easily replaceable by more sophisticated artificial sweeteners.

Table 5.2: Demand for Sweeteners by World Region in 1995 in Millions of Metric Tons (MMT)

	Asia	Europe	NA (1)	CSA (2)	Africa	Oceania
Sugar	33.75	29.75	14.00	17.28	14.70	2.97
Natural S.	2.25	3.50	11.20	0.54	0.15	0.01
Artificial	4.50	1.75	2.80	0.18	0.15	0.02

Source: LMC International, Ltd. (1997).

(1) North America

(2) Central and South America

Since the mid-1960s and amidst rising sugar prices, there has been the industrial development of the alternative sweeteners, both natural and artificial, which today compete with sugar in the global market with varying degrees of success.[8] The most competitive market for artificial sweeteners is in the food industry, and within this sector, the production of non-alcoholic beverages is at the top of the list. Currently, *aspartame* is the most widely used sweetener in this industry, accounting for more than 80 per cent of a total sugar equivalent of almost eight million tons per year. Yet the tendency in the soft drink industry is towards the use of mixtures of high and low intensity artificial sweeteners as a way to cut total costs. This opens possibilities for

---

8   For example, the sweetening capacity of saccharine, an artificial sweetener, is 30 times higher than that of sugar and its price is 90% lower than that of refined sugar. Currently, it is the most consumed artificial sweetener in the world. Saccharine demand is equivalent to approximately eight million tons of sugar, but close to 50% of it is concentrated in China and it is used primarily for direct consumption.

Despite its lower price and higher sweetening capacity, saccharine — as a product for direct consumption — does not appear to have the competitive capabilities that could allow it to displace sugar. Only in China, given its population and its level of per capita income, would it be possible for consumption of a product such as saccharine to grow despite its inferior quality in terms of taste. In certain countries, moreover, saccharine has received much negative publicity because it is considered a carcinogen.

There are high-income consumers that are willing to purchase other artificial sweeteners of low caloric value, which makes it likely that products like aspartame and acesulfame-k will maintain their presence in the direct consumption market. Nevertheless, one should bear in mind that these are artificial products that must overcome environmentalist publicity that promotes the consumption of natural products which is most influential precisely in those consumer markets with the highest per capita income levels.

a diversification of the industrial uses of artificial sweeteners which does not necessarily require rapid growth in consumption.[9]

What's more, the diet beverage industry — an important site for the industrial consumption of artificial sweeteners — has been showing signs of stagnation in recent years. These have been reflected in the levels of demand for its products.[10]

Although artificial sweeteners are penetrating the international sweetener market, sugar's strongest competition comes from another natural sweetener, a fructose-rich corn syrup known as HFCS. It is estimated that HFCS will remain sugar's principal competitor for at least the next ten years. HFCS is a liquid sweetener capable of substituting for sugar in international industrial food and beverage markets. Data for 1997 show that the United States is the leading producer of HCFS, accounting for 75 per cent of a total global sugar-equivalent output of 10.4 million tons, or approximately eight per cent of the entire sweetener market. When the production of HFCS in the United States is compared with production in the rest of the world, a supply increase in the USA is observed, while in the latter, supply remains practically the same, stagnating at levels that oscillate between 2 and 2.4 million sugar-equivalent tons.

Figure 5.1: HFCS Production

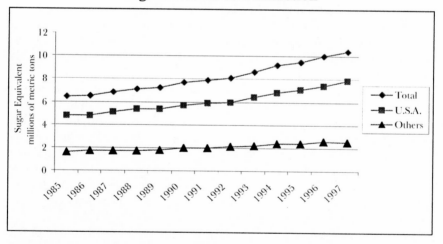

Source: USDA, *Sugar and Sweeteners Situation and Outlook Yearbook* (1999).

9   In April 1998 sucralosa — another high-intensity sweetener that is 600 times more potent than sugar — was approved for use in beverages and food in the United States. Sucralosa is elaborated from sugar and experts expect it to become an important presence in international sweetener markets within a relatively short period of time.

10   ISO (1998a).

Several important factors must be kept in mind when analysing the competitive potential of HFCS in relation to sugar.

In the first place, the primary productive base for this artificial sweetener is corn production. This means that any country that pursues HFCS production must possess either the natural and technological conditions that will allow it to produce this grain at competitive costs, or a protected sugar market that artificially raises its price levels, thus making HFCS production profitable.

Secondly, HFCS production technology, when compared to the technology used in sugar production, is more complex and more capital intensive. This is quite obviously reflected in the relationship between processing costs and the prices at which it is commercialised.

Thirdly, given that the use of HFCS is primarily industrial, its production is only justified if there exists a productive chain within the country or in a neighbouring country that is able to absorb it. In such cases, one must also keep in mind that the costs to transport HFCS are high.[11]

These three arguments suggest that sugar production may be preferable to HFCS production, yet the development of new varieties of HFCS and the growing availability of the product on the market create well-founded fears among sugar producing countries regarding the competitive potential of HFCS in the sweetener market. Some specialists have pointed out, for example, that since 1986 HFCS has been on the market in crystalline form, and that over the last several years there has been a commercial expansion of this product that could very well signal the development of a new technological process with substantially lower and more competitive costs in relation to sugar.[12]

The effects that the supply-demand imbalances of HFCS has on sweetener markets can also not be ignored. On the one hand, the ability of certain industries to substitute sugar with HFCS — as is the case with the soft drink industry in Mexico — carries with it the danger of creating additional surpluses that would then be released into sugar export markets, bringing down its overall price levels. On the other hand, the overestimation of the North American HFCS industry in relation to its internal demand could stimulate the growth of HFCS exports, which would constrain the possibilities for sugar consumption and also generate negative pressure on price levels.

With regards to the effects that government policies applied within the framework of multilateral agreements involving sweeteners may have on sweetener markets, the consensus is that they tend to have little if any real impact. Stated in other terms, it is estimated that in the medium term the sugar industry will continue to be, as it is today, one of the most protected

11 *Ibid.*
12 Evans and Davis (1999).

industries in the world. In fact, the accords adopted at the Uruguay Round regarding the commercialisation of agricultural products, protection for producers and export subsidies, did not have a significant impact on the sugar market in the sense that they did not introduce overarching regulatory norms. In real terms, these accords were only able to establish a certain ceiling on the levels of protection and subsidy for internal producers, which would suggest that their repercussions on sugar markets will be minor.[13]

Changes that could have a positive influence on price levels and commercialisation are also unlikely in the context of regional trade accords in which sugar does play a relevant role, as is the case in the Common Agrarian Policy of the European Union and NAFTA.[14]

Table 5.3: Principal Exporters and Importers of Sugar (millions of metric tons)

Exporters				Importers			
	1990–91	1993–94	1997–98		1990–91	1993–94	1997–98
Cuba	6.8	3.5	2.3	Russia	4.2	5.8	3.8
EU	5.6	6.3	6.2	USA	2.6	1.6	2.0
Thailand	2.7	2.8	2.9	EU	1.8	2.0	1.8
Brazil	1.3	2.3	7.2	Japan	1.8	1.7	1.6
Australia	2.8	3.5	4.6	Korea	1.2	1.3	1.5
Total	32.3	30.0	35.6	Total	27.3	28.8	35.6

Source: USDA, *Sugar and Sweeteners Situation and Outlook Yearbook* (1999).

The table above illustrates the main importers and exporters of sugar in the world over the past ten years. There is no doubt that a change in the tradi-

13   For example, if the agreements made by particular countries with respect to export subsidies are respected, it is estimated that the figure of 7.2 million metric tons of sugar reported as subsidised for the 1986–90 period (which is a highly dubious figure) will decrease to 5.7 million tons in 2001. Even if this figure is attained, the amount of subsidised sugar will remain very high in relation to total world exports, approximately 16% (ISO, 1998) and the decrease will have little if any impact on price levels.

14   We believe that the policy which could have the strongest short-term impact on the behaviour of sugar markets is the one implemented by the Brazilian government with respect to its internal producers and its sugar/alcohol programme. Such a policy could significantly stimulate or restrain increases in the supply of exportable sugar, creating the possibility of a saturated market. Another important factor linked to policy perspectives in specific countries are the forecasts of the recuperation of the Cuban sugar agro-industry. This issue will be taken up later in the chapter.

Development Prospects in Cuba

tional sugar policies implemented by governments in these countries could
have significant repercussions on the behaviour of its world market, yet at
least in the short term, there do not appear to be significant policy changes
on the horizon.[15]

In summary, the competitive prospects of the global sugar market in the
medium term are those of a protected supply-saturated market which is
being challenged by alternative sweeteners that constrain its potential levels
of demand. On the other hand, as has already been seen, the most trustworthy forecasts indicate that sugar will continue to be the most important
sweetener on the market until at least the year 2010, and that both its
demand and its consumption will continue to rise.

Such prospects situate the competitive possibilities of major sugar
exporters in the price-cost relation of its product vis-à-vis the world market.
The following graph shows the behaviour of raw sugar prices on the world
market in the 1990s. As can be observed, the sugar market maintained relatively high and stable prices until 1998, the year in which a very significant
downward trend emerged.

Figure 5.2: Average Monthly Price of Raw Sugar, January 1994–July 1999

Source: Coffee, Sugar, Cocoa Exchange (1999).

The forecast elaborated in the second half of 1999 indicated that prices
would continue to fluctuate between three and five cents per pound in the
short term and between five and eight cents per pound in the medium term.

15   In the case of the European Union there seems to be no need for important changes in the
Common Agricultural Policy, which means that its high subsidies for sugar production and
especially for exports will remain at current levels.

These forecasts were consistent with the oversupply with which demand was met and with the maintenance of protectionist mechanisms for internal production in almost all countries.[16] In the fourth quarter of 2000, however, price levels began to recuperate rapidly despite persistent supply-demand imbalances.

Despite the recent rise in sugar prices, there is little doubt that downward market pressures on prices will continue in the medium term, and this will require further competitive conditioning to the cost-price relations currently present on the world market. The analysis of the cost-revenue relations that are competitive on the world market is a highly controversial subject. At times it appears to be a practically impossible task given the perennial and historical price fluctuations that have characterised this market, and given the differences in the protectionist architecture currently in place in nations that produce and export sugar. These are compounded by statistical inconsistencies as well as distortions in the exchange rates which are used to calculate them.

In spite of these difficulties, it is possible to approach this complex problem using the methods elaborated by Dr James Fry, a specialist at LMC International Ltd., as a valid starting point.[17]

Figure 5.3: Real Price (1994) of One Ton of Sugar

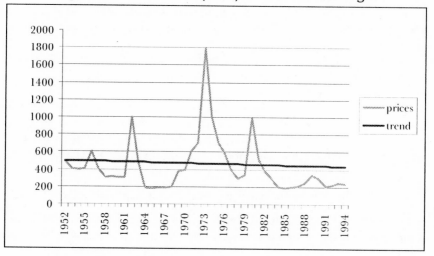

16   Love (1999).
17   Fry (1997).

Figure 5.4: Real Price and Cost of One Ton

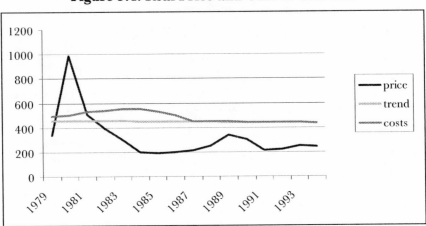

The first graph shows the long-term tendency of the real price (1994) of raw sugar, adjusted for inflation for the years 1952–96. This is a decreasing tendency, declining at an average annual rate of slightly more than 1.5 per cent, which means that a producer that is exposed to world prices would have to be able to lower average production costs at that rate to remain competitive.

The second graph illustrates a long-term comparison of real annual prices for the period 1979–94 and real annual average production costs of raw sugar.

As the graph shows, the average global production cost of cane sugar was higher than the long-term trend of world sugar prices until 1985. Since then both lines have converged.

This price-cost balance suggests that the decreasing trend in costs is a measure of the competitive levels to which each country needs to condition its production within the complex arena of the current global sugar market. It is to this trend then, that the Cuban sugar agro-industry must adjust itself.

The Cuban Sugar Agro-industry and its Competitive Prospects

As was indicated earlier, one of the determining criteria for evaluating the competitive prospects of a country in the world market is the relation of cost to prices and to the current trends of costs on the world market.

There are two factors that complicate the comparison of costs in the Cuban sugar agro-industry with the costs and prices on the global sugar market. The most important of these factors is the lack of an economically determined exchange rate that can make Cuban costs and prices truly comparable to those in the world market. This problem affects not only the sugar industry, but the Cuban economy as a whole.

The second factor, which creates uncertainty when the indicators of the Cuban sugar industry are compared to those of its main competitors, is the absence of the cost of land use in Cuban accounting practice.[18] Along with these difficulties, systematic data regarding the annual production costs of a ton of raw sugar are not available from official Cuban sources, which means they need to be estimated. The following table shows an estimate of costs in the Cuban sugar agro-industry evaluated in pesos (the national currency) at the official exchange rate of one dollar to one peso for the 1997–98 sugar harvest. This estimation was calculated on the basis of agricultural cost data of sugar-cane co-operatives (UBPC), which account for more than 80 per cent of the total agricultural area dedicated to cane cultivation.

Table 5.4: Costs of the Sugar-Cane UBPCs for the 1997–98 Harvest

Agricultural costs of one ton of sugar cane (in pesos)	Agricultural yield in tons of cane/hectare	Costs of one ton of sugar (in pesos) (1)
30.31	35.00	445–482

Source: Sulroca, 1999

(1) Estimated according to a 10.5% industrial yield with 60–65% of agricultural costs in total costs

If one bears in mind that the costs of imported goods required in order to produce one metric ton of sugar — which are calculated at an exchange rate of one dollar to one peso — have fluctuated between 120 and 160 dollars per ton,[19] and that these are part of the total costs previously indicated, the remainder of the costs that are entirely domestic (mainly wages and the amortisation of plant and equipment) vary between 304 (464–160) and 344 (464–120) pesos, assuming that the total cost of a ton of sugar in pesos fluctuates at a level close to the mean (464) within its range of variation (445–482). If these figures are calculated according the average exchange rate currently operative in Cuba's retail market (20 pesos to 1 dollar), the total costs measured in dollars would be very low. An exchange rate of 12–15 pesos to a dollar, however, would yield costs approaching 200 dollars per ton.

According to unofficial information obtained by the author, the figure calculated as the cost of a ton of raw sugar in the so called schemes of 'ter-

18 ECLAC (2000).
19 Lage (1996).

ritorial financing' that involve foreign capital is close to 200 dollars per ton.[20] This is also the figure used to calculate the industry's recuperation strategies.

Finally, the following table shows comparative data for the 'real' costs of the principal exporters of cane sugar and the global average according to the findings of a comparative cost study elaborated by International LMC, Ltd.[21] It is important to keep in mind that this study does not specify the methodology utilised to calculate the exchange rate (in fact, the official national exchange rate is assumed for each country). This study also fails to address the assumptions made in the cost of land rental in the Cuban case. The average cost figures given for the Cuban sugar agro-industry for the 1989–90 to 1994–95 period (434 dollars) are close to the minimum figure for the total estimated cost if a one to one exchange rate is used.

Table 5.5: Average Real Production Costs (adjusted for inflation to 1994 prices) for One Ton of Raw Sugar

	Average 1979/80–1984/85			Average 1984/85–1989/90			Average 1989/90–1994/95		
	Agricult	Ind.(1)	Total(2)	Agricult	Ind.(1)	Total(2)	Agricult	Ind.(1)	Total(2)
Australia	236.1	99.6	386.1	194.5	89.7	326.9	158.4	58.2	249.1
Thailand	272.4	138.4	472.5	163.5	103.7	307.2	172.6	63.9	272.0
Brazil	205.2	119.2	373.1	149.3	107.5	295.3	127.4	50.0	204.0
Cuba	256.6	123.1	436.7	226.1	111.2	388	248.6	128.8	434.0
World	279.3	163.9	509.8	226.2	143.5	425.1	207.0	106.8	360.8

Source: LMC International, Ltd., 1997

(1) Includes an allowance for molasses by product credits, which are assumed to accrue to the factory.
(2) Includes a 15% allowance for administration costs. Thus, Total = Field +Factory + Administration.

As the preceding table illustrates, total costs per ton in the Cuban sugar industry since 1990 are above the average costs on the world market. Furthermore, data show that over the past several decades, the production costs of raw Cuban sugar have been above those of its global competitors.

---

20 Peña and Alvarez (1997).
21 LMC (1997)

The Reform Process in the Sugar Agro-industry

The following table shows the behaviour of the principal indicators of the Cuban sugar agro-industry for a period of slightly more than ten years.

Table 5.6: Key Indicators of the Cuban Sugar Agro-Industry

| | Indicators of Production | | Indicators of Yield | |
| | Sugar | Sugar-Cane | Industrial | Agricult. |
Years	MMT	MMT	(%)	T/H
1988	7.4	67.5	10.9	51.7
1989	8.1	73.9	10.8	54.5
1990	8.0	74.4	10.7	52.0
1901	7.6	71.0	10.6	49.1
1992	7.0	65.4	10.6	44.7
1993	4.3	42.9	9.9	35.3
1994	4.0	43.0	9.3	33.5
1995	3.3	33.2	9.9	28.2
1996	4.5	41.4	10.7	32.5
1997	4.3	42.5	10	32.0
1998	3.2	33.0	9.9	30.2
1999	3.6	34.4	10.5	36.0
2000	4.1	39.4	10.5	37.1

T/H: tons per hectare MMT: million metric tons
Source: MINAZ, 1998. Data for the 1998–2000 harvests are the author's estimates

As the table illustrates, indicators were relatively favourable until 1993, at which time one can see an abrupt decrease in the levels of production and output from which the sugar industry has yet to recover.

In our opinion, there were three determining causes in the crisis of the Cuban sugar industry; the exhaustion of the model of extensive growth of the industry,[22] the highly negative impact that the collapse of socialism in

22   Throughout the 1980s the main indicators of the Cuban sugar agro-industry showed relatively favourable levels. During this decade, the volume of sugar-cane production destined for industrial elaboration averaged 71 million tons. This was 28% above the average for the 1970s and 54% above the average levels of production of the 1960s. The elevated levels of cane production during the 1980s allowed the industry to maintain average production levels that surpassed seven million tons of raw sugar per harvest.

Eastern Europe and the Soviet Union had on the Cuban economy,[23] and the strengthening of the economic embargo imposed on Cuba by the United States.[24]

The new international context which the Cuban economy had to confront starting in the 1990s and the exhaustion of the extensive growth model that

---

The increases in the cane and sugar production of the 1980s, however, were not sustained by increases in agricultural output, but through the implementation of an extensive growth model characterised by large amounts of land under cultivation, high levels of capital investment, low average levels of potential milling capacity, sustained consumption of productive goods, and high costs (Alvarez and Peña Castellanos, 1995).

This extensive growth model has an obvious limitation. It presupposes a growing availability of resources that are inefficiently utilised as well as a growing expansion of the quantities of land under cultivation, and brings with it insoluble problems with respect to agro-technology and to the productive organisation of both agriculture and industry.

In the late 1980s the exhaustion of the extensive growth system was clearly manifested in two important indicators — the drop in investment efficiency (the variation of the value of cane production in relation to investments) and the low levels of agricultural output (Alvarez and Peña Castellanos, 1995).

23   One factor which had a tremendously negative impact on the performance of the Cuban sugar agro-industry in the early 1990s was the radical transformation of the external environment of the Cuban economy.

The collapse of socialism in Eastern Europe and the Soviet Union and the disintegration of CAME resulted in the literal disappearance of the country's principal framework of economic relation, in which it had operated for almost 30 years.

Towards the end of the 1980s Cuba conducted approximately 80% of its international economic transactions with CAME's member nations. This group of countries absorbed the majority of Cuba's total exports (including 63% of its sugar), and was the source of approximately 85% of the country's total imports, including its main sources of fuel, chemical products and machinery and equipment for the sugar industry (Peña Castellanos and Alvarez, 1997).

It is calculated, for example, that between 1989 and 1992, the value of imported productive goods and equipment of the Cuban sugar agro-industry fell by over 70%. Cuba's ties to CAME member nations, moreover, were based on stable and favourable terms for the country within a framework of co-ordinated strategies for resource provision, exports and development loans in which the Cuban sugar agro-industry played an essential role. One figure which illustrates, albeit insufficiently, the importance of these economic relationships for the sugar industry is the following: through its commerce with CAME nations, Cuba obtained revenues that were over 50% higher than those it would have received for its exports at world market prices in the period between 1981 and 1990 (Alvarez González and Fernández Mayo, 1992).

24   The collapse of socialism in Eastern Europe and the Soviet Union strengthened the influence of conservatives in US foreign policy towards Cuba. The prevailing notion in the United States was that a strengthening of the economic embargo against Cuba (in place since the early 1960s) would precipitate the collapse of the Cuban sociopolitical system.

Economic measures against Cuba were strengthened starting in the early 1990s. In October 1992, US Congress passed the so-called 'Cuban Democracy Bill' . This law reiterated the existing prohibitions on the establishment of economic relations with Cuba by US companies and extended them to their subsidiaries in third countries. Furthermore, these measures prompted other governments to adopt similar policies. In the context of this escalation, the president of the United States signed the Helms-Burton Law (named after its congressional sponsors) in March 1996, legally codifying the policies of the economic embargo against Cuba.

had until then predominated in the sugar sector forced a radical transformation in the productive and managerial systems of the industry. Economic reforms in the sugar industry were first implemented in its agricultural sector. The basic problem that had to be confronted in the early 1990s was how to reactivate the industry during a time of severe resource scarcity. The initial response was the elaboration and implementation of a new form of agro-industrial management and organisation that was intended to produce a more efficient use of scarce resources. This became known as the Basic Unit of Co-operative Production (UBPC).[25]

In essence the UBPC is a form of co-operative agricultural production in which *state land* is leased to producers over an indefinite period of time. Co-operative producers, who are legally recognised as the owners of what is produced and of the productive inputs which they purchase through credit, sell harvested cane to industrial processing centres (called Agro-industrial Complexes), and possess relative autonomy over how they use their monetary and productive resources.

Once the UBPC was approved for sugar-cane agriculture, an accelerated process of transformation began sweeping through the sector. In late 1993, practically all state land dedicated to sugar-cane cultivation was reorganised under this new administrative and productive model, and over 98 per cent of workers employed in agricultural cane cultivation became members of the co-operatives.

The conversion of state sugar-cane farms into UBPCs was more than simply nominal. It signalled a profound transformation in the organisation of agricultural production. In early 1993, for example, there were approximately 734 sugar-cane farms operating on 1.2 million hectares of land, with an average farm size of 1,665 hectares.

By December 1993 93 per cent of the total state agricultural lands had been turned over to the UBPCs, which by then numbered 1,556. This meant an average area of 800 hectares per co-operative, and therefore a reduction of more than 50 per cent in the area of land per productive unit.[26]

The second important policy implemented to reactivate the sugar agro-industry was its partial opening to foreign capital. Actually, there had been a

25   In accordance with Law No. 142, the Ministry of Sugar (MINAZ) implemented Resolution No. 160 93 in September 1993 which put in effect the General Ordinance of the UBPCs administered by the MINAZ (MINAZ, 1993). This ordinance established that the UBPCs were to be constituted primarily of sugar farmers linked by labour to the lands destined for the creation of this kind of co-operative, and who expressed a desire to belong to such co-operatives.

The ordinance states, moreover, that the fundamental objective of the UBPC is to develop and increase the production of the high-quality sugar-cane by implementing the agro-technical protocols most appropriate to the soil and climate of each region and through the rigorous application of state-of-the-art technologies in sowing, cultivation and harvesting processes.

26   Alvarez and Peña (1995).

legal framework (Law No. 50) for international economic investment on the books since 1982 yet it was not until 1990 that this legislation was given broader and more extensive use. In September 1995 the Cuban National Assembly approved Law No. 77. Since its promulgation it has served as the legal framework for everything related to the movement and transactions of foreign capital in the country.

In the specific case of the sugar sector, the resolutions regarding foreign capital adopted in the early 1990s only permitted investment or financing agreements for the production and commercialisation of sugar-cane derivatives. In 1994, as a response to the scarcity of resources and the generally difficult situation facing the sugar sector, these restrictions were eliminated and the sugar sector was formally opened to associations with foreign entities. Since then, territorially based financing schemes for sugar production have been the most important means of entry for foreign capital into the sugar sector. Such financing is given annually, although it is possible to negotiate it through medium-term agreements, and is destined to secure the agricultural and industrial inputs needed for the territorial production of sugar under such agreements.

These arrangements were implemented for the first time during the 1995–96 harvest, when nine out of the thirteen sugar producing provinces received foreign financing through such agreements for a total of approximately 300 million dollars.

The agreements established with foreign capital under this arrangement presuppose that the principal, the interest and a portion of revenues will be repaid in sugar, in accordance with production increases above the production average of the harvests selected in specific negotiations, as well as the price fluctuations on the global sugar market. Following this initial experiment, territorial financing arrangements have been maintained, but assuring the timely availability of needed funds at reasonable rates has presented some difficulties. In fact, the rather unstable reactivation of the country's sugar industry and the persistent organisational and efficiency problems in this sector have contributed to the elevation of financing costs.

As several industry officials have pointed out, the terms of credit written into these financing agreements for sugar production have created difficulties for the Cuban economy as a whole. These agreements, however, are indispensable considering the scarcity of other resources and given the critical situation that agro-industrial sugar sector is currently facing.[27] Up to now the reforms implemented in this sector of the sugar industry have not been sufficiently effective. In fact, the recuperation of its production and output indicators has been unstable, with these still far below their historical levels.

---

27   Lage (1995).

The reforms have also been limited and have not been accompanied by the resources necessary for the reconversion of the sugar industry in accordance with the multiple exigencies imposed by the highly competitive conditions of the international market. Dr Carlos Lage, vice-president of the Council of State and secretary of the Executive Committee of the Council of Ministers, referred to this problem in a speech before the Cuban National Assembly for Popular Power in December 1998:

> ... Given the volume produced by the sugar industry, given the need for large-scale investment and modernisation projects, resources have not been available as they have been in the tourist and fishing industries, for example. They have not been available to ensure sugar production in these past few years and they will not be available for the coming harvest either. These funds have not been available on the scale that they are needed and as a result, the next harvest will be a difficult one, one which will take place under very complicated material conditions, and we must take this into account as we evaluate the state of sugar production ...[28]

In the short term at least, the process of recapitalisation of the sugar industry will not be based on domestic investment. At the same time however, there is no evidence that there will be a further opening of the sugar sector to foreign capital, at least as far as the production of raw sugar is concerned. This particular situation generates much uncertainty with regards to the competitive prospects of the industry.

Yet this does not negate the fact that today there are serious efforts to increase the levels of sugar production underway, particularly the levels of cane production. The strengthening of the economic and organisational mechanisms of the UBPCs as well as a gradual extension of these efforts to the Agro-industrial Complexes (CAI) and the Policy of Improvement of Enterprises (*Perfeccionamiento Empresarial*) — which encompasses the entire national economy — seek to reactivate the potential of this sector and recuperate its historical levels of production and revenue.

The following table contains a set of indicators that together illustrate the efficiency of the sugar agro-industry of various nations, among which is Cuba. A column has been added that extrapolates the behaviour of these indicators into an imaginary scenario of a reactivated Cuban sugar industry, calculated for the year 2005.

28   Lage (1998).

Table 5.7: Indicators of the Sugar Agro-Industry, Average for the Years 1993-97, and Forecasts for Cuba, 2005

	Area harvested in thousands of hectares	Agricultural yields in tons/hects.	Cane production in millions of tons	Sugar production in millions of tons	Yearly industrial output in (%)	Sugar per area of cultivation in tons/hects..
Australia	376	95.3	35	4.9	14.2	13.5
Thailand	943	50.6	48	5.2	10.8	5.5
Brazil	1740	61.5	107	12.0	11.2	6.9
Colombia	130	130.0	17	2.0	11.5	15.0
Cuba	1240	36.2	45	4.1	9.2	3.3
Cuba(*)	950	60	57	6.0	10.5	6.3

Source: USDA, 1999

(*) Forecasts of the sugar agro-industry for 2005 elaborated by the author.

One strategy to reactivate the potential of the country's sugar industry which prioritises areas related to agriculture and management — like the one currently being implemented — can raise sectoral production and efficiency levels in the medium term, to volume and revenue levels as high as those shown in the forecasts provided. This, however, does not necessarily mean that costs will be aligned with the competitive tendencies evinced by the world market (-1.5 annual average) that has been cited here. In fact only a strategy leaning towards a technological reconversion of the industry and towards the harnessing of its diversifying potential could have a significant impact on the cost-revenue relation and on the competitive prospects of this sector in the global arena.

The Sugar Agro-Industry and the Prospective Model of Growth of the Cuban Economy

As has been already indicated, the average level maintained by Cuba's sugar exports between 1986–90 was slightly more than six million tons, four million of which were destined for what was then the Soviet Union. Currently, there is widespread debate both inside and outside the country as to whether it is possible for Cuba to find a comparable level of demand in the context of a saturated world market.

The following table shows the results of a simulation conducted by a distinguished Cuban expert in order to prove that it would in fact be possible for Cuba to place approximately six million tons of raw sugar on the world market.

Table 5.8: Simulation: Cuban Sugar Exports to the World — 6 Million Tons

Russia	3,000,000
China	800,000
Arab Countries	700,000
Canada	400,000
Latin America	300,000
Japan	250,000
Bulgaria	150,000
Sub-Saharan Africa	100,000
Vietnam	50,000
Korea	50,000
Others	20,000

Source: Fernández (1997)

Although not stated explicitly by the author, this simulation presupposes the establishment of direct commercial agreements between Cuba and its potential customers. It also presupposes that the average price of sugar on the world market will remain at ten cents per pound.

As already indicated, current forecasts estimate that prices on the world market will fluctuate between eight and ten cents per pound and it is probable that any direct agreements with specific markets will be calculated accordingly. However, even under conditions in which there is a demand for Cuban sugar, the more restrictive cost and price conditions will play a determining role in its commercialisation.

The most immediate potential for increasing the efficiency of the sugar agro-industry lies in the boost of productivity levels in its agricultural sector, which have always been low, considering the benign climatic conditions of the country. Take the following example. In the 1980s, which was the period that registered the highest levels of agricultural output, average agricultural production levels reached only 67 per cent of its minimum potentials, levels which are obtainable without recourse to sophisticated agro-technological methods.[29]

29   Alvarez and Peña (1995).

Raising agricultural output, moreover, is a prerequisite for determining the parameters of the reduction and reconversion of the sugar agro-industry according to the limitations on demand and the scarcity of productive resources that characterise the sector today. In effect, the extensive growth model implemented in the Cuban sugar industry has created productive potential that is above ten million tons of sugar per year, presupposing that national agricultural yields are around 66 tons/hectare and that industrial output is at ten per cent. It does not seem prudent, however, to suppose the existence of export markets that can absorb more than six million tons which, when added to one million for internal consumption, yields a maximum total of six million. The elevation of agricultural output would then allow for a reduction of the agricultural areas destined for sugar-cane cultivation.

A simple estimation, for example, reveals that the agricultural areas destined for sugar-cane cultivation could be reduced by more than 20 per cent. Such a reduction, moreover, would require a reapportionment of the capacity of the industrial sector. Currently, there are 156 sugar-processing centres in Cuba that milled 71 million tons of cane annually between 1986 and 1990. This meant an under-utilisation of median industrial capacity for daily milling above 15 per cent — a calculation based on 150-day harvests and on an 85 per cent median use of industrial capacity.

This means, in theory, that 15 per cent of the country's daily milling capacity could be disposed of without affecting the total capacity necessary for processing harvests of seven million tons. In fact, of all existing sugar mills on the island, 16 per cent have a daily milling capacity that is under 2,300 tons (the median in the country is 4,200) — a milling capacity of questionable economic efficiency. In order to be competitive, however, more drastic reductions are required. The Cuban sugar agro-industry needs to achieve cost levels below ten cents per ton. Sustaining a trend of 1.5 per cent annual cost reductions at real 1994 prices is only possible in modernised industrial plants utilising advanced technology which have an average daily milling capacity above 10,000 tons.

Yet technological reconversion programmes — including automation processes and the reconversion of electrical energy systems which appear to experts in this area[30] as the most realistic and potentially significant ways to develop the potential of the derivative products of Cuban agro-industry — are economically justifiable only in industrial plants with a high milling capacity. Therefore, recuperating the competitiveness of the Cuban sugar agro-industry is a complex and multidimensional process that goes far beyond overcoming the managerial and organisational shortcomings that have characterised this sector for decades.

---

30   Torres and Sieczka (1993).

The necessity of maintaining a competitive strategy in the sugar sector is often identified as an obstacle to 'modernisation', or to the implementation of a new model of economic growth in the context of a global economy. Yet what is really at stake in most debates in Cuba are not precisely the ways in which resources for investment are generated, but the ways in which these are utilised. In this author's view, that equates to a misplaced focus in the analysis of the prospects of the sugar-cane industry in Cuba. It is a fact that a competitive strategy for Cuba's sugar sector cannot overlook the real potential of the market for sugar and sweeteners which, as was pointed out earlier, shows a tendency towards a relative decrease in the quantities of sugar that can be commercialised. Consequently, cost reductions and the modernisation of technology are the conditions for competitiveness imposed by the market, and these can only be implemented through efficient investment.

The failure to elaborate and implement a competitive strategy for the Cuban sugar industry is, it is argued here, the result of an incorrect notion that fails to evaluate objectively the competitive capacity of the country in the world markets as well as the real short-term alternatives with respect to net revenues obtained from the export of goods and services. Such a position also overestimates the macroeconomic relevance of the dynamism of emerging sectors, such as the tourist industry, and their capacity to attract foreign capital.

The gradual reduction of the exaggerated influence of the sugar industry on the country's macroeconomic indicators, specifically in its external sector, needs to be the result of the competitive development of new sectors and branches of the economy and not of cutbacks or limitations on the growth of a sector, like the sugar-cane industry, which has had a competitive potential that has been historically recognised by the market.

Finally, with respect to the possibilities for a sectoral transformation of the sugar agro-industry in the context of a dynamic and competitive insertion of the Cuban economy into the contemporary global economy, the potential of a diversified sugar agro-industry cannot be overlooked.

Currently in Cuba there exists both the accumulated knowledge and the available technological base to develop a diverse array of derivative sugar-cane products of various degrees of complexity. Commercially, the Cuban economy can produce more than 30 derivatives from the remains of pressed sugar-cane, 27 from cane molasses, 14 based on cane alcohol, and four from processed residues. The production of energy by the sugar-cane industry holds important reserves for the industry and for the country's economy more generally, as suggested earlier.[31]

31   ICIDCA (2000).

Conclusions

At present the sugar industry continues to be the most important sector of the Cuban economy although its relative influence has diminished, particularly in the overall trade balance of goods and services. Nevertheless, Cuban sugar exports continue to be an important source of the net foreign revenues in the economy, but its future development will depend on the behaviour of international sugar and sweetener markets and on the internal competitiveness that is achieved. The most trustworthy forecasts indicate that sugar will retain its place as the most important product in the market for sweeteners, although its relative participation will decrease as a result of competition from natural and artificial sweeteners. Forecasts also predict an intensification of the competitive conditions in the international sugar market, reflected in a tendency towards cost reduction to which sugar exporters will have to adjust. It is a given that under such conditions the select group of exporting countries will tend to shrink and that technological modernisation will determine which countries retain membership.

Currently, the Cuban sugar agro-industry retains considerable competitive potential. But the prolongation of its recuperation period as well as the delay of the process of technological modernisation could very well lead to Cuba's definitive displacement from the principal group of sugar exporting nations. The materialisation of a scenario like the one described could be accelerated by a distorted, deterministic and anachronistic vision of the feasibility of the model of economic growth of the Cuban economy in the context of globalisation.

The development of the model for growth and insertion of the Cuban economy into the global world economy must consider a diminishing influence of the sugar agro-industry in the overall intersectoral matrix of the economy and in the external sector. Nevertheless, the sugar industry has diversifying potential that could be efficiently pursued within such a model and that could contribute to a relatively sophisticated insertion (involving industrial upgrading) of the Cuban economy into its global counterpart.

CHAPTER 6

Domestic Markets and the Development Prospects of Cuba

Mauricio de Miranda Parrondo

Introduction

A nalysis of the role of the market in socialist economies has played a very important part in the theoretical and political debate about socialism. The debate's importance has both theoretical and practical connotations.

The experience of the Soviet Union and other socialist countries with building socialism was characterised by an ideological contradiction regarding whether it was appropriate or not to utilise market mechanisms in socialist economies. Starting in the 1960s, timid schemes of economic reform were adopted in the socialist states, especially in Eastern Europe. Several outstanding economists have bequeathed to us a vast body of work concerning this issue, which serves as a point of reference.[1]

Both the reforms of the 1960s and 1970s as well as those of the 1980s and even those carried out in Asia, particularly China and Vietnam, bore the mark of the debate on the market's role in socialist economies. The traditional reformist vision within socialism has advocated increasing the role of the market with an eye toward stimulating the production of goods and services and deploying the potential of the productive forces; this is true even if such advocates sometimes recognise the danger of immanent contradictions within this strategy. Meanwhile, the orthodox vision rejects the market, places faith in the possibilities of central planning and is fearful that the full re-establishment of market exchange relations may lead to the rebirth of capitalism.

The main goal of this chapter is to highlight key aspects of the relevance of the market to the current development prospects of the Cuban economy. To this end, the role of the internal market is examined first, in the light of the new conditions created by the crisis-driven reform measures adopted since 1993. Then attention shifts to discussion of a series of alternative policies by which the role of the internal market in the future development of the Cuban economy could be enhanced.

---

1   Among these works are Brus (1969), Sik (1968) and Lange (1966).

Economic Reform Measures and the Internal Market in the 1990s

The crisis management measures adopted in 1993 and 1994 by Cuba sought to reverse recessionary tendencies, recover budgetary balance, develop alternative sources of foreign exchange and stimulate foreign investment. They have had a relatively positive impact.

The tendency toward decline in the Gross Domestic Product (GDP) was halted. Between 1994 and 2000, Cuba's GDP grew at an average annual rate of 2.8 per cent. If this were to continue, it would mean that only in 2007 — 13 years after the recovery's start — would the country surpass its 1989 GDP level, based on constant 1981 prices. Measured over the past five years, the average annual growth rate has been 3.8 per cent, meaning that only in 2005 will 1985 GDP levels be surpassed.

Other economic indicators also reflect positive trends. In recent years the budget deficit was stabilised at 2.0–2.5 per cent of GDP.[2] Likewise, the proportion of the money supply held by the population as a share of GDP fell from 66.5 per cent to 37.5 per cent in 2000. Both industrial and agricultural production have recovered, with agriculture receiving a significant stimulus from the re-opening of agricultural and livestock markets (albeit still at lower levels than those of 1989). Foreign investment has continued to expand. The exchange rate has stabilised at around 20–21 pesos per dollar. The tourism sector has achieved significant results that have made it into the country's largest generator of foreign exchange.

Nevertheless, macroeconomic recovery and the re-establishment of sectoral growth trajectories have not translated into a significant improvement in living standards. Moreover, recent changes have exacerbated social inequality inasmuch as self-employed workers have been favoured, as have workers employed in those emerging sectors that operate in dollars.

In practice, the measures adopted by the Cuban government to confront the crisis have revitalised the internal market, so much so that the laws of supply and demand prevail in a growing number of processes that characterise economic relations. Nevertheless, the market that is developing contains very dangerous elements of distortion that threaten its own proper functioning, which will be examined below.

Parallel Currencies: the US Dollar and the Cuban Peso

The Cuban internal market has become segmented into two clearly defined components in terms of the currencies governing the circulation of merchandise and services — the dollarised market and the peso market. This has

---

2   De Miranda (2000b).

been the result of the de facto application of a monetary system based on parallel standards. Market segmentation was a clear result of moves in 1993 to legalise foreign exchange holdings and to authorise the parallel circulation of dollars along with pesos as a means for meeting particular obligations or paying for certain services.

This market segmentation has developed with a number of distinctive features. In the first place, an important and growing number of basic necessities are sold in dollars in the various store and supermarket chains, which had initially been intended to serve tourists but which nowadays count Cubans among their main customers. This group of basic goods ranges from foodstuffs of many types to electrical appliances, and also includes clothing and footwear, which are part of the basic family needs of any civilised nation.

All this means that, in principle, those citizens lacking any source from which to obtain foreign exchange are deprived of those products. Those with access to US currency may, in principle, be divided into four groups: (1) workers in the tourism sector and employees of foreign companies or joint ventures who receive tips and bonuses in convertible currency; (2) family members of expatriate Cubans who receive remittances from those countries; (3) professionals who secure temporary contracts abroad and are obliged to pay a certain share of their income to the Cuban state; and (4) self-employed workers who are paid for their services or labour in foreign exchange or in equivalent amounts in pesos based on market exchange rates. This permits these types of workers and their families to earn a considerably greater income than those who continue to work in the public sector.

A second feature of the parallel market is the lack of correspondence between what amounts to a fictitious official exchange rate of 1 US dollar = 1 Cuban peso and the free market rate of 1 US dollar = 20–22 Cuban pesos. Economic theory suggests that the exchange rate should reflect the competitive and relative price conditions that prevail between a country and its trading partners. Under current conditions, continuing to maintain an official exchange rate based on dollar-peso parity constitutes an economic policy error. Exporting companies bring exchange receipts back into the Cuban economy at an overvalued peso rate. What is more, the existence of the so-called foreign exchange market has created the fiction of '*exportaciones en frontera*';[3] this refers to the sale of products in internal markets under conditions of protection that derive from the state's control over commercial distribution and distribution channels, a control which acts as a non-tariff protectionist barrier for nationally produced goods. This is not to deny the importance of privileging domestic production in the internal consumption market, but to argue that this preference should occur under conditions of competition.

---

3   '*Exportaciones en frontera*' means special internal transactions that are in US dollars.

A third feature of market segmentation stems from the state's control over the commercialisation of goods, including those priced in dollars. This control has allowed the state — through high margins that consumers must bear if they want to obtain such goods — to make state enterprises operating in foreign exchange efficient.

A fourth feature of market segmentation concerns government directives requiring that various enterprises and institutions be self-financing in foreign exchange. Such policies have created a situation in which state enterprises undertake foreign exchange transactions even amongst themselves while government institutions demand payment in hard currency for certain services. All this takes place despite the fact that, by law, the Cuban peso is the medium of exchange that serves as 'legal tender and has unlimited acceptance for the payment of all obligations contracted or outstanding on national territory'.[4]

Under such policies, which defy common sense, the position of the national currency has been weakened, and in effect a partial dollarisation of the economy has occurred. This has happened to such an extent that products and services sold in the internal market can be paid for either in dollars or in pesos calculated at prevailing market exchange rates. Meanwhile, most of the Cuban population earns Cuban pesos, at wage rates that do not correspond to the inflationary spiral that the country has had to endure for several decades during which a black market in foreign currency has existed. In fact, current wage rates do not guarantee minimal conditions of survival for the majority of workers and their families.

Rigidities in Internal Markets

Another of the factors distorting markets' proper functioning is their very own rigidities. These are due to the state's absolute control over them, a control which has always tended to give priority to political over economic considerations in defining economic policy.

The *labour market* is one of the most rigid among the country's markets. Ever since private enterprises were nationalised (at the beginning of the 1970s) and the state became the sole employer, the labour market came to be controlled through the demand side. The state sets the wages for the different categories of workers, based on their professional training, but without taking into account the professional's personal conditions. The situation does not allow workers to compete for better paid positions or state entities to hire the most qualified workers. The state even guarantees 'full employment' by placing every young graduate of universities and technological schools in positions that do not necessarily correspond to his or her professional expectations or even the interests of the enterprises.

4   This is inscribed on all peso bills in Cuba.

In the same manner, managers are prevented by the state's mandatory wage scales from competing for the best professional or technical personnel by offering wage differentials. In addition, the legal norms that allowed for self employment initially excluded professionals who, even later on when they were included, were restricted to activities outside their profession. Such restrictions correspond more to political considerations than to a logic of competitive advantages.

Given this state of affairs, it is not surprising that one can observe university-educated professionals holding down unskilled jobs that are, in practice, better remunerated than those available in their own fields. Persistence of this situation would be the worst possible scenario for Cuba's future if one considers that so-called human capital is still today one of the country's main competitive advantages.

Among the country's labour market rigidities it is worth underlining the prohibition on hiring non-family members in micro-enterprises as well as the detailed limitations placed on the size of family firms. These measures restrict demand for labour and in fact limit the growth of productive employment, especially in those activities in which the state has not been sufficiently efficient. This policy reflects a reluctance to authorise privately-owned Cuban enterprises outside of small peasant-held plots of land.

One of the consequences of this situation is that the Cuban state must take on an immense burden of providing work and social benefits. The overwhelming majority of Cuba's workforce — 78 per cent — works for the state, while the domestic private sector employs only 13 per cent of the labour force, four per cent of whom are self-employed.[5] Another consequence is that the state does not facilitate the exit of those who wish to leave the state employment system and enter the private sector. In fact, the state maintains the right to grant or refuse operating licenses for certain self-employed activities.

In terms of the labour market, it is also important to note the archaic character of the pension regime. It does not take into sufficient account the demographic changes occurring in Cuba, particularly the tendency toward an ageing population.

For its part, the *capital market* still does not function in Cuba. Since Foreign Investment Law 77 was adopted in 1995 the country has benefited from foreign direct investment (FDI), although this has been somewhat intermittent. Law 77 gives the state, acting through the Ministry of Foreign Investment and Economic Collaboration, the power to decide whether investment proposals are appropriate. This authority is understandable in light of the interest that any state takes in guiding national economic development and above all in controlling illicit activities. However, even though

5   ONE (2000a).

foreign investment can enter almost all sectors of the Cuban economy (except health, education and defence), in practice individual FDI projects only take place if the government sanctions them as beneficial for the country. This leads to the casting aside of certain investments that, while they might not have a substantial impact on the country's strategic economic course, nevertheless constitute a business option for the country as well as an additional source of employment.

Meanwhile, the prohibition on private national investments is becoming a brake on the country's economic development. As a result of the market opening measures adopted during the economic crisis of the 1990s a small part of the population took advantage of the opportunity to become wealthy. Every time there has been an attempt at market opening in Cuba, however timid and controlled, the scarcity of private sector possibilities has given a special advantage to those few who are able to insert themselves into those markets. This has translated into private internal capital accumulation that has been insufficient to foster sustained development of new ventures.

Under present conditions, existing restrictions on the size and magnitude of self employment activities place limits on the capital accumulation process, negatively affecting economic growth. This is not because the restrictions prevent growth, but rather because they waste growth potential. In practice, excessive restrictions on the development of private activity have created a situation in which it is precisely those engaging in illicit activities who have the most capital accumulation capacity, rather than those who abide by the law.

The limitations imposed on domestic private investment have produced a situation in Cuban society that defies common sense. This is because the complete, or near complete, lack of saving and investing opportunities make this into the kind of consumer society that is so strongly criticised in terms of capitalist societies. If the individual cannot save and invest, the only purpose that savings can have is to increase future consumption, thus establishing consumption as an economic goal. This phenomenon ends up curtailing entrepreneurial initiative and the creativity of individuals and, consequently, that of society as well. Cuban society has clearly turned into a society based on consumerism — an unsatisfied desire for consumption.

In *goods markets* serious rigidities also persist, despite recent liberalising measures. The anachronistic system of rationing of products persists, which aims to protect the minimum consumption levels of the lower-income population. The rationing of so-called 'industrial goods' (consumer goods other than foodstuffs) disappeared with the crisis of the Special Period of the 1990s. Food rationing is not enough on its own to assure nutrition levels that guarantee people's healthy survival. Apparently there persists, due to human solidarity, a space of egalitarian distribution, yet it is still insufficient to enable individuals to lead a healthy life. All this amounts to the fact that, in practice, the everyday life of the great majority of the Cuban people has become a struggle for survival. There is not just a struggle for the survival of socialism in Cuba, but also a struggle for the survival of individuals and families. It is worth considering whether it would be more efficient to adjust relative prices according to market conditions, while at the same time subsidising those low-income people whose living conditions would deteriorate under such an adjustment.

A noteworthy aspect of goods markets is the growth of the relatively new selective distribution schemes being carried out in workplaces, especially those linked to the hard currency sector and even to members of the armed forces and interior ministries. A growing number of public sector workers receive, with varying levels of frequency, indirect income through baskets composed of certain industrial goods or foodstuffs. Other public workers can acquire durable goods at subsidised prices through arrangements made in their respective workplaces. Based on official figures for the year 2000, a total of 1,158,000 workers took part in hard-currency based incentive systems; 1,461,000 received special food assistance; 1,999,000 received clothing and shoes; and more than 700,000 received household cleaning items and other consumer articles.[6] Moreover, it is important to point out that, even though a sizeable share of workers receives this type of benefit, it is still insufficient to guarantee a living standard that goes beyond survival-level conditions for a modern society.

Moreover, one of the still insoluble problems in Cuban society has to do with the absence of a housing market. The housing shortage is probably one of Cuban society's worst problems. The successive housing laws under Cuban socialism have prohibited the buying and selling of real estate, generating a situation that is *sui generis* in the whole world — the exchange of housing units. The state intervenes in this type of transaction, even deciding if such trades will go forward or not. In Cuba, the right to own one's home is recognised. Of course, many families gained title to their homes by paying small fees that are low by world standards, albeit with income levels that also are not comparable to international standards. However, Cuban legislation does not permit the sale of this property through private transactions, but rather only through sale to the state, at the price recognised by the state. The decline in home building has aggravated this problem, whose persistence is the source of more than a few psycho-social conflicts.

Likewise, and for the same reasons mentioned above, the *market for services* suffers from various rigidities that lead to grave social contradictions. The ban on self employment in certain professions that in theory could offer professional services to society creates an inequality of material opportunities, which do not correspond to any contribution to society or to social justice, especially under conditions of difficult survival. While certain serv-

6   Rodríguez (2000).

ice-oriented trades can charge market prices, other categories of professionals must pay such prices for the services they receive but cannot charge what their own services are worth. If this market were liberalised, there would be additional sources of self employment that would help adjust the relative prices of services based on market conditions. Without denying the social importance of certain social services and the achievement that it represents for Cuba to be able to offer them free of charge to the entire population, it should not be forgotten that no good or service can be distributed if it has not been created first. This implies that the free education and healthcare enjoyed by Cuban society are the result of the daily effort of millions of Cubans. However, alongside what the state contributes to this effort, it is worth considering the possibility that these services could be offered privately wherever there is demand for them.

Inadequate Linkages between Domestic and International Markets

The reform measures introduced in Cuba have not managed to overcome the lack of persistent linkages between the internal market and the international market. This is basically because the relative prices of goods and factors of production do not correspond to each other. These prices are distorted by the maintenance of an archaic system of prices and wages in which the market is subordinated to political decisions.

Since the triumph of the Revolution, the political interest in maintaining unchanged price levels for goods so as to chase away the phantom of inflation has widened the gap between domestic and international price levels. Prices could only be kept under control through non-convertibility of the national currency, lest international resources be totally exhausted. As a result, the linkage that establishes the exchange rate between the internal and external markets was severed.

If non-convertibility breaks the linkage between internal and external economic conditions, the establishment of a dual currency regime has helped reinforce this lack of connection. This is because it only makes sense to invest foreign exchange in those activities in which it is possible to recover the investment in hard currency. Nevertheless, for a foreign investor access to the internal market is almost always attractive at the same time that such access may also mean an important possibility for positioning the firm on the international market. Yet the peso-based segment of the Cuban internal market has become a sort of marginal market that consumes the worst products, whereas a significant portion of the goods sold in the country only circulate on the hard currency market.

The immense unsatisfied consumer demand that exists in the internal Cuban goods market holds opportunities for investors who seek to develop production that is indiscriminately targeted at the internal and international markets. However, in order for these opportunities to be realised, the purchasing power of the Cuban population must increase, and this can only occur in the context of a very profound economic reform that the current political leadership is not in a position to adopt.

In contradictory fashion, the need for goods and services is immense in Cuba, but the scarce purchasing power of the majority of the people acts as a brake on the development of production. However, some enterprises that have begun to sell products on the internal market, in hard currency, have managed to achieve a certain level of dynamism. This is true even though their levels of efficiency — given the persistence of a pattern of import substitution under the country's commercial policy — are far from international levels

Some Reflections on the Possibilities of the Internal Market in the Future Economic Development of Cuba

The historical experience of development processes illustrates the important contribution of the internal market. In the case of the developed nations of Europe and the United States, economic development resulted from a dynamic internal market under the conditions of the industrial revolution. In the case of the Asian economies, both Japan as well as the newly industrialised countries, these appeared to have developed by combining accumulation based on an active trade balance with an internal market that grew as their respective external sectors expanded. Moreover, experience also reveals the pivotal role played by industrialisation in the now more developed countries.

In good measure, the majority of the nations now considered developed achieved their development after a stage in which conditions were created in the context of frameworks of protection. It is for that reason that, given the predominant current conditions of globalisation, analysis of the development processes of underdeveloped nations becomes complicated. Present-day development processes must take place within an increasingly globalised economy, and Cuba will not be an exception to these tendencies.

During almost all its economic existence Cuba has been inserted into the world economy based on the advantages deriving from natural resource availability or the presence of specific conditions for natural resource-based development of production. The specialisation of Cuba based on sugar, tobacco and nickel responded to this pattern. Even under current circumstances, in which tourism has become the principal source of foreign exchange (without taking into account unilateral capital transfers), the insertion of Cuba seems to be occurring based on the utilisation of its natural conditions. By contrast, the historical experience of the countries that have obtained a certain level of development even through natural resources demonstrates that this has occurred based on a significant creation of advantages centred on what have been called 'advanced factors'.[7]

Now then, unlike developing nations, Cuba has human resources of relatively good quality in general terms. This competitive advantage consists in the population's level of professional training and its capacity to assimilate advanced technologies and even innovate and generous autochthonous technologies. The country's educational infrastructure could be a factor that would facilitate the necessary flexibility in the process of training and educating human capital. Under such conditions, the country would be able to insert itself into productive processes that are highly technology intensive.

Nevertheless, as was noted above, the low wage levels of Cuban workers seriously threaten to condemn human resources to a growing deterioration that is not only physical and spiritual but also technological. Therefore, *the increasing flexibility of the labour market* becomes imperative, so that the most qualified workers can compete for the relatively well-paid jobs based on their professional training, and firms can attempt to attract the most highly skilled workers based on their diverse technological needs.

The loosening of the labour market should contemplate the elimination of the current system of hiring of workers in joint ventures and foreign enterprises. This system is based on a Cuban state entity (ACOREC), which acts as the sole direct employer, setting a monopolistic restriction on the price of labour and, in practice, participating in the appropriation of surplus value as wages are kept under the true value of labour power. The Cuban state could receive the revenue necessary to fulfil its role as development promoter and income redistributor through a tax policy. This would be an attractive alternative to the direct capture of dollar wages from Cuban workers employed by firms in the 'emerging' sectors, wages which are relatively high compared to those paid in countries at similar levels of development.

Labour market reforms should not mean that the state abandons its regulatory role. A legal minimum wage would be necessary to protect all workers in the country from the danger of depreciation in the value of labour power — a depreciation that is particularly strong currently as a relatively skilled workforce earns paltry wage levels. Moreover, the state could establish, for private enterprises in general and foreign firms in particular, a series of employer contributions that would allow workers to receive indirect income that would guarantee adequate levels of social service coverage. Nevertheless, in its regulatory role the state must be careful not to set excessive taxes that would tend to discourage FDI.

Liberalisation of the labour market should also include a modification of the rigid wage ranges that the state establishes for the diverse occupational

7   Porter (1990).

categories in its own enterprises. This reform would allow state enterprises to adjust their workforces to their needs as well as to provide workers with sufficient incentives so as achieve high productivity and efficiency levels. Moreover, the elimination of current restrictions on hiring workers in the various types of private Cuban enterprises would enhance both workforce mobility and firm expansion.

Contrary to current rhetoric, private property could also play a social role — it could become an economic growth factor and alternative employment source at the same time that it fulfils the fundamental objectives defined by social consensus. Worker rights can be protected by legislation; social market economies constitute paradigms in this respect, as there the worker rights recognised in socialist countries are equalled or even surpassed.[8]

Under such conditions, it would be illogical to maintain the prohibitions on self employment that today prevent professionals from practising their respective professions. Not all professionals will be able to abandon their jobs to set up their own businesses, as demonstrated by experience in every country of the world. This would become particularly evident once wages were re-adjusted to the new relative price conditions.

The loosening of the labour market must be accompanied by the *loosening of the markets for goods, services and capital*. It makes no sense to maintain the fiction of a state market of rationed goods at reduced prices because it does not represent a significant portion of commercial exchange in the Cuban domestic market (and despite the fact that it currently represents a significant volume of consumption for lower-income families). The need to protect disadvantaged and low-income people could be met by creating direct transfers in the form of consumption subsidies, like those that exist in various relatively developed countries. Under such conditions, price liberalisation would allow the necessary relative price adjustments in the national economy to take place. This would facilitate price comparability with the economies of other countries, at the same time that it would foster the integration of domestic and international markets.

The reform of internal markets can only be achieved fully if it is accompanied by a *reform of the monetary system*, aimed at abandoning the parallel circulation of the dollar and the Cuban peso. Certainly, the Cuban peso in current conditions is an extremely weak currency given the weakness of the Cuban economy. For this reason, it would be worthwhile to consider the circulation of a convertible peso, whose convertibility would be adjusted to the economy's capacity to generate foreign exchange; that is to say, this would mean tying the value of the national currency to the availability of international reserves.

8   De Miranda (2000b).

Under the proposed reform, the prices of all goods and services would be set in Cuban pesos that would be fully convertible into hard currency. There would be no need to hold foreign exchange in the treasury as long as parity is maintained. Thus, available foreign exchange could be used in international transactions, rather than a situation — as currently occurs — in which dollars are more easily accepted for transactions in the domestic economy than the national currency. Obviously, this would imply a monetary policy of austerity, as well as support for conditions of macroeconomic equilibrium that would ensure an adequate level of convertibility of the national currency.[9]

In unifying the monetary system, markets would be unified and connecting vessels would begin to form between the various sectors and branches of the national economy. This would produce a process of competitive selection that would make possible the survival of firms that offer quality goods and services at competitive prices.

If the internal market exhibited greater dynamism, productive forces would be unleashed that would allow for greater economic growth. The domestic market is thus an indispensable source for strengthening the level of economic activity. However, the illusion that it is only through the market that Cuba will traverse the path to economic development must be avoided.

The state plays an essential role in the process of economic development insofar as it has the capacity to design, based on economic reality, strategic development guidelines. The state fails in the design of development strategies when it does not heed the objective conditions that define economic processes. Yet, if it uses economic policy instruments it has immense opportunities to stimulate the adaptation of productive forces in sectors that could generate future competitive advantages. Through various available levers, the state could signal the national development course that is desirable, based on the country's present conditions or those that might hold in the future.

During the last four decades in Cuba the state has been the main actor directing the economy. Yet its tradition of excessive centralism and disproportional emphasis on ideological considerations has turned state management into an important obstacle for the development of economic relationships that could accelerate the material progress that contemporary Cuban society needs. The effort to supplant the market in its function as the principal mechanism for the assignment of productive forces has failed, thus generating the disproportions, distortions and the inefficiencies noted above.

For this reason, the state in Cuba should play a new role in economic management. That role should stick closely to guaranteeing the resources

9   Presently there circulates a sort of 'third currency', which has been labelled the 'convertible peso', that is nothing other than a sign of equivalent value in North American currency. By contrast, the proposal advanced by this author is directed toward the creation of conditions of convertibility for the Cuban peso.

necessary to fulfil its most important social functions, namely, guaranteeing the material and social welfare of citizens, defence and national security, administration of justice and support for those sectors and branches of the national economy in which comparative advantages based on advanced factors of production are evident. The latter activities could become pivotal elements in a process of economic advancement that combines a highly skilled workforce, modern technology and fresh capital resources.

The adoption of measures like those described above would certainly create capitalist relations of production. Such relations, in the case of the underdeveloped Cuban economy and with adequate social control, could constitute a factor of development based on greater productive efficiency. With market relations social differences will be sharpened. Thus, the state must utilise fiscal policy mechanisms in order to manage national economic development with an eye toward guaranteeing the resources required by an industrial policy; such a policy would seek to strengthen the productive capacity of the economy and its respective factors of production, including labour, as well as provide the regulation necessary to redistribute resources and thus alleviate the social differences created by the market.[10]

Social differentiation has, in fact, persisted in socialist societies in general and in Cuba in particular. This has been based on the distinctive position of each individual in the hierarchy of state functionaries and on the differential access each has to private use of societal resources. Given this reality, socialist societies have not been able to form an adequate system for harmoniously combining social interests with private interests. Given that inequalities are a reality, albeit greater in some societies than in others, it is possible to imagine a structure of social relations in which wellbeing — the objective of any rational modern society — is directly tied to the increased capacity and creativity of individuals, subject to mechanisms that prevent those differences from excluding any segment of society.

In Cuba's current situation, inequities are based on inequality of opportunities. If these inequalities were corrected by eliminating the current spaces created in the internal market, this would return the country to uncertainty and stagnation and have a severe impact on social wellbeing. However, with the unleashing of market relations Cuba could take advantage of the creativity and entrepreneurial spirit of a population that has a higher educational level than average for countries with a similar, or even greater, level of development. This could be a factor that strengthens wellbeing.

In the same spirit, pragmatic advances must be made toward the *liberalisation of the capital and capital goods markets*. The restrictions on investing in private businesses — even at the level of small and medium enterprises — that are now imposed on Cuban citizens residing in the country not only

---

10   De Miranda (2000a).

constitute a form of discrimination, since foreign citizens can legally accumulate capital. They have also led to a situation in which some established ventures have left the country or turned to lavish consumption due to their inability to invest. Moreover, the impediments on Cubans residing outside Cuba, based on strictly political considerations, imply a real loss of investment resources that could be channelled toward the island. In this sense, the governments of China and Vietnam have shown greater pragmatism, subordinating political considerations to the need to raise economic wellbeing.

It would not be advisable for Cuba to open itself to a torrent of short-term capital, given the speculative effects that this would generate. However, it would be worthwhile to initiate an incipient internal capital market that would seek to channel the population's savings based on the criterion of the highest return. At the same time, such a market should be sufficiently dynamic as to be able to channel temporarily liquid financial resources into productive investment.

Cuba should proceed toward a greater level of economic integration with the world economy, based on a greater participation and adaptation of its economy to both multilateral as well as regional and sub-regional commercial frameworks. Clearly, as long as current US–Cuban hostility continues, there will be many obstacles to the island becoming inserted into a system of trade based on economic considerations. It is likely that, under a scenario of normalisation of US–Cuba ties, there would be a substantial change in the island's external economic relations, and the United States would become its principal trading and financial partner. However, the fact that currently Cuba's foreign economic relations are diversified could become an important consideration in terms of the interest in not repeating the traditional single-market dependence that has characterised Cuba's international economic relations, from the colonial period through the 1990s.

The current system of state import controls ought to pave the way toward a more liberal regime in which import limits are imposed on the basis of economic considerations. Stated differently, it is tariff policy that should be assigned the task of protecting national industry, within the framework accepted under Cuba's obligations to the World Trade Organization (WTO) and based on the establishment of necessary incentives for industrial exports in keeping with industrial policy objectives. Under a framework of greater commercial liberalisation, national private enterprises should be permitted to decide whether to purchase certain goods and services abroad with an eye toward improving their efficiency.

The policy of substitution of industrial imports should aim clearly at the manufacturing of goods that are internationally competitive. It should thus be linked to technology transfer and the contributions of foreign capital. Export orientation would make it possible to produce at the quality and price levels that the international market requires, as well as to avoid the errors of the process of import substituting industrialisation carried out by Latin American and Caribbean countries. Under such a policy framework, changes in the productive structure of the Cuban economy would be reflected in changes in the structure of its international insertion.

Moreover, Cuba needs to strengthen its capacity for international insertion through services. In this sense, it is important to stay on the road toward improving the efficiency of the tourist sector, as well as to achieve through that sector necessary linkages to other sectors of the national economy that could produce inputs. Such linkages could consolidate these sectors' position as producers of internationally tradable goods. However, this option should be accompanied by the strengthening of the financial sector and the development of communications, transportation and infrastructure, aspects in which the country is backward, even compared to underdeveloped market economies.

Finally, development policy should aim to strengthen productive chains that facilitate the country's international insertion as well as the productive integration of the internal market. Cuba is on its way towards requiring an intensive economic growth that can serve as the path to raising society's well-being and achieving greater economic development. To this end, traditional productive sectors that are the basis of Cuba's current international economic insertion need to be consolidated, while at the same time the transformation of the productive structure should be undertaken by favouring the manufacturing of higher value-added and more technologically intensive goods.

In the case of the Cuban economy, the greatest challenges of economic development lie in the liberalisation of markets, the acquisition of new technologies, the development of infrastructure and the greater utilisation of relatively skilled human resources. Market liberalisation would allow entrepreneurial initiative and creativity to combine with the greater intellectual and technical training that characterise both the labour force and an emerging class of individual and collective entrepreneurs. This would translate into a greater supply of goods and services for a market that is currently restricted on the supply side. Likewise, positive stimuli would be generated that represent greater levels of factor productivity, an indispensable condition for a model of intensive growth.

Access to new technologies would permit the reconversion of the bulk of Cuban industry, adapting it to advanced technological conditions. The technological obsolescence of Cuban industrial plants is still evident in a series of branches of the national economy, given that a backward technological pattern prevailed during the decades in which most industrial machinery came from the USSR and the other socialist countries. Cuban authorities are conscious of this necessity of technological upgrading, and thus one of the objectives of the loosening of controls on FDI is to capture not only financial resources but also to transfer more modern technology to the island.

Current infrastructure in terms of communications and transportation is inadequate for the demands of modern times. The transportation system throughout the country is not functional, which has increased geographical distances and created time inefficiencies that affect the national economy as they reduce labour productivity. Solving this problem is thus a fundamental economic priority. The country's ports still exhibit levels of inefficacy that severely raise the costs of loading and unloading ships. The use of computer networks like the internet is still limited in Cuba and highly controlled by the state; this use does not correspond to the educational level of the majority of the population. If Cuba is to advance toward becoming a modern society, it must endeavour to generalise telecommunications and information technology advances to the greatest possible number of people, despite the potential risks that this implies for the present system of information control in the country.

Finally, the current sectoral distribution of the labour force is distorted due to the irregular functioning of markets, the persistence of a dual currency regime and the stimuli that certain sectors generate under conditions of non-existent competition. This phenomenon has become a brake on the efficient use of human resources in the economy based on levels of professional and technical preparation, thus translating in practice into a waste of human capital. That is why there are grounds for believing that the liberalisation of the internal market and the possible deployment of productive potential that it would generate would produce a number of benefits. Among other things, it would allow all human beings to be the true owners of their destiny based on their own effort, and afford them the enjoyment of and responsibility for their liberty; it would permit human resources to be used efficiently from the perspective of individuals and society as a whole even though such harmony is sometimes elusive; and it would allow markets to function efficiently under responsible state regulation.

By Way of Summary

The Cuban economy has suffered a series of important transformations over the course of the 1990s, as a result of an acute crisis. Based on this situation and despite contrary ideological criteria, the direction of the reforms undertaken has been towards the market. It is on that path that, with a few cosmetic changes, the money and exchange relations that had been neglected at the end of the 1980s were re-established.

Reform measures have had positive effects on the whole, although they have not been immune to contradictions.[11] However, the Cuban leadership

11   A critical analysis of the reform measures adopted in Cuba in the 1990s can be found in Mauricio De Miranda, 'Contradicciones y alternativas de la reforma económica en Cuba', Paper presented to the 1998 Congress of the Latin American Studies Association (http://lasa.international.pitt.edu).

faces the dilemma of whether to deepen economic reforms while perhaps undermining the bases of the social and political regime or, alternatively, to continue on the road toward building a market economy in which the state exercises a certain regulatory role that combines growth with equity. If interest in preserving the prevailing social and political order in the short term leads to paralysis or reversal of reforms, over the medium term the economy will undergo a new crisis that will seriously threaten the social gains made in the last four decades and unleash unpredictable internal conflicts.

No society can quietly accept that its welfare be eternally relegated on behalf of an idea that is difficult to achieve. The dissolution of so-called 'really existing socialism' has left a great theoretical vacuum concerning the characteristics of the socialism that can be built in nations that still preserve it as a social regime. Thus, China and Vietnam have opted pragmatically for a system of economic relations that aims to increase material welfare based on the principle that such material welfare will lead to social welfare. For the moment, the large-scale liberalising measures have not been accompanied in either of those Asian countries by political reforms toward open democratic systems. However, the recent historical experience of those countries, above all that of China, demonstrates that political conflicts end up appearing in a society in which the market economy gains sway as a system of social relations. Insofar as the market establishes a certain social segmentation, conditions are created for the clash of interests within society.

This is precisely the great fear awakened in certain sectors of Cuban society by the prospect of a deepening of economic reforms, leading toward a market that is regulated but sufficiently strong to constitute the principal space for the assignment of factors of production. The appearance of a class of successful businessmen, whose living standards exceed those of the rest of society, could signify greater economic independence from the tutelary control of the state, a development which could oblige the state to become more politically independent. This would obviously depend on what characteristics the state might take on under alternative scenarios.

Over more than four decades Cuban society has deferred the possibility of reaching the material wellbeing it so desires, despite the fact that certainly in this period it has managed to reduce levels of absolute poverty. Contributing to this has been the special international situation characterised by the permanent hostility of the United States. But also of great importance has been the programmatic vision that from the beginning imposed on society a material sacrifice, with an eye toward a better future for future generations.

So-called 'real socialism', which constituted the hope of the Revolution, crumbled due to its incapacity to resolve creatively its internal contradictions. Thus, Cuban society faces today the dilemma of either insisting on a socioeconomic model that disappeared due to its economic and even political inviability or, alternatively, producing, in an orderly fashion, the necessary changes to insert itself into modernity with all its contradictions. It falls precisely on the social sciences and, among them, political economy to unravel the knot of contradictions in relations of production, with an eye toward generating viable alternatives that result from consent more than exclusion and that contribute to the objectives of building a developed and sustainable society for all.

CHAPTER 7

Industrial Upgrading and Human Capital in Cuba

Claes Brundenius

Introduction

One of Cuba's assets is its human capital, an essential asset for industrial upgrading and for Cuba's opportunities and possibilities for linking up to regional and global networks in an era of rapid globalisation. Human capital development coupled with impressive physical investment rates was pivotal to the high growth rates recorded in the Cuban economy between 1970 and 1985.

But sustained long-term growth is at stake. After 1985 the economy started stagnating, and after 1989 it declined rapidly, primarily as a result of the demise of the Soviet Union, but also the result of the inertia of an over-centralised command economy. In spite of slow to moderate economic recovery after 1993, domestic investment rates are still lagging behind, and perhaps the most worrying fact is that human capital formation has come to a practical standstill. Enrolment rates have fallen dramatically during the last decade. This chapter discusses this latest Cuban dilemma and the consequences for industrial upgrading and long-term growth.

An Extensive Growth Model with Slow Productivity Growth

Like other socialist models of accumulation the Cuban model has been based on so-called *extensive* growth. That is, economic growth has primarily been the result of a more or less proportional expansion of output with the expansion of factor inputs, i.e. capital and labour.[1] In other words, the economy is growing at the same rate as the expansion of factor inputs. A more *efficient use* of the factors of production results in *intensive* growth. In the West the *extensive* growth model is often referred to as a *factor growth* model, while the *intensive* growth model is equivalent to *factor productivity growth* in western terminology.

A look at Table 7.1 reveals that Cuba has largely followed an extensive growth trajectory. Between 1962 and 1999 Cuban GDP grew at a rate of 2.4 per cent per annum, while gross investments increased at an average rate of 2.8 per cent. Labour inputs increased at a rate of 2.0 per cent, that is, slightly below GDP growth, but labour productivity grew very slowly, at 0.4 per cent. On the other hand, labour productivity increased rather rap-

---

[1]   See, for example, Ofer (1987) and Kornai (1992), pp. 180–6.

idly in the 'golden period of growth' (1970–85), at an average rate of 2.8 per cent, so the picture is perhaps not so clear-cut. What is clear, however, is that the period after 1985 shows clear symptoms of the exhaustion of the extensive growth model. In the period 1985–90 the economy started stagnating in spite of a continuing increase of both capital and labour inputs, with declining labour productivity as a result.

Table 7.1: Cuban Annual Growth Rates: Selected Indicators and Periods, 1962–99

Periods	GDP	GDP/capita	Gross Investments	Occupied Civilian Labour Force	Y/L*
1994–99	4.0	3.3	17.6	-0.3	4.3
1990–94	-9.3	-9.8	-39.0	-0.2	-9.4
1985–90	-1.7	-2.0	3.5	4.1	-3.9
1970–85	5.2	3.8	13.2	2.3	2.8
1962–70	5.2	3.0	2.0	3.6	1.5
1962–99	2.4	1.2	2.8	2.0	0.4

*Y/L= GDP/Occupied Civilian Labour Force

Sources: Series calculated by the author based on JCP (1977); Zimbalist and Brundenius (1989: Table 4A.1); Rodríguez (1990: Table 14); CEE (1990); CEPAL (1997); ONE (1998a); ONE (2000) and CEPAL (2000).

Human Capital in Cuba: a Great but Dwindling Asset

In this section of the chapter an attempt is made to estimate the stock of human capital in Cuba and its development over time. Comparisons with some OECD countries and some developing countries are also made. The most commonly used measure of a country's endowment with human capital is educational attainment.[2] Educational attainment in turn is as a rule measured in two ways. The most straightforward measurement is in terms of the percentage of the population that has completed various levels of education, from primary to secondary to tertiary. The population is usually the working age population (or adult population) or the labour force population. Another common measure is to estimate the average years of schooling of the population.

An advantage of this measure is that it gives an estimate of the stock of human capital in a specific country at a specific point in time. It should, however, be emphasised that this measure is just a proxy and it is slightly

2   See, for example, OECD (1998).

biased since it unrealistically assumes that one additional year of education adds one homogeneous unit of human capital to the stock, irrespective of whether this additional year comes from a primary school child or from a university student. But even so, the measure gives a reasonably good picture of the human capital endowment of a country.

Table 7.2: Educational Attainment of the Cuban Labour Force* by Sex and Level of Education, 1953, 1978, 1986 and 1998

	Total (000)	With University Education	With at Least Upper Secondary	With at Least Lower Secondary
1953				
Total	3,487	1.5%	4.5%	12.4%
1978				
Total	2,540.8	3.9%	20.2%	46.4%
Males	1,778.7	3.5%	16.8%	40.8%
Females	762.1	4.9%	27.9%	58.1%
1986				
Total	3,317.6	8.9%	38.7%	76.5%
Males	2,056.4	7.4%	34.1%	73.3%
Females	1,261.2	11.5%	46.3%	81.5%
1998				
Total	3,753.6	13.7%	52.7%	82.8%
Males	2,354.8	11.2%	45.4%	79.2%
Females	1,398.8	17.9%	65.0%	88.8%
1999				
Total	3,826.3	12.8%	52.7%	83.0%
Males	2,396.2	10.6%	45.6%	79.7%
Females	1,430.1	16.3%	64.5%	88.5%

* Occupied civilian labour force; 1978 and 1986 data refer to the state sector only

Sources: Elaborated by the author from data in CEE (1990); ONE (1998a); ONE (1999); ONE (2000); ONE (2001). Data for 1953 are elaborated by the author from Census data appearing in Appendix Table 1 in Seers et al. (1964)

Table 7.2 shows estimates of the educational attainment levels of the Cuban labour force by sex, in 1953 (that is pre-revolutionary data), 1978, 1986 and 1997.[3] Several interesting observations can be made. Thus, in

3   The data are estimates by the author based on official data on educational attainment of the *occupied civilian labour force* (that is, including the non-state civilian sector) for 1998, while the 1978 and 1986 figures only refer to the occupied *state* labour force.

1953 only 12.4 per cent of the adult population had completed primary education, or the lower secondary level (at that time 8 years of education); only 4.5 per cent had completed upper secondary (12 years), and those with some university education accounted for merely 1.5 per cent of the total. After the Revolution the emphasis was at first on expanding primary education rapidly (including adult education), while gradually also expanding secondary schools and finally higher education.

The proportion of people with a university degree has grown from 3.9 per cent of the labour force in 1978 to 13.7 per cent in 1998, which is quite an achievement in 20 years. The number of people to have completed at least upper secondary school (including vocational schools and preparatory education for university) has also increased rapidly in Cuba. By 1998 no less than 83 per cent of the working population had completed at least lower secondary education. In the case of women the percentage was as high as 89 per cent. Women are also ahead if one considers those having finished at least upper secondary education and those with university degrees. The Cuban educational attainment levels are higher than those in other Latin American countries, and are among the highest in the Third World.[4]

There are, however, worrying signs. The 1999 data indicate that the stock of human capital is stagnating or even in decline in Cuba. Thus, the percentage of the labour force with university education fell for the first time since the Revolution, from 13.7 per cent in 1998 to 12.8 per cent in 1999. This drop is no doubt the inevitable result of declining university enrolments since 1990 (discussed further below).

I shall now turn to the estimate of human capital formation (Table 7.3).[5] It should be stressed that these estimates for Cuba only relate to the *occupied civilian labour force*. There are no figures for educational attainment for the whole population in recent years. It is clear, however, that the educational attainment levels of those in the labour force is somewhat higher than for those who are outside the labour force.[6] The human capital stock has increased at an impressive rate in Cuba since the Revolution, and especially between 1978 and 1986, when it increased at a rate of 4.6 per cent per annum.

---

4   World Bank (2000).

5   The human capital stock is estimated by multiplying the labour force by the average years of schooling. The average years of schooling is arrived at by assigning a number (year of schooling) to each level of education: 6 to primary education, 9 to lower secondary, 12 to upper secondary and 16 to university education.

6   There appears to be only one source in Cuba that gives educational attainment levels for both the adult population and the occupied labour force, and that is a demographic survey from 1979, quoted in Brundenius (1984: Table A1.7). These data reveal the following differences: *total adult population* (above 14): with university education or equivalent, 3.3%; with upper secondary education or more, 18.7%; and with lower secondary education or more, 41.4%; *occupied labour force*: with university education, 4.5%; with upper secondary education or more, 21.6%; and with lower secondary education or more, 48.4%.

**Table 7.3: Estimate of Human Capital Stock* and Growth
Rates in Cuba, 1978, 1986 and 1998**

	Total	Men	Women
1978			
Average Years Schooling	8.1	7.9	8.8
Labour Force (000)	2,934	2,054	880
Human Capital Stock	23.8	16.2	7.7
1986			
Average Years Schooling	9.8	9.5	10.3
Labour Force (000)	3,493	2,166	1327
Human Capital Stock	34.2	20.6	13.7
1998			
Average Years Schooling	10.6	10.2	11.3
Labour Force (000)	3,754	2,355	1,399
Human Capital Stock	39.7	24.0	15.5
Growth Rates			
1978–86			
Labour Force	2.2	0.7	5.2
Human Capital Stock	4.6	3.1	7.4
1986–98			
Labour Force	0.6	0.7	0.4
Human Capital Stock	1.2	1.3	1.0
1978–98			
Labour Force	1.2	0.7	2.4
Human Capital Stock	2.6	2.0	3.6

* million years of schooling
Sources: same as Table 7.2

For women the increase was even more impressive, with an annual rate of growth of 7.4 per cent, compared to 3.1 per cent for men. Since 1986 there has, however, been a slowdown. In the period 1986–98 the growth rate declined to 1.3 per cent for men and to only 1.0 per cent for women. But even so, the rate of growth of human capital formation is impressive in Cuba, even when compared to a 'tiger economy' like Taiwan. While the labour force in Taiwan increased at a rate of 2.8 per cent per year between 1980 and 1986, it is estimated that the human capital stock of the labour force increased by 5.0 per cent annually in the same period.[7] These growth esti-

---

7   Calculated by the author, using the same methodology as above (see note 15), from data in *Statistical Yearbook of the Republic of China* (Executive Yuan, 1996: Table 28).

mates are quite similar to Cuba's in approximately the same period. Between 1986 and 1995 the growth of the labour force in Taiwan slowed to 1.8 per cent per annum, and the growth of human capital formation to 3.5 per cent. In other words, there was, like in the Cuban case in the same period, a clear trend of declining growth rates, but the drop was not as sharp in Taiwan as in the Cuban case. Taken over the whole period, 1980–95, the rates of growth of the labour force and of the human capital stock in Taiwan were 2.2 per cent and 4.1 per cent, respectively. The corresponding growth rates in Cuba, 1978–98, were 1.2 and 2.6 per cent, respectively.

Has Cuba Overinvested in Human Capital?

Has Cuba overinvested in human capital in the past? It is quite clear that Cuba has, in relation to GDP per capita, a much higher density of highly qualified labour than the world average (see Table 7.4). Cuba had at the end of the 1990s an educational attainment level of its labour force that almost equalled many OECD countries, and was equal or higher than that of 'emerging' economies like Taiwan and Chile, countries with considerably higher GDP per capita (measured in US$PPP). But this does not necessarily mean that Cuba has overinvested in human capital formation, and for two major reasons.

First of all, even if it is true — as shown in this chapter — that a large part of the disposable educated labour force actually has not been utilised efficiently recently in Cuba, slow population growth, coupled with the ageing of the Cuban population, means that there is likely to be a *shortage* of highly qualified labour in the near future. Between 1996 and 2000 the working age population (WAP) actually *declined* (from 6,642,000 to 6,618,000), and is expected to grow by only 0.4 per cent per annum until 2005, and then continue at the same rate for at least another five years.[8] This means that a large number of highly educated Cubans will leave the labour force in the coming ten years, and this will put pressure on universities and also require a more efficient utilisation of the labour force. The only short-term solution to increase the working age population in the coming years would be to increase the retirement age to 65 for both men and women (from today's 55 for women and 60 for men). To retire at the age of 65 is quite common in many countries (for instance in most OECD countries), but it might be too drastic a change with accompanying financial implications in Cuba, and it might not be popular among Cubans due to retire.

Second, revolutionary Cuba has traditionally been 'internationalist' in the sense that thousands of skilled young Cubans have volunteered to go to poor areas of the world, assisting with rescue teams in national disasters (like the earthquakes in Peru and Nicaragua, the hurricanes George and Mitch in

8   CEDEM (1995), Table VI.1.

Central America and the landslides in Venezuela) or assisting in social development work. Between 1963 and 1999 no fewer than 41,400 physicians, nurses and other medical personnel, 32,400 teachers, 45,400 construction workers and 19,600 other qualified workers, amounting to 138,800 Cubans in all, have given assistance in other developing countries.[9]

Table 7.4: International Comparison of Educational Attainment and GDP per capita around 1995–98

	Highest Completed Level of Education		Average Number of Years of Schooling of Labour Force	GDP per capita (US$PPP) 1998
	With Upper Secondary Education or More	With University Education or Equivalent		
United States*	86%	33%	13.5	29,605
Denmark*	62%	20%	12.4	24,214
Sweden*	75%	28%	12.1	20,659
United Kingdom*	76%	21%	12.1	20,336
Russia** (1997)	53%	20%	11.9	6,460
Cuba*** (1998)	53%	14%	10.6	3,967
Taiwan** (1995)	54%	9%	9.9	15,752
Chile**** (1992)	43%	18%	9.3	8,787
China** (1997)	16%	3.5%	7.5	3,105
Brazil** (1997)	n.a.	n.a.	6.0	6,625

*   Data refer to population aged 25–64 in 1995
**   Data refer to occupied labour force
***   Data refer to occupied civilian labour force
****   Data refer to economically active population
US$PPP = purchasing power parity in US dollars

Sources: OECD countries: OECD (1998, Table A 2.1); Russia: Goskomstat (1998, Table 7.15); Cuba: ONE (2000, Table V.10); Taiwan: Executive Yuan (1996, Table 28); Chile: INE (1992, Table 9); China: SSB (1998,Table 5–31); Brazil: IBGE (1999, p. 76); GDP figures are taken from UNDP (2000: Appendix Table 1), except the figure for Taiwan which is updated from Maddison (1995: Table D–1e).

9   Figueras (2000).

The number of physicians and nurses sent out by Cuba surpasses by a wide margin the number sent out by the WHO in the same period. It should be stressed that this assistance has been free of charge, an act of solidarity by Cuba.[10] At the same time Cuba has been very generous in offering scholarships (especially to young people in Africa) for tertiary studies in Cuba. Between 1961 and 1999, 15,496 foreign students graduated from Cuban universities, of which there were 10,888 from Africa alone.[11] The study of medicine has an especially high reputation in Cuba, and it was decided in 1999 to set up a Latin American School of Medicine (Escuela Latinoamericana de Ciencias Médicas).[12]

Far from concluding that Cuba has overinvested in human capital, it is in fact suggested that Cuba should make better use of this 'comparative advantage'. Cuba could easily develop regional centres for the training of young people, considering its large stock of teaching staff and educational institutions. The creation of centres like the regional medical school above is a case in point.

Is there a Brain Drain Problem in Cuba?

Brain drain is a serious problem for many developing countries that invest heavily in education, and one would suspect that this would also be a major threat in the Cuban case. It is well known that hundreds of thousands of Cubans have left the island since the Revolution, especially for the United States, but this has also been the case of Mexicans, Salvadorians, Haitians and Puerto Ricans. So in this respect Cuba is far from unique.

The question is, however, whether those who have left Cuba, especially in the last decade, can be considered part of a brain drain or not. Is the share of highly educated people overrepresented in the migrating population? Perhaps surprisingly, this does not seem to be the case. According to the latest United States Survey of the Foreign Born Population, there was a total of 991,000 residents of Cuban origin in the United States in 1996. Of these 772,000 were born in Cuba. 105,000 of these had arrived in the United States after 1990.[13] A closer look at the characteristics of the latter shows that 73 per cent

---

10   Figueras (2000).

11   *Ibid.*

12   1,800 students from 15 countries in Latin America started a two-year course in September 1999, at newly constructed premises in Baracoa (outside Havana). After the initial two years the students were to be allocated to other medical faculties all over Cuba, according to speciality. The Cuban government offers scholarships, covering tuition fee, board and lodging to all the students. The participating Latin American governments only have to meet the travel expenses of their respective students (CEPAL, 2000: p. 283).

13   According to Cuban sources (ONE, 2000), 120,103 Cubans emigrated between 1990 and 1996 which would mean that about 15,000 emigrated to other destinations than the United States, a reasonable assumption.

were of working age (18–64), of whom 8.0 per cent had a university degree and 17.0 per cent had completed senior high school. That is, only 25 per cent of those arriving in the United States after 1990 had attained upper second-ary level or more. This should be compared with the corresponding attain-ment levels of the Cuban labour force shown in 1998 (see Table 7.2) that are considerably higher (13.7 per cent having a university degree and 53 per cent completing at least upper secondary level).

In other words, it was *not* primarily the highly qualified people who were leaving the island in the 1990s. It is difficult to speculate about the reasons for this. One reason could be that it has been more difficult for university trained people to emigrate. In any case an external brain drain does not seem to pose a major problem, relatively speaking. A rough estimate shows that out of a total stock of approximately 500,000 university graduates in Cuba at the beginning of the 1990s, fewer than 10,000 emigrated during the following six years; that is, the total stock was reduced by less than two per cent due to brain drain. However, if one considers the decline in uni-versity enrolments the situation might worsen rapidly in the future. Between 1991–92 and 1997–98 the number of students who graduated from Cuban universities fell from 38,000 to 19,000, or by half.[14] If an average of 2,000 Cubans with a university degree leave the country yearly, then this will no doubt imply a brain drain in the coming years, that is, if the trend is not reversed, both with respect to migration and enrolments.

But if external brain drain does not seem to be an immediate problem, there is another brain drain that is already a serious problem, the *internal* brain drain. A great number of Cubans, especially young people, work in profes-sions other than those for which they were trained. In Cuba there are highly educated people (even medical doctors, researchers and other professionals) who either 'moonlight' (for instance as taxi drivers), or leave their original employment entirely to dedicate themselves to other types of better-remu-nerated 'services' (often related to the booming tourism industry). This will, if the trend continues, amount to a huge waste through misallocated resources.

Dilemma I: Low Productivity Growth with Declining Labour Force Participation

Cuba's problem in a nutshell: low productivity growth with a labour force that is growing slowly as a result of an ageing population, with a stagnating (and by the end of last decade even shrinking) working age population.[15] Thus, a growing segment of the non-active population (those below 15 and

14   ONE (2000), Table XV.10.
15   The population of 65 and over is expected to increase its share of the total population from 9.8% in 1998 (ONE, 2000: Table II.2) to 10.4% in 2005, to 11.6% in 2010 and to 13% in 2015 (CEDEM: Table VI.1).

those above 65) will be dependent on the output (and hence productivity) of a shrinking segment of the economically active population.[16] But in spite of slow population growth and a declining population of working age, labour force participation rates have also declined in the 1990s. Labour force participation rates[17] thus went down from around 75 per cent at the end of the 1980s to 67.6 per cent in 1994 and were only slowly recovering at the end of the last decade (Table 7.5).

Table 7.5: Labour Force Participation Rates by Sex, 1970, 1981 and 1989–98

	Total*	Male*	Female*
1999	71.5	86.3	55.5
1998	70.2	85.0	54.3
1997	69.3	84.0	51.2
1996	67.9	82.3	52.4
1995	68.1	81.9	53.3
1994	67.6	81.9	52.3
1993	69.2	84.2	53.1
1992	70.8	87.0	53.4
1991	73.0	90.3	54.5
1990	74.1	85.1	58.1
1989	75.3	89.3	60.3
1988	75.3	89.9	59.5
1981	70.4	93.7	45.4
1970	63.0	96.1	24.0

* EAP as per cent of working age population (see also note 17)

Sources: Elaborated by the author from data in CEE (1982); JCP (1975); CEE (1990); ONE (1998a); ONE (1999a); ONE (1999b); ONE (2000); and CEE (1986).

Although international comparisons are somewhat tricky (see note 17), it is clear that the Cuban labour force participation rates are about average for

16   For an expansion of this argument see León (1999).
17   Labour force is defined here as the occupied civilian labour force as a percentage of the working age population (which in Cuba is 17–54 years of age for women and 17–59 years of age for men). This complicates international comparisons where country data as a rule refer to EAP (economically active population, which includes unemployed) in relation to the population over 15 years of age.

men and above average for women. According to the ILO (1999), the labour participation rate was 75.0 per cent for men and 36.1 per cent for women in Chile (1998), 81.6 per cent for men and 38.5 per cent for women in Costa Rica (1998), and 86.5 per cent for men and 41.4 per cent for women in the Dominican Republic (1998). In a developed country like Denmark it was 83.1 per cent for men and 73.2 per cent for women (1998).

The crude labour force participation rates estimated for Cuba in Table 7.5 are, however, only part of the picture. The fact that people do not participate in the labour force does not necessarily mean that they are idle, or 'inactive'. They can, for instance, be studying, or in the case of women they can be on maternity leave. Especially student enrolments complicate the picture in the case of Cuba since so much emphasis has been on education since the Revolution. At one point, in the 1980s, it was said that one third of all Cubans were enrolled as students at some level of education (including adult education). In tables 7.6 and 7.7 some characteristics of the working age population (WAP) are illustrated by type of activity. The economically active population (EAP) consists of those occupied (officially registered) in the *civilian* labour force (whether state or non-state), those unemployed (officially registered), those in the *non-civilian* labour force (primarily the armed forces and the security forces). The estimate of 'inactives' is a residual, after subtracting the EAP and students (above 17) from the WAP.

Table 7.6: Characteristics of the Economically Active Population (Labour Force), 1981, 1989, 1994 and 1999

	1981		1989		1994		1999	
	(000)	%	(000)	%	(000)	%	(000)	%
Occup. Civ. LF*	3,068	84.8	3,724	78.8	3,840	85.4	3,826	80.8
State	2,824	78.1	3,527	74.6	3,135	69.7	2,985	63.0
Non-State	244	6.7	197	4.2	705	15.7	841	17.8
Unemployed	122	3.4	372	7.9	301	6.7	284	6.0
Non-Civ. LF**	428	11.8	632	13.4	355	7.9	625	13.2
Total LF***	3,618	100.0	4,728	100.0	4,496	100.0	4,735	100.0

* Occupied Civilian Labour Force
** Non-Civilian Labour Force
*** Labour Force = Economically Active Population

Sources: Elaborated by the author from data in JCP (1975); CEE (1982); CEE (1986); CEE (1990); ONE (1998a); ONE (1999a); ONE (1999b); ONE (2000); and MEP (2000).

Although the accuracy of the estimates can be discussed (thus unemployment figures and the non-civilian labour force are in many cases estimates, especially before 1981), they do suggest a clear trend: there is an increasing number of 'inactive' people of working age after 1989 (Table 7.7). In 1989 the inactivity rate was only 10.4 per cent of the WAP. By 1994 this share had increased to 24.3 per cent but has since fallen slightly. This is also the conclusion that ECLAC draws from a recent study of the Cuban economy.[18] ECLAC uses the term *desempleo equivalente* ('equivalent unemployment'), as a measure of 'real' unemployment, which, according to their estimates, increased from 7.9 per cent in 1989 to 35.2 per cent in 1993, but then fell slowly to 25.1 per cent in 1998.

Table 7.7: Characteristics of the Working Age Population, 1981, 1989, 1994 and 1999

	1981		1989		1994		1999	
	(000)	%	(000)	%	(000)	%	(000)	%
In Labour Force	3,618	70.4	4,728	75.3	4,496	67.6	4,735	71.5
Students	700	13.6	898	14.3	534	8.0	526	7.9
Inactive	822	16.0	655	10.4	1,616	24.3	1,362	20.6
Work Age Population	5,140	100.0	6,281	100.0	6,646	100.0	6,623	100.0

Sources: same as Table 7.6.

Dilemma II: Falling University Enrolments

The Cuban government has mobilised a lot of resources to education since the Revolution: first, in a total mobilisation to eradicate illiteracy in 1961, then in a massive effort to provide primary education to all and then gradually upgrading the population to secondary and higher levels. In the 1970s secondary enrolments skyrocketed, which led to a consecutive boom of university enrolments in the 1980s. Table 7.8 below illustrates this impressive effort by the Cuban government in the field of education. Primary level enrolments have stabilised around one million, not because enrolment rates are going down, but because birth rates are going down. Secondary enrolments have also dropped somewhat in the 1990s but this also has primarily to do with declining numbers in the corresponding age cohort.

18   CEPAL (2000), Table V.2.

Table 7.8: Student Enrolments by Level of Education, Selected Years

	Primary (000)	Secondary (000)	Tertiary (000)
1999–00	987.5	865.4	106.8
1989–90	885.6	1,073.1	243.1
1979–80	1,550.3	1,127.6	147.9
1970–71	1,530.4	272.5	35.1
1956–57	740.5	99.4	15.6

Sources: Based on time series data supplied by ONE (Oficina Nacional de Estadísticas), Havana.

But as seen in the table there has been a dramatic decline in university enrolments and this decline cannot be explained only by a decreasing population in the cohort. University students in Cuba are usually between 20–24 years. Looking at university enrolments in relation to this age group, enrolment rates increased from 6.7 per cent in 1972–73 to 20.8 per cent in 1989–90, then dropped to 17.3 per cent in 1992–93 and to 12.4 per cent in 1998–99. The decline in university enrolments is quite noteworthy, with enrolments in 1998–99 reaching just 42 per cent of the peak level in 1989–90. It is not clear to what extent young people opt not to continue university education because of bleak job opportunities, or for other reasons. It is claimed, however, that one reason for the decline is that the Ministry of Higher Education only admits students to the extent that the state can guarantee employment after completion of studies. If this is so, there should perhaps be even more reason for concern. Instead of continuing a rather uncertain university career, it seems that many young people today deliberately choose not only *not* to enter university, but also that many refrain from joining the legal labour market. This could be a worrying indicator. However, as already mentioned, being 'inactive' in this sense does not necessarily mean that these young people are just lying on their backs doing nothing. It is, on the contrary, quite likely that many of them are very active in 'wheeling and dealing' activities that are today considered illegal, as has been discussed above.

Table 7.9: University Enrolments by Area of Study, 1956–57, 1969–70, 1979–80, 1989–90 and 1998–99

	1956–57	%	1969–70	%	1979–80	%	1989–90	%	1999–00	%
Engineering	1,668	10.7	8,103	23.5	31,013	31.0	34,867	14.3	13,474	12.6
Nat. Sciences	1,176	7.5	3,420	9.9	6,464	4.4	6,399	2.6	4,019	3.8
Medicine	328	2.1	7,977	23.1	13,052	8.8	37,306	15.3	23,457	22.0
Agriculture	571	3.7	5,324	15.4	12,036	8.1	10,254	4.2	4,984	4.7
Economics	4,546	29.1	1,328	3.8	13,253	9.0	15,773	6.5	9,505	8.9
Soc. Sciences	3,597	23.0	2,199	6.4	10,216	6.9	7,958	3.3	6,084	5.7
Pedagogy	3,723	23.9	6,159	17.8	57,389	38.8	115,529	47.5	3,359	34.0
Physical Ed.	–	–	–	–	3,827	2.6	14,052	5.8	8,000	7.5
Art	–	–	–	–	627	0.4	909	0.4	905	0.8
TOTAL	15,609	100.0	34,520	100.0	147,877	100.0	243,057	100.0	106,787	100.0

Sources: Same as Table 7.7.

The fall in enrolment at universities is a fact, however, and the decline is particularly sharp in pedagogy (teacher training) but this is perhaps understandable since pedagogy actually accounted for almost half of all university enrolments at its peak at the end of the 1980s. This dramatic decline might have to do with a deliberate policy of the government to cut down teacher training.

However, in spite of the decline in teacher training, the high pupil-teacher ratios have so far been maintained in both primary and secondary schools. As a matter of fact, the Cuban pupil-teacher ratios were still in 1995 among the lowest in the world, equalling countries like Denmark and Sweden, and lower than countries like Canada and the United States.[19]

Pupil teacher ratios are *one* measure of the *quality* of education. But this is far from the only indicator. As a result of the crisis, the situation for teachers has become critical. They are facing problems 'in terms of low morale, shortages of materials and the inability of the state wage to cover the escalating costs of household survival'.[20] It is quite evident that the difficult situation facing teachers and the lack of incentives affects teacher morale and hence jeopardises the quality of education.

19   UNESCO (1998), table 7.
20   Pearson (1997), p. 695.

An Untapped Potential: The 'Inactive' Working Age Population

If it is clear that the 'inactive' WAP has increased substantially in the last decade in *statistical* terms, it is not so clear *how* 'inactive' they actually are. Or in other words: what do they do when they are 'inactive'? First of all it should be stressed that the economically active population in Cuba only comprises those who are *legally* registered. Thus the 'informal economy',[21] is not recorded in Cuban statistics. It is true that there is also an incipient legal private small-scale sector in Cuba that is slowly growing, especially after 1994 when it was legalised to exercise many professions on an *individual* basis, that is as self-employed (*a cuenta propia*). It is not allowed, however, to hire labourers, except family members to assist in some trades, like private restaurants (*paladares*).

Thus, there is still no significant private sector, in the narrow sense, in Cuba. *Non-state* activities have increased since 1994 (see Table 7.6) but primarily as a result of the transformation of state farms into co-operatives.[22] In 1998 the private sector consisted of 305,000 private farmers (an increase from 188,000 in 1989) and 113,000 self-employed (registered with licenses), an increase from only 25,000 in 1989.[23] This means that the private sector increased from 4.5 per cent of the occupied civilian labour force in 1989 to 11.1 per cent in 1998. But considering that the percentage share was 9.0 per cent in 1995, the growth of the private sector is very slow, and the share of self employment actually decreased, from 3.8 per cent in 1995 to 3.0 per cent in 1998, although again increasing slightly in 1999.

The main reason for the slow growth of registered self employment has no doubt to do with barriers of entry and disincentives to do private business in Cuba. The taxes imposed are prohibitive for many who subsequently become discouraged, and this is no doubt one of the main reasons for the slow growth of the sector.[24] The question then is to what extent those who leave the legal self employment sector continue doing the same business, but do so in a manner that is unregistered, unlicensed and thus illegal. There are, however, unfortunately no data (at least not official ones) that could shed some light on this important issue. It is clear though that as long as the government insists on setting up barriers and creating disincentives rather than incentives to this group of people, the illegal 'informal sector' is bound to continue growing, and so will the problem.

21 For a discussion of the existence or not of an 'informal economy' in Cuba, see, for example, Pérez-López (1995), Mesa-Lago (1998) and Fabienke (2000).
22 For an analysis of the impact of the transformation of state farms into co-operatives, see, for example, Deere (1997).
23 CEPAL (2000), Table A.48.
24 The taxes are applied as flat rates (*cuotas fijas*) that affect the self-employed in a rather arbitrary way with little or no relation to actual income. There are no doubt many who benefit from this system but there are at least as many who simply cannot survive economically with such a tax system.

An Imperative: Reversing the Internal Brain Drain

One reason for the increasing inactivity of the working age population is not only the lack of employment opportunities in the state sector. It is also reflected in the general decline of student enrolments, especially at universities. It is thus worth taking a closer look at people in their twenties. Table 7.10 shows some activity/inactivity characteristics of this age group, with estimates of how many of these young people are in the labour force, how many are students and how many are 'inactive', that is, those who apparently are outside the *formal* labour force and who are not students.

Table 7.10: Characteristics of the 20–29 Age Cohort, 1988, 1996, 1997 and 1998 (thousands)

	1988	1996	1998	1999
Total Age Cohort	2203.4	2122.2	1971.4	1873.9
In Labour Force*	1351.9	1264.5	1103.7	1125.1
Students	250.6	111.6	102.6	106.8
Inactive	600.9	746.1	764.7	642.0
Inactive/Total	27.3%	35.2%	38.8%	34.3%
Males	1112.2	1071.7	995.0	945.5
In Labour Force*	797.6	776.6	676.5	688.0
Students	107.6	44.5	38.8	40.0
Inactive	207.0	250.6	279.7	217.5
Inactive/Total	18.6%	23.4%	28.1%	23.0%
Females	1091.2	1050.5	976.4	928.4
In Labour Force*	554.3	487.9	427.6	437.1
Students	143.0	67.1	63.8	66.8
Inactive	393.9	495.5	485.0	424.5
Inactive/Total	36.1%	47.2%	49.7%	45.7%

* Economically active population (includes unemployed and non-civilian labour force).

Sources: Same as Table 7.6.

The inactivity rates of the 20–29 age group are considerably higher than those of the working population at large, and more important, they have *continued to grow* in spite of the economic recovery that started after 1994. It is also noteworthy that the inactivity rates of the young are increasing in spite of a *decreasing* population in this cohort! While the inactivity rates for the whole working age population increased from 10.4 per cent in 1989 to 24.3 per cent in 1994, they have actually declined slightly since then. In contrast, the inactivity rates of the 20–29 cohort increased from 27.3 per cent in 1988 to 35.2 per cent in 1996, and then jumped to a new record level of 38.8 per cent in 1998. This negative trend now seems to be reversed, however, and the inactivity rates started declining substantially in 1999, both for males and females. But even so, the problem of inactive youth remains. The high inactivity rates among the young might be symptoms of frustration and disenchantment about the future. They could also be a reflection of an internal brain drain, of young educated people preferring to work in the non-registered informal sector.

Combining Higher Education Studies with Social Work — a New Strategy?

A problem for the young has been that they have had few alternatives but to be 'inactive'. Employment opportunities are scarce since there have been few openings in the public sector, and employment possibilities in the private sector have so far been very limited. At the same time university enrolments have drastically decreased during the Special Period (from 251,000 in 1988–89 to 107,000 in 1999–2000). It should be stressed, however, that the downward trend seems to be reversed, and enrolments have started increasing slightly again since 1998.

In a speech in the summer of 2000 Fidel Castro for the first time made observations about the lack of alternatives for many young people. He said it was not fair to limit admissions to higher education just because the state no longer could guarantee a job after graduation. As a matter of fact, there is a decree in Cuba stating that admissions to higher education can only be permitted to the extent that the government (the state) can guarantee jobs after graduation. Since state employment has been decreasing since 1994, declining admissions to university must then have been a self-fulfilling prophecy. At least this was the case until Fidel himself brought the problem up.

As a follow up to Castro's speech, a household survey was carried out by the Communist Youth (UJC) in the poorer districts of suburban Havana. In this survey, 1,300 young people were found to be 'inactive', that is, they were neither working nor studying (many because they had not been admitted to university). 513 of these were given the opportunity to enrol at a new, special pre-university school to train social workers (*Escuela de Trabajadores*

Sociales de La Habana) in Cojímar. The students, 60 per cent of whom were women, graduated in February 2001.[25] A new course started in March 2001 with 600 students, and in September of the same year another started with 1,200 students.

Such courses will be repeated all over Cuba. After graduation the students are to work as social workers (inspiring *inter alia* other young people to follow their own example) and they will also be admitted to social science programs at the university in their free time. In this way the government is trying to tackle social problems in Cuba seriously, and at the same time to provide opportunities for young people to pursue studies at universities.

Scenarios for the Near Future

The Cuban economy has steadily recovered since 1994, and in 2000 GDP grew by 5.6 per cent. Between 1994 and 2000, the economy grew at an average rate of 4.3 per cent. This is much too slow, however. At this rate, Cuban GDP will just about reach the pre-crisis (1989) level by 2005. The question then is to determine what strategies and policies are required in order to achieve higher growth rates in the medium term (until 2005). We have in a recent study made some projections of possible scenarios until 2005, based on different assumptions from a Harrod-Domar perspective.[26] The growth projections of GDP are summarised in Table 7.11 below.

One of the problems of the Cuban economy is the low investment rate so far, which remains inadequate to induce accelerated growth. In 2000 the investment rate was just 8.2 per cent, far below the historical (pre-crisis) rates in Cuba of around 25 per cent. It is true that the investment rate is steadily, but slowly, growing and it is projected that with a gradual increase of the investment rate to 15 per cent by 2005, it will be possible to maintain the present average GDP growth rate of around four per cent per annum. What are then the preconditions for a higher growth rate, say six per cent (Scenario 2)? First of all, the investment rate will have to increase gradually to 20 per cent by 2005. A GDP growth rate of six per cent is a decent one, generally speaking, but not sufficiently strong for an economy still in its recovery phase. With a six per cent growth rate the GDP level would in 2005 surpass the pre-crisis level but not substantially (by 13 per cent in relation to 1989, and by only seven per cent in relation to the peak year 1985).

What would be required to achieve accelerated growth, say 10 per cent until 2005, that is, a growth trajectory that would resemble the 'tiger economies' in East Asia (Scenario 3)? First of all, that would no doubt require a gradual increase of the investment rate to pre-crisis levels, that is,

---

25 *Granma*, 16 January 2000.
26 Brundenius and Monreal (2001).

to around 25 per cent of GDP. With such an accelerated rate, GDP would by 2005 surpass the 1989 level by 36 per cent and the 1985 level by 29 per cent, and with such a high and sustained rate of growth the Cuban economy would, indeed, be moving in the direction of a 'tiger economy'.

Table 7.11: Growth Scenarios for 2005: GDP, Investments, Labour Force and Productivity

	Actual		Projected Scenarios*		
	1997	2000	2005(1)	2005(2)	2005(3)
GDP(million US$)**	19,767	22,434	26,883	29,650	35,581
Gross Inv. (GI)***	1,522	1,834	4,032	5,930	8,895
GI/GDP	7.7%	8.2%	15%	20%	25%
Labour Force (000)	3,705	3,900	4,300	4,300	4,300
Labour Productivity	5,335	5,904	6,252	6,895	8,275

* Scenario 1: Annual average GDP growth remains at four per cent between 2000 and 2005; GI/GDP rate grows to reach 15 per cent by 2005; Scenario 2: Annual average GDP growth increases to six per cent between 2000 and 2005; GI/GDP rate grows to reach 20 per cent by 2005; Scenario 3: Annual average GDP growth increases to ten per cent between 2000 and 2005; GI/GDP rate grows to reach 25 per cent by 2005.

** constant 1997 US$; GDP estimate for 1997 from EIU (2000b).

*** million 1997 US$.

Sources: Brundenius and Monreal (2001: Table 8.3); Actual labour force data from ONE (2001); scenario data on labour force and productivity projections by the author based on assumptions made in text

However, such a growth rate is, of course, not only determined by the rate of investment. High rates of investment can only be achieved through an insertion of the Cuban economy into the global economy, with all its advantages and disadvantages. Such an insertion would imply not only substantially increasing *new* types of exports (involving not only developing such export products, finding markets for them and being able to compete in such markets), and, above all, the deepening of the reform process.[27]

---

27   For a discussion of such implications see, for example, Brundenius and Monreal (2001).

A strategy for achieving high growth rates will also imply changes in the *utilisation* of the labour force and human capital in Cuba (Table 7.11). As mentioned before, one of the dilemmas facing Cuba, in this decade at least, is the stagnation (and for some time even decline) of the working age population. Thus, an increase in the labour force can only be achieved through an *increase in the labour force participation rate.* In order to achieve a continuing rate of expansion of the labour force by two per cent per year (that was the rate of growth between 1997 and 2000,[28] the labour force participation will have to increase from 71.5 per cent (2000) to 79 per cent in 2005. This would mean a record high and thus imply a virtual mobilisation of all disposable labour, also activating many retired people. But expanding the labour force in this way will not be sufficient, at least not in order to achieve the ten per cent growth rate. In order to achieve such an economic growth rate, *labour productivity* would also have to increase substantially, implying a productivity growth of seven per cent between 2000 and 2005. This would mean a systemic change from an *extensive* growth model to an *intensive* one. Considering that labour productivity even before the 'Special Period' was low (even negative between 1985–90), this will be a difficult task.

The only way of achieving a high productivity growth trajectory is first of all to make much more efficient use of the highly qualified labour force than in the past, and, secondly, to invest in and expand so-called *knowledge-intensive* industries.[29] But even having access to a pool of highly qualified labour does not necessarily mean that the university graduates always have the relevant skills to cope with rapidly changing requirements in knowledge-intensive industries (computer science is just a case in point). Cuba has no doubt been successful in creating a solid base of *general* education skills.[30] However, curricula rapidly become *obsolete,* and the same happens to university skills. Engineers and scientists who have been 'inactive' for some years might find it difficult to find their 'niches' in a new, but rapidly changing, knowledge-based economy.

Concluding Remarks

No doubt Cuban economic growth must speed up in the coming years, or else Cuba risks lagging behind other countries in Latin America in the future. Industrial upgrading is a must and the only way of doing this is through linking up to global and regional networks, and by making more efficient use of human capital. In order to do this the investment rate must

---

28   But it should be recalled that the labour force grew on the average by only 0.6% in the period 1986–97.

29   Cuba has already made substantial advances in some fields, such as biotechnology.

30   According to student tests made by UNESCO of primary school students, Cuba's scores are much above those of other Latin American countries in most disciplines.

radically increase. Cuba has a great comparative advantage in having a highly qualified labour force. But, as has been shown in this chapter, this human capital can rapidly be eroded, and Cuba could fast be facing an insoluble dilemma: continuing low productivity growth, persistent low investment rates and with zero growth in human capital formation leading to zero or slow economic growth. Zero growth of human capital formation could occur for two reasons: the low population growth and the ageing of the Cuban population coupled with stagnation or even further decline of enrolment rates at the university level.

However, the situation could be redressed in two ways: first, by giving incentives for young people to continue with higher studies (that is, they can be assured of meaningful employment after graduation); second, that those 'inactive' with high skills are mobilised and given incentives and thus motivated to come back to the labour force, or rather to (re)integrate into the *formal* labour force. In this context, opportunities should also be created for young graduates to set up their own businesses if they so want, not only as tolerated 'fence breaking',[31] but with proactive government support, eliminating disincentives, and instead creating incentives like credit institutions and legal frameworks with clear 'rules of the game'. Finally, it is of utmost importance that the teaching base in Cuba remains intact, that and that it is expanded rather than eroded, thus ensuring maintenance of the *quality of education*. This can only be accomplished if teachers are motivated and feel committed to their jobs.

---

31   This is an expression that originally comes from the private sector development experience in China and Vietnam, where the governments have been forced to tolerate (and finally accept) 'faits accomplis'.

PART 3
THE INTERNATIONAL CONTEXT AND COMPARATIVE PERSPECTIVES

CHAPTER 8

Cuba — The Challenges of Regional Reinsertion: The European Factor

Francisco León*

Foreword

After a decade of international isolation and economic crisis in the 1990s important and unexpected changes have occurred in Cuba's internal conditions as well as in the international context in which the island finds itself. Despite the limitations imposed on Cuba by ongoing conflict with the United States and the latter's continued economic embargo, the Cuban government has succeeded in maintaining the socialist system, stimulating economic growth, remodelling its political system and reinserting itself — albeit modestly — into the global economy. Cuba's international relations have been diversified, and the basic needs growth strategy adopted by both public and foreign enterprises has achieved more impressive results than the survival strategy that predominated during the so-called Special Period. This has helped reinforce the control of the country's political leadership, while obtaining the support or passive acceptance of the population.

At the dawn of the new millennium, regional integration in Latin America has been pursued within the framework of the World Trade Organization (WTO) rules, resulting in the ongoing efforts to establish the Free Trade Area of the Americas (FTAA). Cuba is excluded from the FTAA for political and economic reasons, resulting in a virtual wall isolating the island from its natural regional trading partners and preventing Cuba from acquiring new technologies being disseminated by transnational corporations. The strategies adopted to cope with the crisis of the 1990s — the diversification of Cuba's international relations and the transformation of its economy and its productive apparatus — must now be reoriented to find a way to break through this wall or to minimise the damage caused by Cuba's regional economic isolation.

The role played by the European Union (EU) in the transition of the former socialist countries of Eastern and Central Europe to market economies and in assisting their reinsertion into the international economy provides a

* This chapter is derived from a project, 'Relations between the European Union and Latin America: Biregionalism in a Changing Global System', based at the University of Gissen. The project was developed within the framework of Volkswagen-Stiftung's Priority Area, 'Global Structures and Governance'. The author is grateful to Victor Bulmer-Thomas, Julio Carranza and George Lambie for their comments on an early version of this paper.

possible model for Cuba. The EU has economic interests as well as political influence in Latin America and the Caribbean (LAC), and it can contribute to the construction of an alternative model of economic and political transition in Cuba. The EU countries were also major actors in Cuba's transformation during the 1990s. All these factors mean that the EU could play a potentially decisive role in providing international support for Cuba's integration into the FTAA in this decade.

This chapter is divided into three sections. The first section analyses Cuba in the context of the Caribbean Basin (CB) countries' integration process and its relations with the United States. In the second section, the major challenges facing Cuba are examined and the ways in which the EU could potentially help Cuba confront these challenges are explored. In the final section, a proposal for an agenda of co-operation between the EU and Cuba for the period 2001–2005 is set out.

Cuba, Caribbean Integration and Relations with the United States

The Process of Integration of the Caribbean Basin Countries

Since the time of the Spanish Conquest the CB has evolved into a strategic area of interest. In the eighteenth century the CB became a main producer of sugar, and since the first half of the twentieth century it has become a principal magnet for the international tourism market. During recent decades it has emerged as a major area of international concern due to massive migration flows, drug trafficking and environmental issues. The CB area was dominated politically by the United States, was subject in the first half of the twentieth century to covert and overt military interventions and later became a scenario of Cold War conflict. By the 1990s the United States had become the architect of the commercial, economic and productive integration of the small CB economies via the North America Free Trade Agreement (NAFTA), but it had not developed satisfactory mechanisms to control migration flows, drug trafficking and other security issues.

The CB economies evolved in the 1980s under the influence of external policies such as the Caribbean Basin Initiative (CBI), devised by the US government. These policies were relatively unsuccessful, but today these economies have a second chance, with Mexico's signing of NAFTA in 1994 and a redefinition of the commercial components of the CBI in 2000. Financial support for balance-of-payments deficits, technical assistance and export and investment incentives have been the backbone of the US-sponsored CBI; such programmes are oriented to increase production and export diversification as the basis for the stability and sustained growth of the Caribbean Basin Small Economies (CBSE). The small Caribbean economies were the earliest target group of the US–CBI beginning in 1984, and the Central American Common Market (CACM) countries and Panama were included in 1990. Given the recent history of armed conflict in Central America, as well as the US interventions in Grenada in 1983 and Panama in 1989, security concerns and a desire to support the peace process in Central America had as much to do with US policy decisions as economic criteria.[1] The US-sponsored CBI benefits from earlier integration schemes and processes, such as CARICOM and CACM.

The inclusion of CACM countries in the US–CBI resulted in an increase in the region's export participation in total US imports during the 1990s. The export participation of CARICOM, however, decreased.[2] The primary reason for this is lower labour costs in the CACM countries and the Dominican Republic compared to the CARICOM countries. The US–CBI had a positive influence on GDP growth and employment creation in most of the CACM countries and the Dominican Republic, but this was not the case in the CARICOM countries. Mexico's entrance into NAFTA negatively impacted on the CBSE in terms of the ability of these smaller economies to attract foreign direct investment and produce competitively priced exports. It also undermined the redistribution of industrial factories in the CB area.[3] In response to this, the Clinton Administration established, in June 2000, mechanisms so that the exports of the CBSE would enjoy similar conditions as Mexican exports until negotiations for the FTAA were completed.[4]

Under the impact of globalisation — most directly through NAFTA and CBI — industrial exports from the CBSE and Mexico increasingly resembled each other in economic and productive terms during the 1990s. This led a regional expert to suggest that: 'In the future, as globalisation progresses, it is not going to be possible for any single product, firm or country to stay competitive unless the production process is dispersed throughout the [CB] region so that each aspect is undertaken where it is most cost effective.'[5] Exports from Mexico and the CBI countries, which have fed a booming US economy, have propelled the integration of these countries into an economic and productive system dominated by the United States. One study of the evolution of the garment industry, which represented 49 per cent of the CBI countries'

1   Cynthia Weber (1995) states: 'Intervention as disciplinary power participates in the production of a sovereign foundation so that a state may function in international society as a sign of the political representation of its population' (p. 124). The transformation in the US approach to the Caribbean from military intervention to the CBI programme has been a major and positive transformation in establishing the sovereign foundation of the CBSE countries.
2   CEPAL (2001), cuadro II.3b.
3   CEPAL (2000a), cuadro IV.2. p 67.
4   Klinger Pevida (2000), pp. 35–55.
5   Dr Richard L. Bernal, Jamaican Ambassador to the United States, Statement before the US Congress Subcommittee on the Western Hemisphere. House Committee on International Relations,17 May 2000.

exports to the US market in the 1990s, reveals the role played by firms from the United States, the European Union, South East Asia, the CBSE and Mexico in this integration process.[6]

From the perspective of the United States and the multilateral agreements it has negotiated, the US–CBI — complemented by Mexico's entrance into NAFTA — has created a new economic base for the Caribbean Basin. Meanwhile, regional regulation and control of migration, drug trafficking, security and environmental protection depend on bilateral agreements. However, the growing importance of drug trafficking in the Caribbean Basin — coupled with the current conflict in Colombia and its likely spill-over effects in the rest of the Andean region — may encourage the United States to move from a bilateral approach to a multilateral approach in the regulation of these issues. Indeed, the US government has been working in this direction with the CARICOM and CACM countries since the late 1990s. Along similar lines, the president of Mexico, Vicente Fox, has proposed reviving the Group of Three (G–3), originally created by Colombia, Mexico and Venezuela in Puerto Ordaz, Venezuela, in 1989, which would also, presumably, encourage multilateral negotiations on these issues. Moreover, since regional leaders would be unlikely to accept a system to regulate drug trafficking, migration and security that was formally controlled by the US government, any bilateral efforts dominated by Washington would face strong regional opposition and could drag on for several years.

Tourism development in the CB countries — particularly Belize, Costa Rica, Cuba, Guatemala, Dominican Republic and Mexico — has enlarged the former tourist industry in the small Caribbean islands and Puerto Rico, creating a common tourism product — sun and beach — but an unstructured tourism region. Recently large air and cruise corporations, mainly from the United States, have been able to reverse this trend and impose integrated operations for some components of the Caribbean Basin tourism area, and have emerged as natural partners with CB countries in this growing market area.

The EU countries' Caribbean policy dates from the colonial era and was marked by the granting of Independence in the mid-twentieth century. Since then, the Lomé Convention has been the main instrument dictating the terms of co-operation and trade between EU countries and most former European colonies from the Africa-Caribbean-Pacific (ACP) region. The recent inclusion of Cuba and the Dominican Republic in the ACP area enlarges the actual and potential country coverage of this agreement. The EU has proposed a new Convention to the ACP countries for the next decade (2000–2010) which would provide special technical and financial

---

6   Several articles from the project, 'The North American Free Trade Agreement (NAFTA) and the countries of the Central American Common Market, Belize, Panama and the Republic', selected by the technical co-ordinators Rudolf Buitelaar and Ennio Rodríguez, appeared in an special issue of *Integration & Trade*, no. 11, vol. 4 (May–Aug. 2000).

assistance for the transition to a new economic framework under WTO rules. The CACM countries received preferential treatment in terms of trade, co-operation and technical assistance under the guise of the San José Group to support democratisation and economic growth in the aftermath of the Central America peace process negotiations. In the 1990s, as a consequence of Mexico's entrance into NAFTA, EU exports to this country dropped, which in turn accelerated the conclusion of EU–Mexico free-trade negotiations in March 2000.

In this context, EU policymakers should adopt a larger regional perspective. The assimilation of US–CBI tariffs and trade rules via the extension of NAFTA and the EU–Mexico free-trade agreement have emerged as necessary reference points for the EU and CARICOM countries participating in the post-Lomé negotiations. From the perspective of the CBSE countries, the preferable next step on the part of the EU would be to maintain most current commercial preferences and grant the CBSE countries import-export tariffs similar to those enjoyed by Mexico. Finally, EU co-operation in facilitating the transition of CARICOM countries to the new, more commercially competitive conditions and a redefinition of aspects of the technical assistance programme to the CACM countries would permit CBSE countries to improve their capacity to compete in the global market, attract new foreign investment and compete in the NAFTA and EU markets.

G–3 countries and Canada have also played a role in the emerging CB economic region. Mexico and Venezuela were the forerunners in adopting a petroleum supply and financing agreement (the San José Agreement) with most CBSE countries in 1978. In 2000 Venezuela submitted a complementary agreement with a selected group of eleven Caribbean countries, and Mexico, the CACM countries and Panama have been discussing another agreement on trade and investment. El Salvador, Guatemala and Honduras have formed the Central American Northern Triangle and negotiated a free-trade agreement with Mexico which went into effect in 2001. Finally, Canada has granted market-preference access to the CARICOM countries through CARIBCAN, while also introducing a 'docking clause' to negotiate a free-trade agreement with Costa Rica that allows other Central American countries to join the bilateral agreement and create a Canada-CACM free trade area.

On 7–8 April 2001 the presidents of Colombia, Mexico and Venezuela — the medium-sized powers of the Caribbean Basin — met in Caracas where they decided to reinvigorate the G–3, reinforce mutual trade and create a fund financed by the Inter-American Development Bank (IDB) and the Corporación Andina de Fomento (CAF) to support employment creation, small-enterprise development, poverty alleviation and illiteracy eradication. At the Summit of the Americas held in Quebec on 21–22 April 2001 the G–3 presidents celebrated the integration of their nations as a crucial step in the process of creating the Free Trade Area of the Americas (FTAA), the benchmark of the regional integration process. They also expressed their commitment 'to reactivate their co-operation solidarity with Central America and the Caribbean, individually or as a group'.[7]

An important step in the political dialogue and further integration of the CB countries has been the creation of the Caribbean States Association (CSA). This group is critical for the development by G–3 and CBSE countries of consensual international positions among the CB countries, such as the proposal of a CB Peace Area. It also represents the emergence of a new and magnified Caribbean identity as well as a forum in which the United States is not represented. The medium powers have found in the G–3 an instrument to consolidate their influence in the Caribbean Basin, while the CBSE provides a support group for their specific interests in the regional integration process and in the global economy.[8]

A multi-polar and active economic integration process has developed in the CB area since the 1980s. The previously dominant United States now faces new actors — the EU, the G–3 members and CBSE countries — which have developed the ability to act collectively, particularly through CARICOM and CACM. The integration process is nonetheless vulnerable to important differences between and among countries in each sub-group (G–3, CACM and CARICOM), and their regional allegiances. G–3 countries are far from an agreement on sensitive issues such as Plan Colombia and FTAA negotiations. CARICOM countries are well known for their irreducible individuality, while within the CACM countries, fissures have emerged over the Northern Triangle–Mexico free-trade negotiations. Yet, as evidenced during the recent G–3 meeting, conflicting issues are discussed even if their resolution is deferred.

Cuba's Participation in the CB Countries' Integration Process and Conflict with the United States

The end of the Cold War did not bring about major changes in US–Cuba relations; on the contrary, it opened a new chapter in the long-standing conflict between the two nations. In what became known as the Special Period, Cuba attempted to cope with the economic changes following the demise of the Soviet Union by means of survival strategies. In expectation of a change of regime in Cuba, the US government launched a destabilisation strategy that attempted simultaneously to stimulate internal disaffection while rein-

7   Agencias (2000) 'Pastrana, Chávez y Fox deciden relanzar el G–3', *El Mercurio*, 9 April 2000.
8   It is interesting to note that, in response to initiatives like the CSA, President Clinton chose the Summit of the Americas in Miami in 1994 to declare that the United States is a Caribbean country, and that in the FTAA negotiations, a small economies committee was created in which the CBSE held the majority.

forcing its unilateral economic embargo against Cuba.[9] Paradoxically, the reinforcement of US sanctions helped bolster the popular legitimacy of the political leadership as well as its ability to mobilise the population. At the same time, however, it has served to undermine the economy, which over the long-term weakens the government's day-to-day support and control, as evidenced by the increase in out-migration flows. The Cuban government has adopted a strategy of diversifying its international relations as an alternative to the island's former political and economic dependence on first the USA and subsequently the USSR.

While the US government had hoped to lead an international front to isolate Cuba, its unilateral embargo has in fact served to enhance international solidarity with Cuba. It also helped to stimulate Cuba's diversification strategy, based on reintegration with Latin America and the Caribbean, financial and trade flows from Europe and Canada and, finally, on existing and renewed relations with former and current socialist countries.[10] As a result, during the 1990s, while the CBSE and Mexico increased their already substantial trade with the United States, Cuba has successfully diversified its trade relations, which has permitted it to overcome its commercial dependence, first on the United States (from 1900 to 1960) and then on the Soviet Union (from 1964 to 1991). In 1998 the EU and the Americas, Cuba's main trading partners, represented 40 per cent of total external commerce, while the socialist countries represented one third. Tourism flows are a major component of Cuba's balance-of-payment revenues,[11] with 50 per cent from the EU and 40 per cent from the Americas — including the United States, but primarily from Canada.

So as to complement bilateral negotiations Cuba accepted collective negotiation patterns in commercial issues, and became a full member of ACP and CSA and an observer to CARICOM. Regional trade negotiations were promoted to reinforce the bargaining power of the CB and LAC countries with the United States. Through these integration schemes and associations, Cuba was able to influence the positions of the CSA and LAC countries on trade negotiations. Cuba also joined the Latin American Association for Integration (ALADI) and acceded to the standard bilateral

---

9   The most evident inconsistency of such a strategy is the simultaneous effort to stimulate external migration while also trying to stimulate civil society development.

10   Relations with the former Soviet Union and Eastern European allies were marked by an 'expectation' period, which came to a close with the failed Russian coup in 1993, and was followed by a 'wait and see' strategy. Closer relationships with China, North Korea and Vietnam developed in the early 1990s.

11   In 2000, according to CEPAL (2000b), the amount of exports was US$4,842,000,000 and imports, including tourism, US$5,766,000,000. In 1998, also according to CEPAL (2000); exports of goods were US$1,819,000,000, while tourism contributed revenues of US$1,816,000,000, and total imports were US$4,181,000,000.

trade forms used for all major LAC economies. It did not, however, accede to integration schemes, like MERCOSUR, that increase participation in regional commerce in order to empower their member countries to improve their bargaining positions vis-à-vis FTAA and other international negotiations.

After a period of conflictive relations between 1989 and 1994, the US and Cuban governments initiated a pragmatic negotiation process on day-to-day matters, ranging from migration and drug trafficking to more sensitive issues such as remittances, family travel to Cuba and reunification. In July 2000 the US Congress approved the lifting of the embargo on food and medicine, but the prohibition on US citizen travel to the island remained intact.[12] US Congress also blocked access to import credits from US financial institutions, thus authorising imports from the US market, but without increasing external hard currency income and financial flows. This pragmatic approach led to several important changes. For example, the information exchanges linked with US army and navy exercises in the Caribbean have increased military contacts between Cuba and the United States. This reduces Cuban troop mobilisation and will save the government several million dollars annually. Even more significant are the new rules allowing family remittances from the United States to Cuba. After the circulation of the US dollar was authorised in 1993 these family remittances became the second-largest hard currency input into the economy in the 1990s. Government-to-government negotiations also made possible Cuba's entry into the Caribbean system established by the United States to control and regulate drug traffic and migration flows.

But the progress resulting from these pragmatic relations does not compensate for the damages produced by US economic sanctions, particularly in terms of the threat of sanctions against countries that invest in Cuba, the loss of regular tourism flows from the United States, reduced export opportunities and higher transport costs. The USA–Cuba conflict also created difficulties for Cuba's international reinsertion by excluding the island from CBI benefits, the NAFTA-influenced production and commercial integration process of the Caribbean Basin and FTAA negotiations — all of which represent major handicaps in the era of globalisation.

Nevertheless, active diplomacy and the diversification of its economic activities have permitted Cuba to improve relations with the CBSE. Some of the principal factors are as follows:

- Trade with the CARICOM countries represents only eight per cent of Cuba's external trade. This relationship is significant not because

---

12   As part of its pragmatic approach towards Cuba, the Clinton administration adopted a flexible policy on illegal travel by US citizens, but the amount of estimated visitors to the island (30–50,000 annually for 1998–2000) is rather marginal compared to the potential flow if prohibitions were lifted.

of the quantity of these exchanges, but because of the role CARI-COM plays as a pressure group vis-à-vis the United States, the EU, ACP, the Organization of American States (OAS) and other important economic and political actors. Cuba has benefited from CARI-COM support, particularly in negotiations to enter ACP and to participate in the post-Lomé negotiations,[13] although Cuba withdrew its candidature at the last minute in mid-2000. Several CARICOM heads of state, including the president of Grenada, have visited Havana in the last two years, and their visits were hosted by President Castro. In addition, Cuba participated in the CARIFORUM Summit held in 2000 in the Dominican Republic.[14]

- Cuba's relations with the CACM countries and Panama were at a critical low point during the first decades of the revolutionary regime, but they improved gradually in the aftermath of the Central American peace processes. Recently, solidarity activities after the disaster of Hurricane Mitch, such as the delivery of medical services and cancelling Nicaragua's debt, represent an important step forward.

- The strengthening of political and economic relations with G–3 members and Canada has resulted in a number of agreements. The most recent and most crucial is the petroleum-for-services agreement signed with Venezuela in 2000. The regional impact of Colombia's armed conflict and Cuba's strategic role in the peace process — Havana has served as a neutral meeting ground for many of the high-level encounters between the Colombian government and the different guerrilla movements — has also helped to consolidate Cuba's regional presence.

During the final months of the administration of former President Bill Clinton there were a number of positive modifications in US policy towards Cuba, and there was even pressure on LAC countries to support these policy changes. After the 2000 presidential elections, in which a Republican administration took office, the Second Independent Task Force, sponsored by the Council of Foreign Relations, issued a report (on 12 December 2000) supporting a bipartisan policy towards Cuba, suggesting that 'the US Government can take many useful steps short of lifting economic sanctions and restoring diplomatic relations'.[15] In addition to reintroducing the travel and import authorisation approved by the House but rejected by Congress in

13   Klinger Pevida (2000).
14   Byron (2000) and Henán Yanes (2000). Puerto Rico plays an important role in Cuba's Caribbean policy. Exchanges with important civil society organisations developed between the two countries in the 1990s.
15   Aronson and Rogers (2000), p. 3.

July, the Report proposes co-operation on environmental issues and counter-narcotics operations, low and mid-level military exchanges, collaboration with Cuba on the Colombian peace process, and resolving the expropriation issue directly through joint-venture investments.[16] A few weeks after President George W. Bush took office, the president of the Inter-American Dialogue, Peter Hakim, concluded in a Memorandum on Cuba: 'Despite the growing pressure, a relaxation of US policy towards Cuba is unlikely under the Bush Administration. However, options to toughen policy are limited.'[17]

Hakim's view reflects the belief, shared by US liberals and the Cuban-American community, that political groups who favour changes in US-Cuba relations will be neutralised under the Republican administration. This belief is not shared universally, however, most notably by the Cuban government. The summer of 2001 marked the beginning of a critical test period that will continue until the Florida gubernatorial election in November 2002, as lobbyists seek to persuade the administration to waive sanctions against foreign firms in Cuba that are using property formerly owned by US citizens ('Helms Burton Law', Title 3).

Contributions of the European Union (EU) in the 1990s and the Challenges Facing Cuba

The Contributions of the EU in the 1990s

The end of the Cold War, the spread of globalisation and the impact of the recurring economic and financial crises on emerging economies and Japan in the 1990s permitted the EU to emerge as the dominant actor in Europe and as the main alternative to the role of the United States as the world-wide hegemonic power. These changes in the international system and the inclusion of Central and Eastern Europe into the European integration process 'have obliged the EU to strive to establish itself as a single, coherent political actor in international affairs... [T]he strategies that the EU adopts to pursue that goal will help to determine the future of what used to be called the West, and therefore of the international system.'[18]

The divergences between the EU's approach to economic development and its understanding of political and human rights and those of the United States provide emerging-market nations with an alternative major international partner. Some of these differences — such as the role of the state in domestic policies and international relations, a developmental approach to representative democracy and a multidimensional approach to human

16　*Ibid.*
17　Peter Hakim (2001) Memoradum in Oxford Analytica, April.
18　Crawley (2000), p. 10.

rights — are highly regarded by emerging-market nations, even if the EU considered these components to be mutually dependent and, therefore, pre-conditions to obtain co-operation and trade preferences.

Within the WTO framework, the EU adopted a regional approach to international economic relations in the 1990s,[19] offering its own experience as a model. The EU has developed closer links with Eastern and Central European countries, LAC and the ACP region.[20] Regional dialogue has been institutionalised through a plethora of regional associations, and in the FTAA negotiations LAC countries have come to see the EU as a regional alternative or complement to the United States. Moreover, the leading role played by the European Union (EU) in Eastern and Central Europe is a marked contrast with the lack of initiative and the reactive strategy seen in LAC before and after the Rio Summit held in 2000.[21]

After the difficult period of the 1960s, the EU countries assumed an active role in promoting Cuba's reincorporation into the international financial institutions developed by the market economies. The EU countries became Cuba's primary source of credit from the mid-1970s until 1986, when the island stopped external debt payments. Nevertheless, a decade later, the EU became Cuba's main commercial partner. Politically, the EU saw Cuba as a strategic partner in the Central America peace process and strongly favoured its participation in the negotiations. The EU also encouraged efforts of LAC countries to normalise diplomatic relations with Cuba and reintegrate the island into the regional system — in opposition to the US government's efforts to isolate Cuba and its policy of economic sanctions. Between 1960 and 1998 EU–Cuba relations were dominated by bilateral agreements, and these ties remained important even after a common position was reached in 1998.[22]

Since 1990 EU countries have approached Cuba's economic crisis as an opportunity for a transition to a market economy, representative democracy and international reinsertion. The EU countries were committed to helping Cuba find a solution to its economic crisis and believed that a successful transition was most viable under the helm of the current leadership, which would assure equity and social development as well as national sovereignty. Two phases can be identified in the EU strategy: the initial phase, which dominated between 1991 and 1996, and the current phase, from 1997 to the present.

In the initial phase President Castro's leadership was considered both viable and legitimating, and the selection or replacement and training of civil servants a natural foundation for a stable succession of leadership. Spain played the leading role, with Felipe González and his finance minister Javier

19   Bulmer-Thomas (2000) and León (2000).
20   IRELA (1997) .
21   IRELA (1999).
22   IRELA (2000).

Solchaga as the instrumental figures. LAC participation was welcomed as a strategic complement to EU participation, and the Ibero-American Summits served as fora for dialogue with the Cuban president on transition issues. Carlos Salinas, the former Mexican president, acted as an EU partner in these negotiations by virtue of the historical and political links between Cuba and Mexico, as well as the important commercial ties between the two nations. Canada acted as the EU's North American partner given their shared interest and commitment in developing a constructive approach to relations with Cuba. The EU and Cuba agreed to keep the United States informed about the transition process, and high-ranking government officials from the EU invested considerable effort to this end.

To address Cuba's economic crisis of 1991–93 the EU countries supported an adjustment programme and the implementation of structural reforms designed to promote direct investment, assure government credit, the creation of joint ventures between the Cuban state and foreign firms, and commercial exchanges. Tourism flows also increased as these institutional changes advanced and the economy stabilised.[23] This was facilitated by a generational change in economic leadership, as well as by the commitment on the part of the Cuban armed forces to participate in transformation and management activities in strategic sectors and in the state firms participating in joint ventures.

After 1997 a new phase was adopted by the EU. Consistent with WTO rules, this new strategy opposed the unilateral economic sanctions imposed by the US government, and in the end helped to convince President Clinton to waive retaliatory measures against firms operating properties in Cuba that were formerly owned by US citizens. This helped stimulate a move towards institutionalising the authority of official reformers over economic affairs, as well as modest moves toward democratisation and a revision of human rights legislation. Cuba sought acceptance into the ACP as well as in the post-Lomé discussions, but political obstacles emerged. The EU understanding of representative democracy and human rights was reinforced by the definition of democracy adopted at the Ibero-American Summits in Santiago de Chile in 1997 and Havana in 1999. Spain continues to play a leading role in EU–Cuba relations, but the means and objectives have changed with the inauguration of a conservative government. Relations between President Castro and Spain's new prime minister, José María Aznar, were strained at best, and eventually King Juan Carlos and the vastly experienced president of the regional government of Galicia, Manuel Fraga, replaced President Aznar in the negotiations. Italy, mean-

23   According to CEPAL (2000), Anexo Estadístico Cuadros A 42 y 43, the number of joint ven-
       tures created annually increased from 21 in 1992 to a median of close to 50 in 1994–96, and
       official import and export credits surpassed those from financial institutions, mostly from EU
       countries, as a proportion of the also increased total external financial flows.

while, developed an increasing economic presence in Cuba. Relations between Mexico and Cuba deteriorated after President Ernest Zedillo (1994–2000) adopted a critical tone towards Cuba and several Mexican investors left the island, fearing retaliation by the United States.

The conflict between Cuba and the EU in the United Nations Human Rights Commission[24] and the negotiations over EU–Cuba co-operation in the late 1990s must be evaluated historically and in terms of the development of a much more complex international situation. Cuba and the EU countries shared common interests and goals in the Central American and Colombian peace processes, establishing an enduring association in the negotiation of conflict resolution in LAC.[25] One of the achievements of the Colombian peace negotiations has been an agreement between the government and the National Liberation Army (ELN) in 2000, which was to lead to the establishment of an area under the territorial control of the guerrillas in 2001 to facilitate further negotiations. Cuba, France, Germany, Norway, Spain, Switzerland and Venezuela have played a mediating role in this process, with Havana as the site of negotiations. Cuba and the EU nations have participated in joint humanitarian activities in Central American countries affected by Hurricane Mitch in the late 1990s. For example, Cuban medical services were delivered in association or co-ordination with EU countries.

EU countries have introduced creative formulae, such as inter-firm agreements and legal retaliation measures,[26] to bypass or neutralise US sanctions. Cuba has almost completed the bilateral debt renegotiation process with the EU, and in the late 1990s it launched external debt renegotiations in Paris — in which the International Monetary Fund (IMF) did not participate — a process reminiscent of the failed experience of the 1980s. This suggests that economic authorities will accept an economic programme based on price stability, exchange rate and fiscal deficit targets, and further structural reforms.

Finally, Cuba has been following a 'two steps forward, one step back' strategy to conform to UN and EU human rights regulations and proce-

24   Cuba–EU differences on human rights, including civil society development, must be understood in a broader context. The Cuban leadership has opposed the US government's Track Two initiative to promote civil society organisation, which led it to associate the initiatives of the EU and Canada to promote civil society to an international conspiracy to overthrow or weaken the government and the control of the Cuban Communist Party's civil organisations.

25   As is well known, the participation of the EU in the Central America peace process has been a long, gradual process. The first step was the creation of the Contadora Group, which later became the Rio Group and the basis of EU–LAC biregional relations. The EU has favoured Cuba as an observer to the process and, even if this did not materialise, it did enjoy full participation in the Group in the second half of the 1990s.

26   STET International (Italy) participates with the Cuban state in a joint venture of the Cuban telephone company, which signed a rental agreement with ITT that allows the legal use of the electrical infrastructure and equipment expropriated in 1960.

dures. Relative progress in this regard — compared to 2000 — helps explain the closeness of the April 2001 vote concerning Cuba in the UN Human Rights Commission.

These events have not changed the short-term international relations objectives and priorities of the Cuban authorities. During 2000, energies were focused on bilateral negotiations with Russia and Venezuela and building momentum in favour of lifting the US food and medicine embargo and authorising tourist travel. In particular, Cuban authorities adopted a more pragmatic approach to US relations, as indicated by evaluations of the potential impact of a partial lift of the embargo published by experts from the government and Communist Party think tanks. One such source stated: 'an end to the hostilities, the initiation of a dialogue and the establishment of a foundation for respectful relations ... would be the correct alternative from the perspective of the national interest of both [Cuba and the United States]'. It is estimated that if the US embargo were lifted, there would be an annual increase in commercial transactions in the first few years of between six to eight billion dollars, half in trade and half in credit and investments.[27] Such an increase would probably amount to 55 to 75 per cent of total current commercial transactions.[28] Several Cuban authorities prefer a lifting of the US embargo to participation in FTAA, even though exclusion from the free-trade agreement would have a negative impact on the Cuban economy.[29] For example, the Cuban foreign minister, Pérez Roque, recently stated that the lifting of the embargo 'would pose a great risk to us — political, ideological — that we are willing to take on'. Analysts who suggest that the island's leaders benefit politically from the US embargo and secretly prefer it to remain in place 'are mistaken'.[30]

Cuban authorities and specialists are also aware that as far as commercial integration schemes go, the LAC nations favour the FTAA negotiations. The announcement that Chile and the United States would begin bilateral free-trade negotiations and its impact on MERCOSUR and the rest of LAC is the most recent evidence of the weight of the FTAA negotiation process in Latin America and the Caribbean, and of NAFTA in the FTAA.[31] As Victor Bulmer-Thomas (2000) indicates in reference to MERCOSUR–EU free-trade negotiations: 'MERCOSUR is currently negotiating with 30 other

---

27   Aguilar Trujillo (2000), pp. 78 and 79.
28   CEPAL (2000b).
29   Regueiro (2000); the author has developed a complementary view of the subject in León (1998). The publication included a selection of the papers presented to Encuentro Internacional: Globalización, América Latina y la Segunda Cumbre de las Américas, organised by the Latin American and Caribbean Center, Florida International University and FLACSO–Chile just before the Second Summit of the Americas in Santiago de Chile (1998).
30   Goering (2001).
31   NAFTA represents 83 per cent of the commerce and 87 per cent of the GDP of the American region.

countries a Free Trade Area of the Americas (FTAA). These negotiations are not expected to end before 2005, at the earliest, so it is unlikely MER-COSUR will want to end negotiations with the EU beforehand. The reason is that MERCOSUR countries, particularly Brazil, see negotiations with the EU as one of their strongest weapons in extracting concessions from the United States.'[32]

MERCOSUR and Brazil see international reinsertion or preferred trade treatment from the EU as a weapon in negotiations with the United States; this is clearly also the case for Cuba, as it represents an alternative to the lifting of the US embargo, and could be a useful tool for negotiation. To date, the commercial interests of Caribbean tourism firms and the electoral weight of the Cuban Americans in Florida have outweighed the desire of Midwestern grain producers and US pharmaceutical firms to exploit the Cuban market and potential joint research ventures, as indicated clearly by the approval of a series of amendments to the Helms-Burton Law and the events after the 2000 US presidential election.

Cuba's success in bilateral negotiations has been achieved using a complex combination of symbolic, commercial, technical and security factors to compensate for its marginal commercial importance. It has concentrated building its regional trade and integration ties with Canada and the CB and LAC countries. A December 2000 visit to Cuba saw Vladimir Putin and President Castro announce an agreement to complete the construction of the Cienfuegos thermonuclear plant. This decision was not based simply on economic or financial factors, but also reflected the critical factor of security within the larger framework of negotiations between Cuba, Russia and the United States.[33] It also demonstrated the importance of joining forces in multilateral negotiations in order to obtain desired objectives from the dominant partner. Furthermore, Cuba's CBSE integration efforts through CARICOM and CACM should be instrumental to empowering the integration schemes or associations in the post-Lomé negotiations.[34]

A recent example of Cuba's foreign relations strategy is the rekindling of favourable Mexico–Cuba relations after the deterioration of bilateral relations during the administration of former Mexican president, Ernesto Zedillo. The Mexican ambassador in Havana, Ricardo Pescoe, who was

---

32   Bulmer-Thomas (2000), p 2.
33   Some interest and political groups in Florida were concerned by the security problem associated with the Cienfuegos thermonuclear plant technology, given the plant's location and precedents such as Chernobyl. Florida representatives in the US Congress actively opposed the project and Russian participation in it. Just prior to Putin's visit the Cuban government signed the Venezuela petroleum agreement, which includes 11 CBSE beneficiaries. This agreement guaranteeing financial support and a petroleum supply, along with the economic evaluation of the project, were also factors in the Cuba Russia decision.
34   IDS (1999).

nominated and backed by President Vicente Fox and his foreign minister, Jorge Castañeda, is promoting far-reaching initiatives to rebuild commercial relations between the two countries. He is also — unexpectedly — involved in the question of leadership succession and has had close public contact with President Castro. Some of these initiatives, such as the creation of the post of prime minister, resemble Carlos Aldana's 1990 proposal for political reforms.

Finally, after Cuba enters ALADI, commercial integration through standard bilateral agreements is an open possibility, but only until the FTAA negotiations are concluded in December 2005. The framework established under ALADI will be subsumed under the FTAA framework. Moreover, Argentina — the largest holder of Cuban debt in LAC — and Brazil have manifested their interest in pursuing ongoing projects, particularly in industrial agriculture, pharmaceutical research and development, technology exchanges and the creation of joint ventures. Chile and Uruguay have developed close political links with Cuba, thanks to Cuba's policy of providing safe haven to political exiles from these countries during the authoritarian military regimes of the 1970s and 1980s. In addition, the social democratic leanings of the current presidents of these two countries and current contacts with the Cuban leadership indicate that Chile and Uruguay will be supportive of efforts by the government to advance representative democracy, and the current Cuba–Mexico approach is a viable model in this regard.

Challenges Facing Cuba

Regional integration will be crucial for Cuba, given the commitment of the Cuban government and the Cuban Communist Party (CCP) to the economic strategy adopted since 1993–95 and the new challenges the country will face. Major results on this front could be obtained during the period of FTAA negotiations, which have already begun and are scheduled to be completed on 31 December 2005. A representative group of these challenges includes: increasing national investment and external financial flows; upgrading the tourism industry and diffusing its economic impact; addressing increasing social inequities and reversing vulnerability; and assuring an orderly succession in political leadership.

a) Increasing National Investment and External Flows

Between 1995 and 2000 annual national investment was under ten per cent of GDP,[35] half the amount required for moderate sustained growth in LAC countries. Several factors helped compensate for the shortage in investment in the past, including idle production capacity and human capital availabil-

---

35   See CEPAL (2000) ; (2000 a); and (2000b) .

ity, natural capital incorporation and the 'war economy' discipline.[36] Most of these factors have been exhausted or will have limited effects in the future. Meanwhile, other factors, such as improved firm management through decentralisation, joint ventures between the public and private sectors and the recruitment of experienced managers, have been reinforced and will contribute to future growth.

Analysis of Cuba's ability to attract investment suggests several new policies and policy reforms will be necessary to meet the objective of increasing investment. Such policy reforms are underway in the sugar industry, which is in the midst of a complete restructuring programme aimed at improving its economic viability and international competitiveness, and which will potentially make this sector attractive to Foreign Direct Investment (FDI).[37] Because this industry's direct and indirect contribution to total employment is close to 50 per cent and employees are paid partially in convertible pesos, if this strategy were successful, it would bolster the argument for significant reductions of the impact of the currency diversity (Cuban peso, US dollars and convertible pesos) on labour market segmentation. Greater diffusion of the impact of the tourism industry is another example (see below).

A transition from the dual currency regime (Cuban peso/US dollar) to a unified currency — a necessary if not sufficient condition for upgrading Cuba's economy — requires the normalisation of external financial flows and external debt payments, which in turn requires an increase in gross national investment. As Mercedes García has noted: 'The strategy to address the financial crisis will include elements affecting the functioning of the entire national economic structure and will depend on the flexibility of the debtor countries and on internal efforts to design and apply a comprehensive programme to face the critical situation of external finance.'[38]

In the past, a programme relying on such external requirements would have exceeded national economic capacity or met resistance from the political leadership. The US position remains that external debt negotiations and increased financial flows require political and economic transitions which, though they would provide Cuba with direct access to the US market, are unacceptable to the leadership. Given the firmness of the Cuban leadership position and the lessons it has drawn from the experiences of post-communist countries, experts eager to see an upgrading of Cuba's economy realise that the solutions will not be simple. As Adrian Smith and John Pickles have concluded after a ten-year evaluation of post-communist countries:

---

36   As Hubert Escaith (1999) indicated: 'the success of the Cuban stabilisation was possible because of the authorities' capacity to compensate the monetarisation of the fiscal deficit by the forced savings of Cuban households ... resulting in an increase in GNP from 16 per cent to 47 per cent (1993–1999)' (p. 73).

37   George Carriazo (1996) noted early on how economic reform measures would generate a transformation process that might reach an increasing number of sectors.

38   See García R. (1999).

Transition is not a one-way process of change from one hegemonic system to another. Rather, transition constitutes a complex reworking of old social relations in the light of processes distinct to one of the boldest projects in contemporary history — the attempt to construct a form of capitalism on top of and within the ruins of the communist system.[39]

b) Upgrading the Tourism Industry and Diffusing its Economic Impact

The growth of the tourism industry is the main factor in the process of economic transformation in the 1990s. There was high and sustained growth in tourist flows, representing over 15 per cent annually in 1995–2000. Investments before 1995 had an immediate impact on the reactivation of construction activities, but transportation and activities linked to the hotel industry took several years to develop, particularly until the negative effects of inflation and the exchange value of the Cuban peso were neutralised. The need for the construction of hotel rooms was addressed in the late 1990s, through the reassignment and remodelling of buildings and foreign-management contracting. The industry was first to experience full decentralisation in 1994 through the creation of several state-owned corporations (Cubanacán, Gran Caribe, Islazul, Gaviota y Puertosol), and the establishment of specialised tourism enclaves (for example, Puertosol). However, since the decentralisation of other sectors has not followed the same pace, diffusion of the economic impact of the tourism industry has suffered.

Based on the current programme for 2001–2010, Tourism Deputy Minister Carlos Gómez estimated in April 2000 that five million tourists would visit Cuba, and that 78,000 rooms would be available by 2010, requiring $6.6 billion in investment. Considering that the Cuban government retains 50 per cent of the shares in tourism investment, which is derived mainly from internal savings, the tourism sector in terms of hotel construction alone will need twice the amount of FDI obtained between 1991 and 2000.[40] To face such a tremendous challenge investment in other sectors should be curtailed, or the redistribution of investment to the other components of the tourism industry must be stimulated. Whichever option is chosen, it will have a decisive influence on the impact of this sector's growth on the rest of the economy.

Given the diversified nature of tourism flows to Cuba in terms of country origins, the annual growth rate of 20 per cent in the last five years and a tourism market product similar to that of the Dominican Republic, these estimates appear to be well founded. But, in order to meet investment requirements a diversification of the actual product might be necessary, expanding

39   Smith and Pickles (1998), p.2.
40   'Cuba aspira a grandes inversiones en turismo', *El Nuevo Herald*, 15 April 2000.

from the current beach-and-sun product in confined parts of the country to a more integrated national tourism product which would combine hotel facilities, private residence lodging and time-share apartments. This would require policy changes to attract foreign investors and firms to the tourist sector.

The main changes required in tourism investment include improvement in infrastructure, such as roads, airport maintenance and construction, and water and sewage maintenance. It would also probably include the expansion of tourist cities like Cárdenas–Varadero and reconstruction in Havana. Airport maintenance and construction could be addressed with the current joint-venture policies, and be managed and financed by foreign firms, as has been the case with the Havana and Varadero airports. In other tourist destinations, the construction of additional airports is scheduled for the next several years.[41]

There may be some difficulties in terms of financing infrastructure maintenance and construction. The contributions made by the local population in Cuban pesos will represent an exchange rate barrier that does not arise in passenger/cargo airports, where fees are paid in US dollars. If current economic policies are not modified — for example, in the expansion and modernisation of the Cárdenas and Varadero water and sewage system — the alternative is likely to be the segmentation of such services into one system for the local population and another for the tourism industry, which would increase social inequality. Another possible alternative is to charge extremely high fees for facilities serving the hotel and tourism industry to finance the entire operation.

c) *Increasing Social Inequities and Reversing Vulnerability*

The fact that the tourism and export sectors were largely dependent on external factors and had reduced impact on the rest of the economy, together with the dual Cuban peso–US dollar economy, were largely responsible for imbalances in the Cuban economy and inequities in the process of economic growth. Economic liberalisation, the decentralisation of firms and activities, and measures legalising the circulation of hard currency 'allowed fluctuation in the prices of traded goods but did not require official exchange rate modifications to stimulate economic growth; moreover, this introduced elements of dualism in the economy, in employment and, therefore, in income distribution'.[42] The initial success of the revaluation of the Cuban peso in 1994–95 has not continued, and the exchange rate of 20 to one in 1996–2000 consolidates social inequality between Cubans who earn their wages in pesos and those who earn wages in pesos and convertible pesos, and between those who receive hard currency remittances from abroad and

---

41   Information obtained by the author in the First Latin American–European Airport Dialogue, Privatisation, Co-operation and Business Opportunities, sponsored by CONSAL, IRELA and Business Association for Latin America, Spain and Portugal. Berlin, 7–8 June 2000.

42   CEPAL (2000 a), p. 204 *passim*.

those who do not. As President Castro noted in a December 2000 CNN interview, 'A minister earns in one month the same amount in pesos that a Cohiba hotel bellhop earns in a day, in hard currency equivalent'. Such income differences between Cubans represents an ideological inconsistency as well as major social equity and political problems that have to be faced.

Revaluation of the Cuban peso, which is urgently needed on social and political grounds, would also help to overcome other important economic problems. The revaluation of the peso which occurred in 1994–95 had a positive influence on the economy, resulting in an increase in remittances. A revaluation in the near future would thus provide supplementary funds that could be used to reduce fiscal deficit vulnerability generated by increasing health services and pension payments.

d) *Stable Political Leadership Succession*

Political leadership succession has been a factor of insecurity in socialist regimes, particularly when it involves the founding fathers of the socialist regime and/or highly personalised leadership. This was the case in Cuba in 1989, and it remains an issue today.

Foreign governments and foreign investors are as worried as the Cuban people about the challenge of succession. After the 1989–91 crisis, European, Canadian and Latin American governments began to subscribe to the hypothesis that only Fidel Castro himself could guarantee an orderly transition. The United States was of the opposite opinion, conditioning the normalisation of relations between the two countries — as stipulated by the Helms-Burton Law — on the end of personalised leadership and the celebration of open elections.

There have been noteworthy changes in the political structure in Cuba since the 1989 crisis. Even those who criticise the regime agree that the Cuban elites succeeded in reconfiguring themselves throughout the 1990s. Key government officials, including members of the Finance and Foreign Affairs Ministry, have been replaced periodically. Castro has also encouraged periodic renewal of national and regional officials so as to avoid the type of crisis that decimated the communist parties in Central and Eastern Europe. But, critics argue, all of this has happened 'without changing the ingrained bounds of charismatic authority'.[43] Castro has held his posts as first secretary of the Cuban Communist Party, president of the State Council and president of the Cabinet, since 1976. He has, however, increasingly delegated authority on day-to-day affairs, as well as important trade

---

43   The US Government has implemented — quite unsuccessfully — a succession-crisis approach that already includes the first two stages outlined by Robert Pastor (1992): 'i) isolate the dictatorship through a clear, multilateral human rights policy; and ii) facilitate the dictator's exit through negotiations that reflects its full understanding of his weakness and needs.' (chapter 7, p. 144).

and debt negotiations to high-level officials such as State Council Vice President Carlos Lage. In response to pressure from abroad, Castro has also allowed officials in charge of foreign direct investment to develop legal guarantees for foreigners doing business in Cuba.

At the inauguration dinner of the Havana office of the *Chicago Tribune*, at which President Castro and Foreign Minister Felipe Pérez Roque were in attendance, President Castro indicated that he had not selected a successor, and Minister Pérez Roque stated that the government and Party authorities had a five-year contingency succession plan.[44] These statements by the president and foreign minister — selected from a number of diverse statements on the subject by high-ranking government and Party officials — suggest that the succession challenge persists and is in fact growing in importance given an ageing President Castro. In a high-risk investment country like Cuba, any step forward on the subject will be welcomed by foreign debt holders, investors and firms, and will probably translate into greater confidence and boldness in making investment decisions. Perhaps this explains why the above-mentioned announcements were addressed to reporters of the most important business journal in the Midwest of the United States.

Stable leadership succession — even if it is not equated to regime change and a transition to democracy — is also necessary as a confidence-building measure for government and Cuban Communist Party supporters and the population at large, both inside Cuba and without. A succession procedure will be announced while Castro is still head of state — in order to bolster regime legitimacy, a measure that was not necessary in other successions in collective leadership or socialist regimes.[45] The political situation in Cuba has changed dramatically since 1989, due to renewed out-migration flows, visits and exchanges by Cubans and Cuba-born residents who live outside Cuba, and the coincidence of the crisis of communist ideology and the globalisation of information and communication. Government supporters and Party members have to work within the context of the development of civil society and an internal political opposition that constrains them to a public debate of crucial issues such as leadership succession.[46]

e) *Regional Integration*

As noted by Lourdes M. Regueiro, an influential Cuban social scientist close to the CCP official line, Cuba has distanced itself from integration schemes,

44   Goering (2001).

45   One author's analysis of the subject appeared in León (1996), pp. 101–11.

46   Other than internal opposition and dissidents, such diverse out-migrant groups and organisations as the Cuban American Foundation, the Cuban Committee for Democracy and Encuentro's Circle agreed to promote civil society and regime transition. See *Miami Herald* (2001) 'An Activist Cuba Policy', 10 February; and Alejandro Portes 'Strategic Neglect', *The American Prospect* (2000), Sept. 25–Oct. 9.

favouring bilateral accords with individual states. Under present economic conditions the main problem may not be market access but the country's limited export products. In conclusion, the author asserts that 'in the short term it would be better to find a solution to the US embargo ... than to participate in the FTAA'.[47] Regueiro either represents a political sector that continues to disregard regional integration alternatives,[48] or reflects doubts about Cuba's capacity or interest in accepting conditions, including macro-economic co-ordination, that will take nearly a decade to obtain through a comprehensive structural-reform programme.

In addition, there are physical and functional integration links among the Caribbean islands, such as container distribution ports, environmental protection and third-level medical centres, which Cuba and other Caribbean nations might exploit collectively. Tourism is a common sector of interest for Cuba, CARICOM countries and Mexico, and it is a growing activity in some CACM countries. Therefore, a larger and more diversified product and image marketing in the CB could be developed in tandem. Cuba and the Dominican Republic, as tourism destinations and traditional agricultural exporters, might play an important role as links between CARICOM and the CACM countries.

Cuba will also be interested in membership in regional schemes formed to act as pressure groups or for the purpose of creating greater access to larger markets, such as CARICOM and CSA. CBSE integration schemes, particularly CARICOM, would not require meeting democratic or macro-economic co-ordination conditionality; they also favour preferential access to the EU market, participation on the post-Lomé negotiations and EU co-operation during the transition to a liberalised and regional commercial agreement between 2000 and 2010. Meanwhile, acceptance by the EU would imply conditionality in terms of human rights and democratic governance; MERCOSUR and FTAA demand these conditions as well as macroeconomic requirements.

The individual or sub-regional integration schemes (CARICOM, CACM, MERCOSUR) that offer Cuba an alternative to integration into FTAA or NAFTA are generally accepted in LAC. The Cuban government participated in the process of developing a consensus on this issue, adopting a minority position favouring LAC integration as a necessary step to integration into FTAA or NAFTA. President Castro and Venezuelan President Chávez were strong supporters of Brazilian President Fernando Henrique Cardoso's South America FTA initiative and the Brasilia Presidential Summit in August 2000. Cuban Foreign Affairs Minister Felipe Pérez Roque indicated Cuba's interest in MERCOSUR membership dur-

---

47   Regueiro (2000), quotation from pp. 28–30.
48   It has been this way since 1991–92. See León (1995).

ing his visit to Brazil in December 2000, but President Cardoso deemed his words 'a good will gesture, but far from a commercial reality'.[49] At the meeting the Cuban foreign minister criticised the decision of the Chilean government to launch bilateral free-trade negotiations with the United States as an indication of the lack of solidarity among the LAC nations in regional negotiations — despite the fact that Cuba's bilateral agreements with Canada and Mexico are similar to Chile's bilateralism.

The EU–Cuba Agenda: An Incomplete Proposal, 2001–2005

Overcoming Differences on Human Rights

EU–Cuba relations suffer due to different conceptions of human rights, particularly in terms of civil and political rights. The EU is a leading player in the movement to internationalise human rights by creating a system based on universal jurisdiction, which will reinforce the ability of national judicial systems to protect and promote human rights while aggressively pursuing justice for those guilty of crimes against humanity. After years of US efforts to use the human rights issue to isolate Cuba in the international community, the Cuban government identifies most initiatives on this front — including EU efforts — as part of an international conspiracy orchestrated by Washington. Cuba's participation in ongoing or future humanitarian activities in common priority regions, including Africa, the Caribbean and Central America, would help create a context of greater trust and confidence, and would help to overcome these differences and conflicts over the human rights issue. In such a context, the EU–Cuba differences on the human rights issue could be aired and solutions identified, which could in turn increase the political will and capacity of the Cuban government to comply with universal norms and practices, thereby furthering Cuba's international reinsertion.

The EU and Cuba are both committed to providing humanitarian aid to the world's poorest countries. Both also identify the origin of violence and internal armed conflict with 'ancient [and emerging] inequities that have never been redressed', and both 'accord to the state a prominent domestic role, notably as a source of such social goods as publicly funded healthcare and education'.[50] The EU celebrates Cuba's achievements in social development and equity, and has committed humanitarian aid to alleviate the dramatic deterioration of living conditions of vulnerable populations, primarily infants and the elderly, during the so-called Special Period.[51] During this

49   The *World Street Journal Americas*, reproduced in *El Mercurio* (Santiago, Chile), 29 Dec. 2000, p. B7.
50   Crawley (2000).
51   See Pérez Izquierdo (2000).

period, continuity in the training of health services personnel generated a large surplus in personnel, especially in the medical sector, relative to the country's needs; some of this personnel has been assigned to humanitarian missions or contracted on a personnel basis to poor countries. Such international activities have included the education and training of health personnel[52] and the creation of health centres specialising in the health needs of foreign patients.

The EU and Cuba could devise co-operation agreements to establish or participate in multilateral programmes, such as Cairo's approved Action Plan on poverty reduction in Africa, that focus on primary health care, combating treatable diseases such as malaria, and AIDS prevention and treatment.[53] Programmes based in Cuba should welcome the participation of the EU countries in the Latin American Medical Sciences School based in Baracoa, Havana, and jointly promote both the replication of the school in Africa, Central America and the Caribbean, and the participation of other countries in such endeavours.

Similarly, human rights programmes focusing on civil and political rights would be implemented, including the evaluation of the experiences of different countries — Cuba, the socialist countries, and the LAC nations — in terms of systemic changes in the design of their legal systems. Key decisions of the Cuban government would focus on civil society and the legitimisation of the national opposition. LAC countries — particularly Mexico — could offer invaluable co-operation on how to accomplish simultaneously the affirmation of national sovereignty and the legalisation of the political opposition in countries neighbouring the United States that have a long history of US intervention and interference in their internal affairs.

International Reinsertion through Commercial Integration

EU–Cuba co-operation on the transition from post-Lomé to an EU–Caribbean regional commercial agreement based on a WTO framework could be an alternative to the lifting of the US embargo. This, according to Alejandro Trujillo Aguilar, would be more interesting than even entrance into the FTAA in the medium term because 'the outcome of integration depends on certain domestic preconditions and on the adoption of the correct policies. As long as these are not fulfilled, the external global conditions

---

52   See a brief description of the Latin American Medical Sciences School in CEPAL (2000), p 283, recuadro VI.1.

53   EU countries contributed US$1.1 million to such UN programmes in Central America in 1999. Several EU countries (Germany, Spain and Sweden) joined the Cooperation Group in Central America, created after Hurricane Mitch. The group, which meets annually, met on 18–19 January 2001 in Madrid to discuss future activities, some of them related to the 14 January earthquake and programmes for alleviating the damage caused to the local population, and to reconstruct housing and infrastructure.

imposed [on Cuba] can weaken the country's ability to benefit from liberalisation'.[54] As the lifting of the US embargo is not likely in the foreseeable future, EU co-operation with Cuba and its assignation as a post-Lomé beneficiary would be the alternative to entrance into the FTAA.

Cuba could be a strategic ally of the EU in terms of the NAFTA-dominant integration process of the CBSE countries, even if its exports to the United States remain embargoed. One option is to allow an 'integration viability period' in which Cuba would export its products and seek integration with EU, the rest of the CB and the South American countries. This solution could be interesting for the EU if it favours improving the competitiveness of the Caribbean Small Economies, and if Cuba obtains access to the benefits the EU extended in March 1998 to other less-developed economies. [55]

The G–3 countries and Canada would be asked to participate in Cuba's 'integration viability period' to create an export market large enough to increase FDI interest in the island's exports. The participation of the EU, the G–3 and Canada would neutralise the likely negative reaction to this initiative by the United States. Cuba should complement such market expansion by reinforcing its current commercial agreements with South American nations, particularly Brazil and Argentina. Both of these nations, along with several EU countries, are important holders of Cuba's external debt as well as potential joint-venture partners for research and development as well as production in the pharmaceutical industry and in industrial agriculture. The main differences between the 'integration viability period' alternative and the lifting of the US embargo are that economic growth would have a broader sector base; the increase of tourism flows would be low but the impact of the industry's development in the economy broader; and the IMF, World Bank and Inter-American Development Bank (IDB) would not play a role in the transition period.[56]

Structural Reforms, Debt Renegotiation and Economic Upgrading

Barriers to regional commercial integration have played an important role in preventing Cuba from advancing structural reforms, as Escaith and Morley (2000) concluded in a recent study of reforms in LAC:

> When structural reforms are desegregated into their respective components relative to trade, tax, financial liberalisation, privatisation and

54   Escaith (2001).
55   A new post-Lomé partnership agreement between ACP and EU came into effect on 1 March 2000, and in eight years it will move from preferential access to trading conditions in full accordance with the WTO.
56   An Inter-American Dialogue project, 'Cuba and the International Financial Institutions (IFIs)', launched in 2001, started to provide the Cuban government with contacts and technical advice from those institutions.

capital account opening, the speed of trade liberalisation is definitively one of the main culprits of the negative impact of implementing non-gradual reforms.[57]

The EU countries are Cuba's main external creditors and, as stated above, have been discussing with the Cuban authorities a variant of the Paris Club debt renegotiation of the 1980s, which was designed to resolve the 1986 debt crisis. The 'integration viability period' proposal would create favourable external conditions that could encourage the Cuban government to overcome its current opposition to further structural reforms.

Cuba's economic authorities are aware of the successes and failures of the structural reform process experienced by LAC and the former socialist countries, and Cuba's own economic crisis and reactivation have been a learning process for government authorities. The EU countries have more than ten years to evaluate these experiences. In addition, several 'blue ribbon teams' and individual experts have produced a shopping list of options for a structural reform programme in Cuba.

To meet the final requirements for debt negotiations, a structural reform and macroeconomic programme must be approved and implemented by Cuba. Cuban economic authorities could encourage the emerging private sector within Cuba as well as FDI by introducing some pending economic changes on such sensitive issues as small and medium-size enterprises and labour-market institutional development.[58]

57   'The Impact of Structural Reforms on Growth in Latin America and the Caribbean: An Empirical Estimation', CEPAL Serie en macroeconomía y desarrollo, November.
58   See Julio Carranza Valdés, Luis Gutiérrez Urdaneta, Pedro Monreal González (1999): 'La petite et moyenne entreprise à Cuba: le point de vue de trois èconomistes cubains', *Cahiers des Amèriques latines*, 31/32 pp. 103 a 121. For the author's ideas on the latter, see Francisco León (2001) 'Foreign Investment and Labor Relations in Cuba Today: Challenges of an Upgrading Strategy', Looking Ahead (NPA, Washington). Special issue on the Current State of Foreign Investment and Workers Rights in Cuba. vol. XXII, no. 2, January, pp.11–17.

CHAPTER 9

Markets and Reforms in China, Vietnam and Cuba

Julio Díaz Vázquez

Introduction

The market as an economic category has been closely associated with the problems of development and with the practices of what was called 'real socialist economies'. The radical changes that are taking place to a greater or lesser extent in China, Vietnam and Cuba suggest the emergence of development strategies that are very distant from the theoretical-practical heritage of the classic socialist economic model.

Thus, it is worth exploring, if only in a condensed manner, the similarities and differences of these experiences, two of which follow models that move toward socialist market economies, one of which incorporates the market as an element outside of socialism. In reality there are several socialist models, rather than a universal strategy.

The prevailing tendencies indicate that pluralities flourish in each country, depending on the changing situations heralded by the course of the newly begun twenty-first century. The socialist legacy of the past century will have to assimilate that experience from different perspectives. The most important issue involves transcending the requirements imposed by the industrial revolution to meet those demanded by the knowledge society.

The classic model took as its premise a centralised economy that excluded an active role for market mechanisms and had only a passive role for currency. Politically, the model featured the single party and the dictatorship of the proletariat as the most advanced manifestation of democracy. Social policy assured education, health, work, housing, vacations and social security for all citizens. The state and the government were fused under the unquestionable subordination to the party.

This alternative project to capitalism was yoked to a model that made ideology the integrating factor of social relations. The actions of economic /political/social institutions initiated in the ideological sphere, moved to the political sphere, and from there to the economy. Ideology acted as the support and unifying entity for political, economic and state areas.

There are sufficient theoretical and empirical bases to affirm that centralised socialist economies lacked inherent self-correcting properties. The unwanted diversions that cropped up in economic development had to be alleviated with periodic reforms. There is consensus that the conflicts and distortions originated from within the model.

At the same time, there is convincing and overwhelming evidence that supports the view that the market becomes irrational in a socialist economy when it is assimilated merely through formal monetary-financial mechanisms. As an instrument to make economic relations viable, the market needs properly institutionalised spaces and a legal-economic framework sufficient for normal functioning.

Moreover, historically, the classic model demonstrated in excess the deforming effect of mercantile measures that were vertically grafted onto centralised economic links.

It bears recalling that, originally, that model justified state ownership in terms of economic efficiency. Evidence shows that state property, as the right to dispose of economic surpluses and make decisions about the distribution of resources, is not essential to making the economy more efficient.

With the above provisos as background, this chapter will examine the general and specific aspects of the currently developing markets in China, Vietnam and Cuba.

China's Market Economy

The turn in China's economy and society over the last 22 years began in the Second Plenary Session of the IX Central Committee of the Chinese Communist Party (30 December 1978), when Deng Xiaoping's proposals for the 'four modernisations' were approved. The outlined objectives were to restructure agriculture, industry, science and technology and defence.[1] This was complemented with the corollary of introducing an open door policy to foreign investment.

In the 1970s in China there were concurrent internal, external, political and economic factors that both favoured the proposed reform and made it urgent. The country had been able to consolidate a sovereign state, unify the continent and achieve power and international recognition.

China had significant industrial development, including a powerful military-space industry. There were large hydraulic works and infrastructure in agriculture, although not to a sufficient extent, given that China possesses more than a fifth of the world population, and less than ten per cent of the territory is used in food production.

However, despite the ambitious economic objectives and achievements, China was poor, backward and underdeveloped. In 1978 per capita income was only ten per cent that of the Soviet Union and two per cent that of the United States. Almost 100 million people lived on the edge of starvation. Indices such as the average salary in industry and the housing space per inhabitant were equal to or less than 1950s levels.

---

1   The project resuscitated the ideas of Zhon Enlai presented, but not accepted, at the National
     Popular Assembly III–IV in 1964 and 1975.

To perceptive and informed observers, the weaknesses and limitations of 'real socialism' were evident by the mid-1970s. The international economic crisis of 1973–74 was a point of rupture that defined the subsequent evolution of Soviet-European socialism. China did not choose, as it had 25 years earlier, to go back to that experience.

Within China's geographic proximity there were sufficient examples of dynamic development models that featured the state as protagonist in the economy, economic planning anchored in active mercantilist measures, and primary orientation toward the international export market. Of course, these models included multiple authoritarian ingredients in different variants.

The 'Chinese formula' initially rested on three guiding principles: decentralisation of the economy, opening to the international economy and social stability. The directives that defined economic policy up to the end of 1978 emphasised several objectives.

It was emphasised that economic management suffered from excessive centralisation, that state planning should be harmonised, and that there should be more delegation of authority, including autonomy in local governance, businesses and agricultural units. Simplification of economic administration and transfer of more functions to business corporations and entities were of primary importance. Another innovation was that the Party would no longer have the responsibility of all levels of management.

In 1979 an experimental agricultural policy, the system of responsibility by family contract, was introduced. Land was granted with usufruct rights (the state kept ownership) based on the household members, soil type and fertility, location, etc., in an effort to provide all the 'productive cells' with similar conditions. Incentives were created through the distribution of profits.

The state–family contract specified the size of the parcel, number of persons and crops for cultivation. Production to be sold to the state at an established price was not to exceed 30 per cent of the harvest. Inputs, services, etc., and their costs, were specified. Production above the contracted levels could be sold in the free market or purchased by the state at higher rates.

The duration of the contract evolved over time until it was finally extended to 50 years with permission to transfer, divide or rent. Between 1979 and 1984 the new form of production was generalised. The volume of grain production went from 305 million tons in 1978 to more than 500 million in recent years.

At the end of the 1980s the agricultural markets made up 60 per cent of the production. Currently, only a small number of farms for industrial use are under contract, the rest of production in this sector, about 95 per cent, are sold at market prices.

The foreign sector has been revolutionised by foreign direct investment (FDI), the creation of sites within the national territory with favourable conditions for attracting foreign resources, as well as by the restructuring of the channels and mechanisms for foreign trade.

FDI in China has several modalities. Joint ventures of state enterprises (which may include other types of ownership) and foreign entities are the most common. Other established forms include agreements for co-operation, contract corporations or the so-called mixed co-operative corporations, and businesses wholly owned by international capital.

Joint development corporations of foreign investors and the state have been created for the exploration and exploitation of natural resources, and the state has contracted with foreign entities to construct, operate and transfer large public works.

National firms produce raw materials and assemble components and parts with materials supplied by foreign businesses. The international firms then distribute the products in their traditional markets.

The geographic-spatial-economic forms created between 1979 and 1995 were highly innovative. These include the Special Economic Zones (SEZ), which initially appeared as industrial parks with special status in cities, municipalities and provinces. Foreign businesses integrated with national partners through mixed investments and other types of participation.

Subsequently, coastal cities were opened to foreign investment, as well as a number of urban and provincial developments in large river deltas, urban centres, districts and settlements bordering other countries and autonomous interior provincial and regional capitals. Duty free and economic-technical zones enriched the variety of forms for attracting foreign capital.

To support this wide range of FDI, investors were allowed to participate in modern infrastructural projects, and facilities for obtaining raw materials, energy, labour and attractive taxation terms were offered. A legal framework was created through the Law of Mixed Enterprises with National and International Capital and its successive extensions, modifications and delegations of prerogatives, and the 1984 Constitution and subsequent amendments (1988–1993–1999).

FDI acted as a bridge and a window to promote economic modernisation in China. It served gradually to assimilate the most advanced elements of mercantilist production. These initiatives became laboratories to test the introduction of reform measures. Serving as actual training schools, they contributed to the introduction of management and marketing techniques with international standards. Moreover, additional sources of accumulation were facilitated.

The state industrial sector in China is quite complex. The so-called public industrial sector includes large state enterprises, which are relatively small in number but have a large share of the value of production in that sector and are subordinated to government agencies, state enterprises subject to territorial governments, communal entities governed by central agencies and businesses created by local authorities (municipalities, districts, counties, etc.).

The non-state sector is composed of urban and rural co-operatives, private and individual activities, mixed foreign and state capital enterprises and wholly foreign owned entities.

Businesses that employ up to seven workers are classified as 'personal enterprises'. The majority of these are made up of family members or close relatives. Firms that employ a greater number of workers are private. Since 1984 'individual' entities can hire up to eight employees. In special cases this number may be increased.

In sum, industrial restructuring had several stages. From 1979 to 1982 business management was separated from Party committees. Retention of some profits at pre-established levels was authorised. The 1985 fiscal reform substituted direct rent transfers to the state with a utility tax.

Introduction of the contract transformed industry and introduced a dual price system. Businesses received some resources assigned by the plan and obtained others in the market. Centrally located firms had lower prices. Part of the final product was delivered to the state according to the plan; the rest was sold in the free market. The presence of the market began to influence the industrial sector.

The percentage returned directly to the firms increased constantly. The fixed prices gradually approximated market prices. Since the end of 1994 several dozen goods and prices have remained fixed or have been negotiated within a band determined by the state. Currently, only five categories are centrally controlled.

This mechanism had a positive influence on the continuous improvement in efficiency and production. At first it was applied to the consumer goods and then to intermediate goods. There were very few macroeconomic disturbances after prices were freed, and industrial as well as agricultural products were allowed to converge with market prices.

In 1987, industry decentralisation advanced and enterprises were allowed to retain earnings above the contractual amounts that were previously agreed upon. Subsequently, in another step toward promoting efficiency and competitiveness, firms were made responsible for their gains and losses.

Between 1996 and 2000, in an expansion of the 'socialist market', 14,000 businesses were reorganised into totally independent firms without any administrative ties, including the liberalisation of social obligations.

This process brought along with it the creation and improvement of the legal and institutional framework necessary to support the new policies. The growing importance of the market for economic entities induced the introduction of macroeconomic controls.

Instruments such as credit, interest rates, taxation, fiscal measures, reorganisation and establishment of a central bank, a network of specialised financial and banking agencies, government bonds, stock exchange, floating exchange rate and partially convertible currency were among the mechanisms that strengthened the monetary-mercantilist relations in the economy.

The economy moved from centralised planning to planning as macro-economic regulation and control. Effort was deployed in maintaining over-all supply and demand as principal economic equilibria. Integrally using economic levers to stimulate development and viable and balanced rapid growth became the centre of economic policy. The dichotomy between planning and market disappeared.

China more than doubled its Gross National Product (GNP) between 1980 and 2000. It grew at annual rates close to ten per cent from 1980 to 1996, and at eight per cent in the subsequent four years. According to national indicators, poverty (measured at an income of US$80 annually) has been eliminated.

Reform in Vietnam

The transformation initiated with the Sixth Communist Party Congress in 1986 is affected by a series of historical accidents that have not been fully overcome. The country was divided for more than 20 years into two sepa-rate states. The Democratic Republic of Vietnam established north of the eighteenth parallel in 1954 adopted the classic socialist model and its eco-nomic development component: accelerated industrialisation and agricul-tural co-operation.

The country suffered a bloody fight for reunification, independence and rejection of North American neo-colonialist pretensions with the creation of the Republic of Vietnam in the south and the destruction of the state in the north.

Upon reunification, the Socialist Republic of Vietnam was established in July 1976 and the next 25 years were a period of tensions and economic dis-asters. The new state was faced with surmounting obstacles that were the con-sequence of almost 30 years of war, natural calamities and social unrest in the south resulting from an effort to institute the development model of the north.

Between 1976 and 1985 economic management was rooted in the north, which was aggravated by the legacy of centralisation from the guer-rilla war. Among the most noteworthy errors were the emphasis on the cre-ation of heavy industry, insufficient attention to production of consumer goods, acceleration of the abolition of non-socialist property and the forced march to 'co-operativisation' in the agricultural sector.

Subsidies to unprofitable sectors and artificially low prices for raw materi-als made it impossible to sustain industrial production and popular consump-tion in the newly reunified nation. Price dislocation, disorganised salary struc-ture and an increase in circulating currency without material backing gave rise to uncontrollable galloping inflation. Corruption emerged throughout Vietnamese society.

The socioeconomic crisis was complicated by political and economic changes in Vietnam's principal partners. The country received close to 80 per cent of its income from the Council of Mutual Economic Assistance (COMECON), with the Soviet Union the greatest contributor.

Thus, the situation created in 1987–88 made radical measures in economic policy an urgent necessity. Three large programmes were implemented: production of foodstuffs, expansion of the availability of consumer goods and increase in exports. Large projects that did not contribute to this effort were halted.

At the same time, within Asia, the 'four dragons' (Hong Kong, Taiwan, Singapore and South Korea) experienced phenomenal success in the international economy. Thailand, the Philippines and Malaysia had economic growth and China was undergoing its 'reform or revolution' changes.

The internal situation, the transformations in the region and the difficulties attendant on the loss of Central European partners made an abrupt reform of the economic model in place an absolute necessity. As in China, this reform began with the production of foodstuffs.

The family contract and piecework were introduced in agriculture. The nature of the contract varied according to the specific conditions within the country (63 provinces), natural resources, fertility, relative abundance of land, family structure, etc. The time period for the contract varied with experiences obtained, from between 20 and 50 years. Rent was paid in kind, 450 kilos of rice per hectare or the equivalent in currency at the market price.

The role of different types of ownership was reconsidered. With state property as the central link of the economy, the sphere of activity for co-operatives and private ownership was expanded. The right of any citizen to become a producer or marketer was recognised and legally protected without any limitations on the amount of resources that must be mobilised, the number of employees or the purchase of shares in newly created loan businesses.

Management of the economy was reformed. Centralisation was limited, prices freed, mandated distribution suppressed, business and price subsidies lowered and more space for the market was created. Opportunities for all economic actors were equalised. Demand and supply was embraced to regulate the relationships among the different market competitors.

The banking system was remodelled with the creation of a Central Bank and sectoral and specialised banking entities with powers to set and control interest, credits and loans. The tax and fiscal system underwent deep restructuring and became a regulating tool for income. Production and marketing activities developed.

The economy opened up to the international sphere and companies were granted the right to determine the destinations of exports and imports. The first Law for Foreign Investment (FDI) in 1987 stimulated this process. In subsequent years (1990, 1992, 1996, 2000) the level of foreign capital was raised and extended, and transactions achieved international market parameters. The first Open Economic Zone (OEZ) is being established with an initial investment from several sources, including domestic private and state sources.

The crisis in Russia and Asia in 1997–98 slowed the flow of FDI to Vietnam. In almost 55 industrial parks and infrastructural and social projects nearly US$40 billion has been committed by foreign sources, particularly for energy, agriculture, fishery, industry, banking and services. Half of these funds have been disbursed.

But the Vietnamese economy is encumbered by a number of adverse factors. There is insufficient material infrastructure; the central agencies of the state, which have been restructured and reduced, are inadequate to establish reliable economic controls; there is a lack of developed markets, and monetary and financial tools (credit, exchange and interest rates, taxes) are inefficient; and finally, there is lack of fiscal discipline, especially in fulfilling budgetary obligations.

State enterprises are being reorganised in accordance with the new Corporations Law, making them independent through the creation of shares and transferring unprofitable businesses to co-operatives and through sales. Thus, the National Economic Plan orients development objectives indirectly through macroeconomic aggregates, balanced budget and investments.

After relatively high increases in GNP from 1990 to 1995 of over seven per cent, Vietnam experienced slower growth due to the impact of the Asian crisis of around five per cent annually. Financial reserves and readjustments and incentives to FDI presage a recovery of between six and eight per cent in the short and medium term.

Cuba's Economic Adjustment

With the triumph of the Revolution in 1959, the structure of the neo-colonial state was mined from within without traumatic changes.[2] The legal order and infrastructure was designed to create institutions that replaced the old ones, assumed their functions, and founded the supporting bases for the new socialist model.

The National Institute for Agrarian Reform (INRA) had a central role in this effort. The financing requirements of this agency absorbed state assets and led to the creation of a centralised fund for the sugar harvest of 1961. A similar policy was applied to the group of industrial activities administered by the Department of Industries of the INRA.

This experience was the origin of the Budget Financing System, managed by Ernesto Che Guevara. The system, which was extended to the Ministry of Industries created in 1962, was characterised by centralised planning.

2   Vilariño and Domenech (1986).

Productive units covered their expenses from a budget fund, and income went directly to the state coffers. Intermediate products circulated among enterprises without ever becoming 'merchandise', expenses were transferred, and the conversion into 'merchandise' occurred when there was an exchange of 'property'. Economic efficiency was measured by the reduction of costs.

Enterprises were organised in groups of units that used similar technologies under strict administrative supervision. This high level of central control[3] restricted economic leverage, commercial relationships and material incentives.[4]

Because of the dependence on climate factors and the particularities of agricultural and livestock production, the farming sector had greater autonomy in forming business linkages. A type of 'economic calculation' with a lesser degree of centralisation which acted in a partial and very limited way was established in that sector.

By the mid- to late 1960s a confluence of economic and political factors distanced economic organisation and management from those early practices. For example, around 1964 a programme was adopted with the goal of producing ten million tons of sugar in 1970, which subordinated the organisational and productive efforts of the country to this objective.

In the political sphere, party and state functions overlapped. Ambitious economic achievements, in addition to promoting the fusion of state–party activities, consecrated the 'Caribbean way', which was a utopian effort for the 'parallel construction of socialism and communism' as an immediate goal for Cuban society.

A novel form of economic management arose from this fantastic aspiration that was far from the innovative trend of budget financing and the variant of economic calculation implemented in the economies of real socialism. In 1967 the Economic Registry System appeared, which eliminated charges and payments to socialist enterprises, among other characteristics, as providing a 'refreshed vision' of Marxism. Commercial exchanges among state entities were interpreted as excessively capitalist.

Assignment of monetary resources for salaries, purchases and sales in the private sector and credits to farmers substituted for the state budget. The National Bank restructured its functions, eliminating other agencies of the State Central Administration. The experiment involved other issues; it expanded the policy of free services and delinked salary from work, ending overtime pay and diffusing voluntary scheduling.

---

3   Tablada (1987).

4   The theory was discussed by Che Guevara in 'On the Concept of Value', 'Considerations on the Costs of Production as the Basis for Economic Analysis of the Enterprises under the Budget System', 'On the Budget Financing System', and 'The Meaning of Socialist Planning'. See: *Nuestra Industria*, no. 3 (Havana, 1964); *Economía y Desarrollo*, no. 7 (Havana, 1971).

The big productive leaps envisioned were not obtained. From the 'years of mere survival of the revolutionary government'[5] followed the proclamation of the 'knowing how to bravely rectify the errors of idealism committed in managing the economy'.[6] Thus, 1971–75 initiated a rectification phase that created the bases for institutionalisation and the establishment of mechanisms that unified the functioning of the economy.

In 1975 the First Congress of the Communist Party of Cuba (PCC) approved a resolution to establish an appropriate System for Management and Planning of the Economy (SDPE). This system departed from the practices of the European socialist countries, especially the USSR. The idea was 'to gather this experience in a realistic manner and try to adapt it to our conditions, with great care and more conservative criteria'.[7]

The most detailed theoretical treatment of the adopted SDPE was defined as Restricted Economic Calculation.[8] That qualification separated the approach from its original formulation in the USSR, and the application in Central European countries, as well as from the reforms of the 1960s in those countries. But its basic core was still close to the classic socialist economic model.

Additionally, the Cuban economy had a combination of factors that distinguished it from the other members of COMECON. There was no comparable role of the state within or outside socialist experiences. The state controlled 92 per cent of the basic funds in agriculture, while in industry, construction, transportation (with the exception of a small group of private operators), in wholesale, retail and international trade, finance, etc., state entities held 100 per cent.[9]

Thus, the 1976–80 period was described as 'sowing' the principal categories and mechanisms contained in the SDPE, with the subsequent period, 1981–85, as the 'harvest'. Nevertheless, three factors converged to disrupt the economy. Extensive economic growth hit bottom with increases in the consumption of energy and raw materials, distortions in investment and sustained accumulation and, in the absence of sufficient national resources, growing dependence on external financing.[10]

Deficiencies in applying the SDPE mechanisms multiplied. There was a decline in housing construction and public works; yield indices predominated over the provision of goods; there was an increase in food imports, and there was a lack of correspondence between the investment fund and the outputs. At the enterprise level, payment for results became distorted,

5   Dorticós (1972).
6   Castro (1973).
7   Castro (1975).
8   Acosta (1982).
9   Rodríguez (1990).
10   Díaz (1998).

rewards were not always associated with their effects and enterprise independence was increasingly less viable.[11]

At the beginning of 1986 economic and social distortions became evident. A process of 'rectification of errors and negative tendencies' was initiated. The most exhaustive treatments of the period show that this was preceded by two years of reflection, criticism and warnings by the leadership to alert the masses of the need for the introduction and employment of new work methods and styles.[12]

The 'rectification' was centred on eliminating the mediocre and bureaucratic practices in planning, challenging the import mentality, improving investment and increasing public works. It also sought to suppress the farmers' free markets, bring back 'hydraulic will' (construction of dams, reservoirs and irrigation systems), build roads and reinvigorate the materials and construction industry.

New forms of work organisation, called 'compelling forces' (*contingentes*), were created and expanded which were bearers of values, concepts and mechanisms to renovate work incentives and attention to the individual. Procedures for incorporating scientific-technical advances in biotechnology, genetic engineering and microelectronics were implemented.

Mobilisation of the labour force was achieved through the resuscitation of 'voluntary work' and the revitalisation of 'microbrigades' for housing construction. In social development, tourist and food programmes and the 'Turquino Plan' in mountainous zones were created, and experiments in the business sphere were introduced.

Nevertheless, the cold report of the numbers showed that total efficiency in 1985–89 left much to be desired.[13] In 1989, the Gross Social Product (PSG) was 1.2 per cent lower than in 1985; the National Created Income (INC) per capita declined from 1,382 pesos to 1,216; the surplus rate fell from 1,574 to 1,145 pesos (1988); labour productivity fell from 6,281 pesos to 5,127. Other indicators, such as the return on basic investment, material consumed per unit of INC and the total costs for the value of the PSG experienced serious deterioration.

The analyses, discussions and adaptations introduced into enterprise management placed greater restrictions on the already formalised commercial relationships of the enterprise system. There was no substantial movement toward the creation of an alternative to the 'economic calculation' model.

In 1990 historical accidents submerged the Cuban economy into the most profound crisis the country had experienced up to that point. The disappearance of Central European socialism (1989) and the subsequent disintegration of the USSR (1991) quickly erased the international insertion

11   García Valdés (1998).
12   Machado (1993), García Valdés (1998).
13   CEE (1990).

upon which Cuba had relied. Additionally, the crisis brought to light the inefficiencies inherent in the Cuban economic model. The generous financial treatment Cuba had enjoyed from its European partners, especially the USSR, evaporated.

The last decade of the twentieth century brought the Cuban economy to unprecedented paths. After 30 years of divorce from the international market, the country did not have apparent advantages for taking on a task of that magnitude. Gross Domestic Product (GDP) fell by more than 35 per cent, foreign trade decreased by about 30 per cent, and the economy reached the edge of total collapse.

The policies implemented to overcome the crisis after 1990 were, in short: opening to foreign capital, decriminalisation of holding foreign currency, transformation of the agrarian model with the transformation of most state farms into a new type of co-operative (Basic Units for Co-operative Production), and granting of land to families and individuals to cultivate export products (tobacco, coffee, cacao, etc.). Farmers' markets were created for the sale of agricultural surplus and artisan products (state and private), and individual businesses, including restaurants, were authorised.

Macroeconomic reform was carried out with the creation of a central bank and specialised financial entities and the introduction of taxes and tariffs. Adjustments to balance domestic finances were based on social criteria; prices of luxury goods, tobacco and alcohol were raised and the free distribution of many goods was eliminated without affecting the most vulnerable groups in the population. The state budget deficit was reduced to between 2–3 per cent of GDP.

Commerce took place in segmented markets,[14] including regulated distribution (55 per cent of foodstuffs), markets for produce (mostly non-state participation) and craft and industrial goods (2–5 per cent private), sale of state goods at market prices, incentive stores in domestic and international currency for workers, commercial networks in foreign currency, dollar markets, individual service providers (including restaurants), and housing rentals and informal or black markets where unauthorised goods and goods removed from state channels are sold.

The ministries running the economy were reduced (from 50 to 32), structures were simplified, and enterprises were decentralised and granted more autonomy. The monopoly on foreign trade was eliminated and planning went from equilibria in 'material balances' to the concentration on contributions in foreign currency and the importance of financing to regulate and control the economy.[15]

---

14   Ferriol (2000). Market segmentation has rules of access for buyers and sellers, differentiated parameters in pricing (commercial rates, benefits, taxes, etc.), types of currency, and different mechanisms for capturing surpluses in specific spheres.

15   Vascos (1997).

However, the measure considered to be most significant to the subsequent consolidation of economic recovery and the basis for development is the enterprise improvement process (*perfeccionamiento empresarial*).[16]

Of approximately 3,000 state enterprises, 1,103 are in one or another phase of implementation, 650 have certified accounting systems, 520 have been approved and are preparing the final report, 186 have completed the documentation and submitted it to the national group in charge of evaluating applications, and more than 50 are applying the enterprise improvement.

In the 1994–2000 period the crisis was transcended with GDP growth averaging 4.4 per cent (85 per cent of the 1989 level). Official assessments stress two factors: 'the strategy of resistance planned by Fidel and taken up with unparalleled heroism by the people';[17] and 'the existence of a phased economic policy'.[18]

Final Reflections

A comparison of the economic transformations in China, Vietnam and Cuba involves a number of factors, including time and reforming pressures, geographical situation, territorial dimensions, population, characteristics of the historical processes in each country, factors emerging from the changes underway, cultural elements, and particularities of the revolutionary processes that engendered the respective socialist paths taken.

The reforms did not coincide in time and space. In the Chinese case, initiation of reform was predicated on a change in the Party and state leadership. In Vietnam, however, it was instigated by the leaders of the Revolution and the Party. It was not a process undertaken by the next generation of leadership. The Vietnamese 'renovation' did not entail a rupture with party and state agencies.

In Cuba, transformations which were conducive to a socialist economy demonstrated that the replacement of the initial bourgeois democracy and anti-imperialist phase of socialism did not bring about a change in the political leadership.[19] Economic policies and strategies applied to overcome the 'special period in peacetime', as the economic crisis was designated, is led by the founders of the Revolution supported by younger political cadres.

The changes initiated in China beginning in 1978 were not a direct result of imminent socioeconomic crises. Thus, the initial premises were not tied to the eradication of urgent disequilibria nor potential social schisms. Even though the country had alarming levels of 'underdevelopment', it also had factors that facilitated popular understanding of the newly designed policies.

16   Decree-Law of 19 August 1998, published in the *Official Gazette* on 14 Sept. 1998.
17   Lage (2000a).
18   Rodríguez (2000).
19   Rodríguez et. al. (1985).

Vietnam and Cuba faced challenges derived from situations created by both internal and external factors. In Vietnam, there was a combination of economic policy errors, voluntarisms, natural disasters, effects of a long war, imbalances in foreign economic relations and changes accelerated by the specific regional economic context (a high growth area). In the case of Cuba, the key factor for changes was the abrupt loss of supports constructed by over 30 years of co-operation and strategic links (80 per cent of trade) with the COMECON countries.

The processes of all three countries did not involve an ex ante delineated strategy. In China it was the logic of the 'four modernisations', begun with the 'contract' that initiated the changes which resulted in a 'second revolution'. The Chinese experience was also marked by advances, retreats and struggles among reformers and conservatives.

As the market began to play an increasingly important role, political alignments were reflected in the interpretations and connections formed surrounding ongoing events. At first, it was recognised that the 'plan was the most important' and the market secondary. Then, the vision advanced to the state regulating the market, and the market regulating the behaviour of firms. Finally, the formation of a socialist market economy was considered.

The acceptance of the role of the market, and especially, the consolidation of the reform, entailed a harsh ideological conflict that was settled primarily in economic theory. The foundation of the theory was presented as 'socialism with Chinese characteristics' and the notion of 'the first phase of socialism'. China could not elude or skip over the mercantilist phase of economic and social development.

In Vietnam the tense situation in 1987–88 catalysed the renovating impulse. Because the situation was pressing, the social climate and management of the economy had to be rapidly changed. This rapid departure began with reassessment of agricultural policy and diffusion of the 'contract' to co-operatives.

Unlike China, there were no conflicts stemming from political currents that questioned the gravity or urgency of introducing changes to the economic model. The course of renovation was not based on theory; rather, pragmatism and proof were the distinctive orientations for moving towards a socialist market economy.

Speed is the factor that distinguished the Chinese reform and the Vietnamese renovation. The majority of analysts note that gradualism was a positive element in the Chinese experience. Meanwhile, the particular political-economic-social circumstances ushered in a more liberal and accelerated pace in the Vietnamese reforms.

This does not negate the integral nature that the Chinese experience would finally assume. It advanced through pragmatism and experimentation before extending new methods of macro and microeconomic control and management.

Cuba's experience has a difference from the reforms undertaken in Asia, which were adopted from the beginning from the classical model of socialism that was in place. The island did not follow this practice until a correction (inspired by the classical model) was actually undertaken in 1971, based on a unique variant of economic calculation. Nevertheless, in essence, all of its components did not achieve full application.

Hindsight suggests that the adoption in Cuba of the restrictive version of the programme of economic calculation — practised then in most socialist countries — eliminated all its innovation potential, if it in fact had any. Of course, the country did not have a critical mass of researchers, economic practice, qualified personnel, specialised publications, etc., that would support a rigorous analysis of the possible advantages and limitations of the proposed model.

Foreign investment, which was integrated organically into the Chinese and Vietnamese processes, is the initial purveyor of the 'market' in Cuba. This market operates in foreign currency and is connected to the domestic economy through 'bridging' enterprises. By 1993 there was a very polarised dual economy on the island with two currencies: foreign and national. Currently it is considered a 'semi-integrated' economy.[20]

The market is accepted conjuncturally, a necessity of coexisting in a fortress under siege by the capitalist economy, or of tolerating the new situations created by a socialist economy's insertion into the market.[21] The influences of the past appear to be alive in the rejection of monetary-mercantilist relations, since they are associated with capitalism.

The lack of integration and of a legal-institutional framework for assimilating the market has been widely noted in Cuba. It is observed that mercantilism without adequate control leads to social stratification and can exacerbate corruption.[22]

The geographic differences in the Asian and Cuban experiences should not be trivialised. Asia has become the most dynamic economic region. Growth and development is imperative in order not to be left behind. China and Vietnam have chosen to accept the challenge of globalisation and enter into the competition with those rules of the game. Cuba, in Latin America, faces the globalising challenge excluded by the hostility of the US blockade[23] and the relative stagnation of the continent battered by the consequences of neoliberal policies.

---

20   González (1998).
21   González (2000).
22   Carranza, Gutiérrez and Monreal (1995); Díaz (1998).
23   The term blockade and not 'embargo' is used because the United States does not merely refuse to trade with Cuba, but influences third parties to impede commercial and political relations with the island.

In Cuba 80 per cent of the population is urban, whereas China's population is 32 per cent urban and in Vietnam only 20 per cent is urban. The modernising and organisational effort required to structure a mercantile economy is much greater in China and Vietnam than in Cuba.

The territorial and population dimensions are also relevant. Regional differences, zones of poverty, communications, infrastructure, etc., are influential in accelerating or retarding innovative policies. China presents the greatest challenges: disparities in economic development between the southern coast and the absolute and relative backwardness in the central and western parts of the country.

Vietnam is facing the growing breach in development between the north and south. Commercial practices have had greater assimilation in Ho Chi Minh City and the Mekong Delta than in the north. These regional disparities have not occurred in Cuba, although it is recognised that the eastern part of the country requires greater employment generation.

Culture is also an important factor. China has reopened the debate from the end of the nineteenth and beginning of the twentieth centuries over the diffusion of intellectual influences resulting from opening the country to the west in obtaining technology and democratic institutions. Vietnam, which had been a French colony for many years, is more open to those tendencies. There are foundations for the resurgence of nationalisms, either coming out of national minorities, or as a political mechanism promoted by the social groups holding power.

Predictably, China is on its way to creating a social model that currently does not have its rough edges completely defined. It does not correspond to real socialism, its patterns are far from state socialism, and the 'first phase of socialism' appears to be a transitional stage. Objectively, the Chinese reform can be called capitalism, in that various forms of capital and socialism can coexist for long periods.

Vietnam is still at a relatively early stage of the process of transformation and thus it has, at best, a 'model in construction'. There are some indications, however, that suggest that Vietnam could follow a trajectory of transformations similar to China.

Describing an economic profile of Cuba is more complicated. The economy has a symbiotic or syncretic character. The theoretical arsenal of classical, neoclassical, neoliberal or even orthodox Marxist economics do not easily explain the nature of transformations taking place in Cuba. The description could include: liberalisation, adjustment, transition, reform, opening and adjustment, deregulation, movement towards a market economy, etc.

Academic and professional experts agree that it is not possible to return to past models, if they can be called that. In 40 years of socialism Cuba has not had an 'economic model that is systematically integrated in every respect'.

It is a relief that reclaiming the supremacy of efficiency in state enterprises may make it possible to 'gradually overcome the causes that brought on the special period and take up more than ever the construction of socialism'.[24] At the same time, 'economic policy, market mechanisms, new parameters of planning ...' are objects for continued study.[25]

Finally, the incorporation of 'segmented markets' on the island led to positive results; 'there were no precipitous or spontaneous measures. Not even in the most difficult days were decisions adopted without careful consideration and a well thought out strategy. Fidel's leadership in economic policy during the years of the special period has been masterly'.[26] Thus, it is premature to label the economic model that finally will take the economy out of crisis and direct it towards new paths to economic development.

24   Lage (2001).
25   Rodríguez (1999).
26   Lage (2000a).

CHAPTER 10

Vietnam: So Much Done, So Much to Do!

David Dapice

Introduction

One of the most distinctive aspects of the last quarter-century in economics has been the ability of many Asian countries, including India and China, to begin and sustain rapid economic growth. These growth rates, of around 4–5 per cent per capita per year, will quadruple real incomes in a generation. While not all Asian countries have managed to join this elite and desirable group, many have. They seem to rely on a mixture of common-sense policies that include low inflation, promotion of manufactured exports and attention (where relevant) to a strong rural economy. By raising savings and investment rates and allowing competitive markets to direct an increasing share of capital, they ensure sufficient efficiency to convert growth in human and physical capital into real output growth. Many have wondered why, with few exceptions, there have been only a limited number of similar success stories outside of Asia. Aside from Chile and some small African nations, it is difficult to find any other nations that have been able to sustain rapid GDP growth for at least 20 years. The reasons why many can sprint but few can sustain a marathon are of interest to all, but perhaps especially to Vietnam.

Vietnam is unusual in that it decided on its own that it had to reform its economy in the 1980s, just when the Soviet Union was disintegrating. With little western foreign aid until the mid-1990s, and in spite of the collapse of its main trading partner and aid giver, it managed to move to a more market oriented system. The surprising result was that it boosted its real growth rates to among the highest in the world. The transition was marked by a rural policy that essentially re-established family and private farms, macroeconomic reforms that brought about market prices and low inflation and a welcoming of foreign investment. It was able to take advantage of growing oil exports, the boom up to 1997 in capital flows to Asia and growing western development aid. However, the Asian crisis slowed real growth in 1998 and 1999, and prospects for 2000 and 2001 seem to indicate a rebound to 6–7 per cent growth, helped in part by favourable oil prices and volumes. Is this recent recovery due to short-term factors, or have they found a fundamental solution to move from recovery to long-term sustainable economic growth?

The Recovery in Asia

The period through 1995 was one of rapid GDP growth and growing capital inflows in much of East and Southeast Asia. Excluding China, a slowdown began in 1996–97, followed by a sharp recession in 1998, and then recovery in 1999 and afterwards. South Asia experienced moderate growth in the period to 1995, and then India actually accelerated afterwards to 6–7 per cent. The data for China need special discussion, in that from 1986 to 1998 GDP growth seems to be at least three per cent a year too high in the official series.[1] It is difficult to make precise adjustments for these problems, as they change year-by-year. Perhaps it is enough to say that even with plausible adjustments, growth in China has still been very rapid, with adjusted per capita GDP growth of five per cent from 1986 to 1998. This performance is all the more remarkable given Japan's sluggish growth in the 1990s. Table 10.1 shows growth rates for several Asian nations.

Table 10.1: Real GDP Growth in Selected Nations, Average Annual Rates

Nation	1990–95	1996–97	1998	1999–2000
Japan	1.0	3.3	-2.5	0.8
China*	9.8	6.7	7.5	7.3
S. Korea	7.2	5.9	-6.7	10.0
Taiwan	7.1	6.2	4.6	6.1
Hong Kong	5.6	4.8	-5.3	5.8
Singapore	8.7	8.0	0.4	6.7
Indonesia	7.6	6.4	-13.2	3.8
Malaysia	8.7	8.0	-7.5	6.6
Philippines	2.3	5.5	-0.5	3.5
Thailand	8.4	1.9	-10.2	4.3
Vietnam	8.3	8.8	4.4	5.4
India	4.6	6.0	6.8	6.7

Notes: Most nations are taken from the Update of the *Asian Development Outlook, 2000,* from the Asian Development Bank, Table 1. *China is taken from A. Young's NBER Working Paper 7856, except for 1999–2000, which is the ADB source. Japan is taken from the IMF *World Economic Outlook, October 2000.* Taiwan data from 1990–96 comes from the *Taiwan Statistical Data Book 2000.*

1   See Alwyn Young (2000), p. 17

The general pattern has been a 'V' shaped recovery for most of the crisis-affected nations, except for Indonesia with its peculiar problems. China, India and Japan all seem to march to different drummers. This is not surprising given their large internal economies and low trade/GDP ratios. Vietnam is a curious hybrid. It certainly slowed sharply in 1998, but much less so than its Association of Southeast Asian Nations (ASEAN) neighbours. However, its recovery has been rather slow given its low per capita income and oil exports. Both of these factors might have led to a faster recovery than noted so far. (However, growth in 2001 was expected to be about seven per cent.) Both as competitors in export markets and as customers, the growth of Asian nations is important to Vietnam. There was much concern that the considerable real currency devaluations of ASEAN nations in 1997–98 would hurt their export growth, but this effect was short-lived. However, there has been a considerable decline in FDI commitments and inflows, even though these have risen in much of Asia. To understand why Vietnam has performed the way it has, it is useful to go back to the reasons for its reforms and their results, before going into a deeper analysis of current trends and prospects.

The Period Leading to *Doi Moi*

The situation in Vietnam in 1986–87 was very difficult, even grim. Inflation of 20 per cent a month (several hundred per cent a year) combined with poor harvests to create food shortages. The Soviet Union, Vietnam's major aid source and trading partner, was undergoing major changes likely to reduce aid for Vietnam. Exports were low (about $600 million) and mainly directed to the Soviet bloc. Imports were double exports, and prospects poor for non-Soviet aid or commercial loans. It was a time of intense discussion and introspection. Reality had to be faced and conclusions drawn from it. This was done and *Doi Moi* was the result. A period of reform followed that resulted in a decade of rapid growth, lower inflation, soaring exports and high levels of direct foreign investment. In the decade after 1988, Vietnam's economy was one of the best in the world.

There had been prior hints that reform would emerge. 'Fence breaking' had occurred at the local level since the late 1970s, and in times of crisis the Party would endorse pragmatic steps taken to cope with difficult conditions. The central planning model adopted by North Vietnam in the 1950s and applied nationwide after unification in 1975 aimed to develop heavy industry at the expense of agriculture, services and light industry. In this model prices played no role in allocating scarce resources, and capital was used lavishly on firms and projects of low productivity. These problems were set aside during the war against the United States, but re-emerged after 1975. The withdrawal of major aid by all parties but the Soviet bloc, the Chinese invasion in response to Vietnam's incursion into Cambodia and the stagnation and declines in output created a critical situation in the early 1980s. As a Swedish essay said, 'This crisis was in essence a crisis of the economic system, and revealed the weak foundations of the centrally planned state economy. At the same time, the parallel or second economy, which had never been effectively quelled, gained momentum. At a party congress in 1982 the first tentative steps towards economic reform were formalised. However, these fell far short of the concerted effort needed to address the fundamental problems and imbalances in the economy.'[2]

Agricultural Reforms and Growth

However, the late 1980s needed more than local responses. Food output per capita was well below the 1982–86 average in 1987, and hunger began to be a problem in some localities. Soviet aid was clearly going to decrease as economic troubles and political change combined to reduce the willingness and ability of the USSR to continue providing generous levels of support. While the Sixth Party Congress in 1986 had criticised aspects of the central planning model, it was only after the food shortages of 1987 that sweeping reforms were put in place. These reforms had both structural and macroeconomic aspects. Agriculture was fundamentally changed, as land was taken from the collective farms and distributed to the collective members. They got land use rights rather than land ownership, but for a long term. They could transfer these rights or use them as collateral. They could increasingly plant what they chose and sell their products to any buyer they chose. The family farm had returned.

At the same time, most prices were set in markets; the exchange rate was changed from 425 dong to a market-based 4,500 dong to the dollar and the printing of money was curtailed. Government spending was cut, thus ending most food subsidies. However, food output grew 11 per cent in 1988 and ten per cent in 1989. Food supply per capita became more plentiful than at any prolonged period since before World War II. Millions of tons of exports of rice replaced imports. Inflation (Dec. to Dec.) collapsed from nearly 400 per cent in 1988 to 35 per cent in 1989. A reinvigorated agricultural sector had ended the crisis.

Broadly speaking, the move towards family farms and voluntary forms of co-operation brought policy back to where it had been in the mid-1950s, after the land reforms in the North but prior to the forced collectivisation in 1958. The willingness to allow a market-based exchange rate and relatively free prices for agricultural products allowed the underlying benefits of trade to be enjoyed by farmers. In addition, there were supportive investments in

---

2   Ronnas and Sjoberg (1990).

irrigation, roads and other infrastructure. Trade policies allowed inputs to be available, and bank loans at market rates to many farmers ensured they could apply fertiliser. The success of agriculture had far-reaching implications, for it was broadly based and allowed improved food and incomes in both the North and the South. In 1992–93, a Living Standards Survey found just over half of the population in poverty by a World Bank standard, down from 70 per cent in the mid-1980s. By 1997, the same poverty line and survey approach suggested only 37 per cent poverty levels. By any measure, life was much better than before for most people. Caloric intake per capita per day rose from 2,192 in 1987 to 2,422 in 1998, a gain of over ten per cent. People had more to eat, in spite of net grain trade shifting from imports of over half a million tons to exports of over 3.5 million tons.

It was not only rice output that grew. Sugar-cane output jumped from 5.4 million tons in 1987 to 13.8 million tons in 1998; coffee from 20,000 tons to 362,000 tons; and rubber from 50,000 tons to 225,000 tons in the same period. Real GDP in agriculture grew over five per cent a year from 1989 to 1998. Population growth was about two per cent a year in the entire nation, while the agricultural labour force grew 1.8 per cent a year. Thus, there was a sustained and significant increase in farm output per worker for the 70 per cent of the population living in rural areas, and also per capita for all of Vietnam.

However, Vietnam is a land-poor country. There are about eight million hectares of farmed land for 80 million people, a ratio of only 0.1 hectares per person. While increasing farm output per hectare and per worker is essential, it is not sufficient to propel Vietnam's economy to the levels now enjoyed by its neighbours. Indeed, agriculture has fallen from about two-fifths of GDP a decade ago to only a quarter in 1998. It is in industry and services that the future wealth of Vietnam will be built. As the declining share of farm output suggests, these other sectors did grow remarkably fast in the last decade.

Trade and Industrial Growth

The pattern of industrial growth is especially interesting, since a larger industrial sector and deeper industrial structure usually provide the capacity to increase exports and employment. Real industrial growth was negative in 1989 and only three per cent in 1990, as Vietnam lost its Soviet markets. However, two sources of demand were quickly found. There was a rapid shift to production for hard currency markets, mainly in Asia and Europe. These products tended to be garments and shoes and other light industrial products. The other source was import substitution, the replacement of import demand by domestic production. These products tended to be in heavy industry such as cement, steel, sugar and various types of machinery and vehicle assembly. Special fast-growing products included oil, which was produced mainly by a Russian joint venture and exported, and electricity, which is not widely traded. In 1991 industrial output grew nine per cent and at 13–14 per cent in 1992–96. However, industrial growth slowed to 8.3 per cent in 1998 and only 7.7 per cent in 1999, reflecting problems with both exports and weaknesses in the high-cost import-substituting products.[3]

The most dynamic industrial sector by ownership has been the foreign-invested sector. Its share in industry grew from 11 per cent (mainly oil) in 1990 to 37 per cent in January 2001. The domestic non-state sector has had a steadily falling share of industrial output, from 32 per cent in 1990 to only 23 per cent in January 2001. The state sector (excluding joint ventures with foreign firms) share fell from 57 per cent in 1990 to 40 per cent in January 2001. In recent years, the foreign industrial sector has been growing at over 20 per cent a year while both state and domestic non-state growth rates were half as much in 1995–97, and only 6–8 per cent in 1998. In 1999 state firms grew at only 4.5 per cent, while foreign firms grew at 20 per cent. If that trend were to continue for five more years, the state sector's share in industry would fall to 30 per cent, while the foreign sector's share would rise to over 50 per cent. Thus, trends observed from 1993–2000 will produce an industrial sector that is predominantly foreign-owned.[4]

Manufactured exports — mainly garments, shoes and electronics — have grown very rapidly though from a low base. They were only US$100 million in 1988, but had surpassed US$1 billion by 1993. By 2000, processed exports (including processed foods) reached about US$6 billion, of which foreign enterprises accounted for two-thirds. In 2000, garments had an export value of US$1.9 billion while footwear accounted for US$1.5 billion and electronics US$800 million. The value added of labour-intensive industries is low, with labour and other domestic costs taking only 10–20 per cent of the export value. Total exports in 2000 were US$14.4 billion, nearly double those of 1996. The ratio of manufactured to total exports was just over two-fifths in 2000. This is only a little lower than Indonesia's ratio (51 per cent in 1996), but well below that of Thailand, the Philippines or China whose ratios are three-quarters or more.

The reason manufactured exports are viewed as important is that they are likely to have better market prospects than many raw materials, and their growth is not tied to a specific amount or quality of land. If labour intensive, they allow for labour to be withdrawn from low productivity jobs in rural areas. They often stimulate the growth of supplier industries and

---

3   It is not unusual for import-substituting goods to cost consumers two to three times their import price. Locally-made steel, cement, sugar, fertiliser, motorbikes, cars and machinery all cost much more than their pre-tariff/quota imported equivalents. The extra costs to consumers are high, over US$1 billion a year.

4   The recent jump in domestic private industry is too new to include in this data, but it could indicate a different pattern of growth with more domestic private participation in the next several years.

other services, and lead to technology transfer and a greater familiarity with foreign markets. The most successful Asian nations have used manufactured exports as an 'engine of growth' to sustain rapid and equitable growth. Any slowdown in total and labour-intensive exports is of concern because it slows the overall growth rate, reduces the growth in demand for workers and slows the increase in earnings of much needed foreign exchange. However, Vietnam has increased its total exports from US$730 million to over US$7.3 billion in the 1987–96 period. Even from 1996 to 2000 the annual growth rate of 18 per cent is very strong. The new deal with trade opening the US market should help speed growth even more. If policies promote further rapid growth in manufactured exports, this will be a massively important support for the economy.

One important point is that manufactured exports normally require an extremely high level of managerial attention to be profitable.[5] Manufactured exporters must be fiercely efficient to survive. In all other countries that have sustained rapid export growth, it has been the private or non-state sector that has supplied most of that growth. This is true in Vietnam, except it is foreign-owned and managed firms that have played this role. However, to sustain progress, it may be necessary for Vietnam to create conditions that would allow domestic non-state suppliers to assume a larger role. The official policy has been one of supporting a multi-sector economy for some time, though with a leading role for the state. However, in reality there have been a number of obstacles to the growth of domestic private businesses of any size. With a slowly growing state sector, a stronger domestic private sector is the only way to make industrial growth less reliant on foreign sources. Foreign investors have been the major source of manufactured exports in Malaysia and Singapore, but Vietnam may prefer to resemble Taiwan or Korea, where the role of foreign exporters is much less.

Foreign Direct Investment

There has been a great deal of foreign investor interest expressed in Vietnam and billions of dollars of foreign investment has been put in place. At the end of 1998 there had been US$35.5 billion in approved foreign direct investment (FDI) (125 per cent of 1999 GDP), and an official US$10

5   There are examples of garment quota being allocated from the European Union through the Ministry of Trade or Light Industry in Hanoi to individual, mainly state-owned, firms. These firms have the right to sign contracts and deliver on them with EU customers, while other factories (even if better) cannot if they lack the quota. This quota system, which is being phased out under the World Trade Organization (WTO), does provide an element of protection or subsidy for less efficient firms. However, even now, over half of garment exports are outside of quotas. They do not exist for shoes or electronics, the other two major manufactured export items.

billion of realised inflows by mid-1999 on a balance of payments basis. In 1997 foreign direct investment was estimated to have accounted for 28 per cent of the total of US$7.2 billion in gross investment. This includes the share of domestic partners in joint ventures, but is a high number by any measure. (Correcting the official data for certain biases discussed below would reduce foreign investment totals by an amount between one-third and one-half, depending on the year.[6] Total gross domestic investment would also fall if these corrections were included.)

The situation with regard to data on FDI is complicated. Until recently, most foreign investors were effectively forced to set up joint ventures with state enterprises. The share of the Vietnamese partner was frequently set at 30 per cent, even if their contribution (usually only land) was not worth that much. The response of the foreign partner was to overstate the value of the physical capital, so as to maximise the reported depreciation and interest cost. This would increase the estimated costs of the enterprise and reduce apparent profits that had to be shared. In the last few years, some provinces have allowed 100 per cent private investments to be set up, and these do not suffer from the same problems. Firms setting up in export processing zones have always been able to have 100 per cent ownership, but now this option is becoming more widespread. However, this past behaviour pattern for joint ventures has resulted in the data tending to be inflated on both the local and foreign partner sides. This is true for both approved and realised FDI.

Another difficulty in evaluating trends in FDI data is the tendency of the authorities to approve projects that have a low probability of finding finance, or of ever appearing in the form they are approved. In 1998, for example, over half of the US$4 billion in approved FDI came from two dubious projects. One was a US$1.3 billion oil refinery in the middle of the country. Western and Korean companies had evaluated this project and found it to be unprofitable. Finally, a Russian oil company with virtually no financial standing was selected. It is unlikely that the refinery will be financed unless oil exports of Vietnam are used to provide collateral for needed loans. Since technology can be licensed, it is not clear in what sense that refinery will be a 'foreign' investment. The other project, a US$700 million resort centre in Da Lat, is unlikely to appear in its licensed form. With excess capacity even at first class hotels and generalised excess tourist capacity in Asia, it is all but certain that only a fraction of the project will be implemented. If these two items are excluded, there was only US$2 billion in other FDI in 1998. This is a decline

---

6   In 1998, reported imports of capital goods by foreign enterprises were US$637 million, while estimated FDI inflows in the balance of payments were over US$1,800 million. It is hard to reconcile these two figures, even allowing for EPZ and oil investment and other sources unlikely to be in the US$637 million figure.

of more than 75 per cent from the reported 1996 level of FDI approvals and less than half of the 1997 level.[7]

Most of the FDI has flowed to the Hanoi–Haiphong area in the North and the area in and around Ho Chi Minh City in the South. At the end of 1998, there had been US$33.9 billion of approved FDI allocated to provinces. Hanoi and Haiphong accounted for nearly US$9 billion of this, while the HCMC area accounted for US$17.7 billion. Together, these two areas accounted for four-fifths of the total FDI, or slightly more if the two doubtful 1998 projects are excluded. This heavy regional concentration is not surprising and may even be higher if implementation rather than approvals were to be considered. Many of the approved projects will never be implemented because the profitability anticipated at eight per cent GDP growth in a dynamic region disappears with four per cent Vietnamese GDP growth in a slower growing region plagued by excess capacity, smuggling, and excess stockpiles.

It is uncertain if industrial FDI will increase any time soon. There is still strong interest in some provinces among export-oriented foreign investors. These tend to be southern provinces in which the local governments have worked hard to cut red tape, ease licensing requirements and promote problem solving in customs, labour supply, congestion, etc. The Fujitsu factory in Dong Nai, for example, is expected to provide US$1 billion in electronic exports itself in a year or two. Nike, the largest employer in Vietnam with tens of thousands of employees, is also located in this region. When the trade pact is finally concluded with the United States, it and/or other shoe manufacturers should eventually increase production for the US market. This should provide immediate benefits to business-friendly provinces, mainly in the South.

Prospects in the northern provinces are currently less promising. The well-equipped Nomura industrial zone in Haiphong has few investors and none in the last year. Problems with customs and local administration have blunted the natural advantages of low labour costs, good port facilities, very good quality land and infrastructure and a strategic position in the Red River Delta. If a combination of commitments to the ASEAN Free Trade Area (AFTA) and the WTO, along with smuggling, reduce protection, it is likely that there will be less investment in highly protected import substituting industries. Investments in services will be sensitive to the stringency and quality of regulation and the overall rate of economic growth. On balance, prospects for FDI inspired industrial growth in the South are brighter than elsewhere unless there is a change in regulatory practices.

7   Expansions of existing foreign investments amounted to an additional US$769 million. These are likely to be genuine, if somewhat overstated. Still, 'real' FDI approvals fell sharply in 1998–2000 relative to 1997 or 1996. A large gas investment in 2000 is an exception to this trend.

In the past probably only a third of industrial FDI (an eighth of total FDI) went to export-oriented manufacturing firms. Two-fifths of total FDI went to hotels, processing zones and other real estate. So long as there is excess capacity in real estate and import substituting industries, the lift from export FDI may not be enough to offset the drag from the weaker sectors. Over the longer term, if Vietnam can further reform its economy and procedures effectively, it is likely that this will generate profitable opportunities and overall FDI would then again increase and play a major, and more productive, role.

State Enterprises and Equitisation

In Vietnam, there is a very small proportion of employment in state enterprises. Employment in all state enterprises is 1.9 million in a workforce of 39 million, or about five per cent of total workers. This level of employment has changed very little in the 1990s. In terms of output, the state sector accounts for two-fifths of total output. This ratio has changed little in five years. The state sector dominates heavy industry, foreign trade, energy, and utilities such as telephones. These have more capital per worker than most other businesses or farms. Two-thirds of workers are in agriculture where the proportion of state activity or workers is very low. Thus, capital and output per worker in the state sector is much higher than in the private domestic sector, even with agriculture excluded.

There were 5,450 state owned enterprises (SOEs) in 1999 and about one-half are thought to be profitable.[8] It is likely that slow growth and pricing pressures will continue to force adjustments. There have been rising levels of SOE debts. At the end of 1997, these debts amounted to VD 170,000 billion, more than half of that year's GDP. Fully 44 per cent of the debts, or VD 75,000 billion ($6 billion), were then past due. There are constant complaints about the efficiency of most SOEs, the lack of capital and modern technology and the quality of their management. This is in spite of SOEs having better access to capital and educated workers than private firms. Domestic private firms in the same industry with the same capital have one-half to one-third as many workers as SOEs. Growth rates of state industry have been slowing, and were less than either foreign or private domestic industrial growth in 2000.

The debt/equity ratios of SOEs are high. The World Bank reported that at the end of 1997, the three-fifths of SOEs surveyed which were unprofitable had debts about double their state capital. There were 686,000 workers in these firms. The profitable SOEs had debts equal to 116 per cent

---

8   According to an article in the Nov. 2000 *Vietnam Economic Review*, about half of SOEs may have earned a profit in fact in 1999. See 'Vietnamese Enterprises' by Nguyen Thi Hoai Le, p. 18.

of equity and altogether had 929,000 workers. Average employee income in the profitable firms was 85 per cent higher than in the unprofitable ones.[9]

One major question is what to do with the SOEs that are failing. The choices are to merge them with a healthy firm, allow the sick firm to go bankrupt and close, keep the failing firm alive in its current form or equitise it. The last step creates a joint stock holding structure in which employees, other state enterprises, the government and private investors (local and foreign) can hold shares. The hope is that better management and perhaps more capital will create a healthy and competitive firm. The danger from the overall government perspective is that the SOE may be sold for less than its real value, thereby creating unearned windfalls for major initial shareholders. The greater problem is that many SOE managers do not want to equitise. They prefer the security of being a SOE to the prospect of their firm living or dying with the competitiveness of their products. They also fear, not unreasonably, that their parent ministries or local peoples' committees would no longer support them. Their access to bank loans and favourable regulation would then end and they would be at a distinct disadvantage relative to private firms that have learned to grow in spite of these limitations. This helps explain the very slow progress of equitisation from 1994 through 1998. Only 370 small SOEs had been equitised during 1995–99. The equitisation targets have been set high (1,000 for the year 2000) and generally not met. Even if they were, it would be the smallest and least valuable state enterprises that would be equitised, accounting for a small fraction (a tenth or so) of total SOE output or employment.

It is also unclear what such a process would accomplish, at least in terms of the fate of the transformed firms. The first ten or 20 equitised firms did well, but these were small, healthy companies to begin with. Many of those now slated for equitisation are in deep financial trouble, and many may collapse without the support they now receive. Even the larger SOEs seem to require high prices to function. If the larger, profitable and better run state enterprises are having problems, the smaller ones slated for equitisation are likely to face even greater difficulties. Some, of course, will survive. Many will merge or close. It is crucial to maintain a safety net for workers likely to be displaced. If aid were used wisely, this would be feasible. If 600,000 workers had to be laid off, three years of salary in severance payments would cost about US$600 million, or half of one year's aid disbursements. Compared to China, this is a manageable burden.

---

9   Being profitable is not the same as being efficient. Many state enterprises are monopolies or have other one-sided advantages that allow profits to be recorded even if costs are far higher than similar companies in other countries or private firms in Vietnam. If they had to face deregulation, many of the profitable SOEs would face considerable pressure. Telephone charges, for example, are among the highest in the world.

The fate of the larger state enterprises is likely to be resolved more slowly than the smaller ones. Many of them have been placed in one of several dozen general corporations. These are basically cartels that are grouped around a particular product. They control production, and influence imports, so as to maintain a high price. The idea behind them is that they would become large enough to compete as 'national champions' rather like the Korean *chaebol*. These corporations formed before many of the Korean firms collapsed or had to restructure. Even if the idea of the *chaebol* had been sound in Korea, it was unlikely to succeed in Vietnam. The Vietnamese market is only one-third the size of Korea's a quarter century ago. There is weak control over the creation of excess capacity in key industries, and as yet little effective pressure on these companies to reduce costs to world levels. Smuggling is a major concern, undercutting the ability of any industrial group to hold prices high and maintain output growth, except for monopolies such as telephone charges. (Vietnam's international and internet charges are among the highest in the world.) Finally, these firms are still behaving as state enterprises. They prefer, or are forced, to keep output high and stockpile, rather than adjust output to market demand. If trade barriers are lowered, as committed, in the next five years, they will either be forced to change or require ever-greater subsidies to continue as they now are. Perhaps some will be taken over by foreign investors, as a stock market develops and restrictions on foreign ownership are eased. The general corporations in their current form will either persist and slow the growth of that part of Vietnam's industrial sector, or change into something more globally competitive.

It is seldom that one finds state enterprises that manage to transform their management and compete globally. It is easier in nations such as Singapore that are small and have a strong technocratic leadership. It is much harder in larger nations that are subject to the normal pressures of political and bureaucratic lobbying. Without strong oversight, it is very difficult to create even acceptable performance without the prod of competition, the threat of bankruptcy or changed management and the pressure of shareholders wanting management to earn a good return on their investment. Vietnam is at a very early stage in arranging for any, much less for most, of its corporations to be in a position where they are able to compete fairly and be rewarded if they do well. A major concern is and remains that Vietnam's neighbours will create these conditions more quickly and thoroughly than Vietnam, further setting back any likelihood of Vietnam catching up.

Capital Markets

It is often said that capital is the blood of a market economy. Its circulation is central to the process of economic growth. Financial intermediaries gather savings, aggregate them, change their risk, liquidity and maturity, and then allocate them to their best use. This process does not yet exist in Vietnam, and the lack of such market-based intermediation is a major barrier to economic growth.

There are commercial banks. They provide loans, but nearly half of the funds go to state enterprises whose condition has been described above. Aside from some rural lending, the private loans are also deeply troubled. Much of the infrastructure needed for a functional credit system is only getting started in Vietnam. Central credit registries, credit rating, reliable financial statements and recovery of assets by lenders are either inadequate or unreliable. Fraud, which is vigorously prosecuted, is a major problem. The official figure for overdue loans is ten to fifteen per cent of total loans, but this is likely to understate the magnitude of the actual problem. It would not be surprising if Vietnam's banks resembled China's, where the proportion of bad loans are between a quarter and two-fifths of total loans. In either case, the state banks are insolvent and will require government support to remain operational.

There is a curious advantage to the relatively underdeveloped state of the Vietnamese banking system. In most other Asian countries the amount of bank loans outstanding is about equal to or even more than the value of GDP. In Vietnam, bank loans are only about one-fifth of GDP. Thus, even if overdue loans were at Chinese levels, they would only be about seven per cent of GDP, and not all of those loans will be a total loss. If allowance is made for recovery of one-third to one-half of the overdue loans, the amount to be made up is only about US$1 billion. Over a few years, with the use of foreign aid, this will not be a crushing burden. The existing problem is highly manageable, if it does not get worse.

The problem is that a bailout of banks would be destructive if fundamental reforms in lending practices were not part of the package. Currently, loans are made even to loss-making state enterprises. Banks are still instructed to make loans to projects chosen by the government, even if they have a tenuous economic feasibility. Many foreign exchange loans are made to firms to import goods, not to firms that export them. The former firms usually earn dong and are highly vulnerable if the dong devalues. The latter firms earn dollars and would be less exposed to depreciation of the dong. Thus, pumping money into the banking system with unchanged current practices would almost certainly lead to further losses. Until there are changes, few efficient firms will be likely to get loans; few banks will necessarily know which loans are sound; and the banking system will remain vulnerable to macroeconomic shocks and micro-level fraud and abuse.

There is a distinct reluctance to allow foreign banks to compete with domestic banks. Various regulations restrict the ability of foreign banks to gather deposits or make loans with a prospect for repayment. They have been losing market share and even shrinking their deposits and loans.[10] Many

---

10   *VIR*, 21–27 June 1999, p. 16.

claim to be losing money, even with the help of fee-earning activities such as issuing letters of credit. Increasing restrictions on foreign exchange are also a factor limiting their ability to function normally. These restrictions also limit the transfer of expertise in credit analysis, market intelligence and other knowledge that would prove helpful to the borrowing firms. If these restrictions persist, foreign banks will play a marginal role in Vietnam's financial intermediation, and the improvement in the existing (mainly state-owned) banks will determine the rate of progress. At present, the rate of progress is slow, as it depends on the resolution of the equitisation question. So long as there are thousands of state-owned enterprises with special access to loans, even if they are in poor financial condition, it will be difficult to transform the lending process to one that is commercially based. Similarly, unless firms begin to produce meaningful financial statements, it will be hard to switch from collateral based lending to that based on the prospective profitability of a firm. This will skew growth to those firms that have collateral and away from those that do not, even if they could grow rapidly with loans.

The state of other forms of intermediation is at a formative stage. Insurance is not widely used to accumulate assets. The stock market, recently started, is very small. There are few firms now able to list and currency controls will limit foreign interest. Bond issuance, outside the government, is also very limited. There is also no central place to trade bonds. An attempt by one bank to set up a secondary market in government bonds was squelched by the government. Leasing firms operate at a low level because of regulations restricting their operation.

The situation with respect to rural credit is mixed. The state-owned Bank for Agriculture and Rural Development has boosted lending to farmers up to VD 18,000 billion ($1.3 billion) and to other borrowers (for example, sugar mills) to VD 11,000 ($0.8 billion). However, some of the loans to farmers were made in response to natural disasters and were not so much loans as relief payments. The repayment rate from people who borrowed to rebuild their flood-destroyed homes is low. In addition, many sugar mills and rubber processors report facing high costs and are unable to repay. In addition to this bank, there are a number of credit unions and co-operatives that operate on a small, local scale. There is also a large amount of informal rural lending, but at interest rates of several per cent per month. A misnamed 'Bank for the Poor' is a soft loan window of the Agricultural Bank, but it gets loan funds mainly from aid or budget sources and lends to poor people at low rates. Many of these poor families lack collateral and have low prospects for repaying their loans. The loans are made by Agricultural Bank staff and often face repayment problems. Even if all loans were repaid, it is unlikely that all actual operating costs would be covered. Overall, private and budget (often aid) funds provide finance for planting tree crops such as coffee or extending irrigation, but there is a distinct shortage of medium to long term rural credit for farmers. Working capital is widely available, and chemical fertiliser use has grown over 80 per cent since 1990 to nearly 4.5 million tons in 1998.

The prospects for improved financial intermediation remain murky. Bank deposits or domestic credit relative to GDP were not very different in 1998 than 1991. This in itself is not promising, since so many other developing countries have much higher ratios and fairly rapid growth towards its neighbours' levels might be expected if financial development were truly underway. Beyond the low quantity of credit, there is a low quality of allocation. This judgement is based more on inference than knowledge, since real information about the status of a firm's finances is rare. In addition, the status of bank loan portfolios is closely guarded. However, the troubled position of state-owned enterprises and well publicised problems of private banks and firms suggest that a combination of little experience and limited information make it hard for banks to allocate capital efficiently. It will take further reforms to change this, but it is not clear when they will be implemented. If FDI remains low, no major source of funds will be available to finance the growth of efficient firms except for internal funds.

How Big is Vietnam's Trade Deficit?

Vietnam's official import and export data have shown large but diminishing trade deficits in the 1995–98 period. There is some degree of smuggling, but estimates vary widely as to its extent. Naturally, the official data do not include smuggled imports. There is one independent source of information, the *Direction of Trade*, or DOT. This statistical source is compiled and published by the International Monetary Fund. In addition to the official data, it also uses data from trading partners as a check. For example, imports of Vietnam from Hong Kong should equal Hong Kong exports to Vietnam, plus trade and transport charges of about 10 per cent. The DOT data are only available through 1997. In the table below, official and DOT trade data are shown for 1995–97 (in US$ millions)

Table 10.2: Import and Export Data for Vietnam

	1995	1996	1997		1995	1996	1997
DOT Imports	11,803	13,919	14,165	Official Imports	8,155	11,144	11,622
DOT Exports	5,723	7,156	8,722	Official Exports	5,449	7,256	9,145
DOT Deficits	6,181	6,763	5,443	Official Deficits	2,706	3,888	2,477

The results show quite large differences. The cumulative deficit is US$18.4 billion from the DOT, but only US$9.1 billion in the official version. *This is a difference of over 100 per cent of the official deficit figure!* If the IMF based data are correct, then the trade deficit in 1995–97 was equal to over 75 per cent of 1997 GDP. This is an astonishingly high level, even if allowance is made for US$1 billion or so a year in gifts. It suggests a much higher debt level is being carried than is officially recorded. Extreme caution in adding to debt would be in order if debt/export ratios were actually at 200 per cent or more. This would put Vietnam into the class of 'highly indebted poor countries' that need debt relief. More research is needed to understand the reasons for these differences. However, it is already clear that exports are virtually the same, so the differences in imports will be crucial in finding a reason for the discrepancy. In addition, other ASEAN economies show much smaller differences between official and DOT data, so this very large gap is unusual. This shows the difficulty of using foreign capital flows when the statistical network is not capable of providing essential data in judging the risk of further borrowing or lending.

Government Taxation and Spending

Vietnam has recently released official data on past and projected levels of government spending and taxation. The general pattern for revenues, expenditures and deficits is for all to rise relative to GDP from 1991 to 1994, level off, and then give up about half of the gains by 1998. These patterns are shown below. There has been relatively modest structural change in the sources of revenues. The most notable is a sharp rise in trade taxes offsetting a decline in transfers from state enterprises. There has been a protracted effort to implement a value-added tax, but the design is complex and is supposed to cover many small establishments. This has created many difficulties. Income taxes are frequently adjusted, and have such high rates at such low-income levels that foreign firms often find it cheaper to hire foreign rather than local workers. (Income taxes have different schedules for foreign and local workers.) As state enterprises face continued difficulties it is likely that this source of tax revenue — still a quarter of the total — will fall or increase only very slowly. Thus, the importance of making the value added tax work will take on increased importance. With all these problems, Vietnam has lifted its revenue collections to the same range, relative to GDP, as its neighbours who all have collections of 16 per cent to 20 per cent of GDP. Thus, the problem is one of finding efficient ways to raise the same relative amounts, not increase the proportion collected. As problems with VAT implementation are worked out, and perhaps greater stress put on urban real estate taxes, it should be possible to collect taxes without distorting economic activity.

Table 10.3: Government Revenue and Spending in Vietnam
(percentage of GDP)

	1991	1992	1993	1994	1995	1996	1998	2000*
Total Revenue	14.4	18.3	21.6	24.0	23.3	22.9	20.2	17.5
Total Spending	15.7	19.8	25.8	25.2	24.1	23.6	22.2	22.3
Budget Deficit	1.3%	1.5	4.2	1.2	0.8	0.7	2.0	4.7

Source: IMF Report on Vietnam from 8–2000 for 1995–2000. World Bank Reports are used for 1991–94. Revenue figure excludes grants, which are normally about 0.7% of GDP. These can be used to reduce the borrowing impact of the deficit.

*The 2000 figures are budget figures, not realisations. High oil prices may have reduced the actual deficit.

On the spending side, capital spending has usually been one fifth to one quarter of total spending. Debt service has fluctuated but was an eighth of total spending in 1998. Education spending rose by two per cent as a share of total spending while administrative expenses fell by a large 4.3 per cent and healthcare spending fell by a surprising 1.6 per cent. There is a need to find ways to employ these expenditures more efficiently. This is perhaps most obvious in the choice of investment projects. Under the old system projects were chosen if they fit the plan and were financed largely by aid. In practice, the plan responded to a variety of administrative and political pressures rather than economic or market influences. This is still the case in many instances. For example, the World Bank's 1999 study of the transportation sector stated:

> Making full use of existing [port] facilities should be paramount prior to any considerations on investing Vietnam's limited resources (even when provided by grants or bilateral assistance programmes) in major expansion of port facilities. Requirements generated increased shipborne traffic and changes in cargo packaging and handling technologies should firstly be met by optimising the use of existing facilities and systems; secondly, by rehabilitation and minor expansion of existing facilities; and lastly, by construction of new port facilities.[11]

In spite of this pointed analysis, there are plans to invest large amounts in a number of little used ports. Other examples of an uneconomic oil refinery or a bridge over the Mekong River (when upgraded ferries would provide

11   World Bank (1999), p. 110.

adequate service for three per cent of the bridge cost) all suggest that neither the donor nor the borrower side has yet gained control over the public investment process. Rather, there is control, but it is not aimed primarily at investing efficiently. The result is a considerable level of debt accumulation, but slow progress in key urban and rural infrastructure due to a 'shortage of funds' created by the poor investment choices. Rectifying this situation is a key challenge to donor and government officials. This is especially true if the IMF rather than the official trade data are more nearly correct and debt is higher than generally estimated.

There is also a regional dimension to public finance. The wealthier regions in the South and Hanoi–Haiphong pay far more in taxes than they receive from the federal budget. It is not unusual to get only one dong in return for every five or six paid. This helps the other provinces with much lower incomes, but also starves the fastest growing areas of funds to invest in infrastructure. They need to overcome this constraint, or else the policy will result in 'starving the healthy to feed the sick'. The shortcomings in the aid process and the lack of a national capital market make this issue all the more urgent.

Social Indicators

One of the proudest achievements of Vietnam in its central planning period was its relatively high levels of health and education, especially considering its low income per capita. There has been a distinct shift away from a 'one size fits all' fully subsidised approach towards one that is more complex, with significant levels of user finance. The obvious concern is that too many people would fall through the cracks and health and education levels would suffer. In practice, this has not happened. Rather, social indicators have matched or exceeded levels from the middle 1980s to the later 1990s.

- Vaccination rates for young children have risen from 27 per cent to 94 per cent

- K–12 enrolments have grown by 40 per cent from 1986–98; child population by 28 per cent

- Secondary (6–12) enrolments have grown by 114 per cent since 1992

- Adult literacy exceeds 90 per cent, as does the net primary enrolment rate

- Infant mortality has fallen from 69 to 31 per 1000 live births

- Life expectancy has risen from 64 to 68 years

- Fertility is falling steadily from 4.6 to under 3 children per woman

There remain challenges that need to be addressed. The percentage of children under five years of age with underweight status is 45 per cent, compared to only 26 per cent in Thailand, though a five-year action plan aims to reduce this to 25 per cent in five years. Access to clean water and sanitation remains low, though improving. Iodine deficiency is widespread. Very poor families take their children out of school at an early stage, and child labour in those families is widespread. Pre-natal care needs to be extended. These and other priorities have been outlined by UNICEF.[12] However, these programmes — if well designed and implemented — will not be very costly and can easily be financed in a growing economy. Indeed, the improving levels of food intake and discretionary income for health and education probably explain much of the observed improvements in the social indicators. At the same time, the government acknowledges the need to provide for those left behind, especially in isolated or disaster-prone areas. By combining public and private resources, it should be possible to build on past progress and continue to improve the lives of most people. Economic progress reduces poverty and increases the impact of targeted programmes.

Beyond the prospect for improving the lives of people, there are other challenges to the educational system in Vietnam. It needs to improve the quality of education as well as make it available more widely. Preparing today's children for tomorrow's jobs as Vietnam integrates with the global economy will require a review of curricula and teacher training. This will become more important as enrolments, already fairly high, improve even more. This challenge extends to universities and R&D as well. However, progress on the supply side will need to be matched by progress on the demand side. There are too few profitable firms that use the skills of trained graduates and pay a reasonable wage for them. Social and economic investments and growth ultimately are bound together, especially in the long term.

Questions of Current Interest

The Asian Crisis has intensified a debate in Vietnam about the best path to take. While there is a general agreement that integration with the world is necessary, even inevitable, there is uncertainty about the best way to pursue this. It is not just a matter of slow versus fast, but also a question of how much economic control by the state is compatible with an opening to the world. This debate takes place against a background of concern with falling FDI, but generally healthy overall growth. However, export-led growth has been concentrated in the South, while the North relies on more problematic protected industry.

12   UNICEF (1997).

Perhaps no clearer indication of the real problem comes from a comparison of the Nomura Export Processing Zone (EPZ) in Haiphong and the highly successful zones in Dong Nai and neighbouring provinces. In spite of excellent location and infrastructure, Nomura has only six investors not associated with the running of the zone itself, and none have entered in the last year. Only 800 workers are in the zone, which has been operating since 1997. Haiphong has developed a bad reputation among investors for its cumbersome customs, aggressive tax authorities and other unhelpful regulatory procedures. It has a bad brand name and investors avoid it. However, the leadership in Haiphong knows it has a problem, though it is finding it difficult to make the necessary changes.[13]

In contrast, Dong Nai's exports in 1999 were US$1.2 billion, or more than Hanoi's. Foreign firms accounted for most of the province's exports. The garment and shoe companies employed over 70,000 local workers. The province has a dozen industrial zones operating or coming on line soon, and over US$4 billion in foreign investment has been approved. While recent investment approvals have been low, the momentum of past approvals and expansions of existing plants propel output and employment growth.

Dong Nai has a good reputation among investors as a place where the authorities want to help solve problems, not create them. Some have criticised its willingness to allow 100 per cent private ownership, but this criticism is misplaced. Rather than aim for a small number of large, costly and inefficient projects with few jobs, provinces like Dong Nai get many, smaller, low-cost producers that can tap export markets. An ability to export means that capital is used carefully and labour is used more intensively. It also means that sales are limited by the efficiency of the producer, not the size of the small local market. Above all, it creates a kind of stability. If one factory closes, it is often true that another will open. It is a model more like Taiwan's, which has done well through this Asian crisis. It is less like South Korea's *chaebol*. With the collapse of even Daewoo,[14] this model is now viewed as risky and vulnerable. (South Korea's rapid recovery, while welcome, is not certain to persist unless further reforms are taken to allow small and medium firms to compete more equally with the largest ones.)

13   In contrast, the province of Thanh Hoa continues to plan for high cost industries such as sugar, oil refining and cement, along with high cost aid projects for ports, industrial zones and dams. It is unlikely that any of these would be undertaken if a reasonable economic rate of return were required. Even the rural road-paving scheme has extremely high projected costs. Aid could be used more efficiently to support growth.

14   Daewoo is the second largest Korean conglomerate with sales equal to Vietnam's GDP. Its debts are so high that only a government guarantee will persuade lenders to hold off foreclosure. A Reuters story said, 'Without government backing, few if any market-based institutions would be willing ... to extend four trillion won ($3.3 billion) in fresh credits.' The story quoted one analyst as saying, 'None of the Daewoo companies is a frontrunner in its industry.' (from CNNfn website, 27 July 1999).

In general, the rapid growth of small and medium firms in Vietnam would be profoundly stabilising. They would generate many jobs, require no subsidies, use scarce capital carefully and be flexible enough to find activities that fit the very different conditions throughout the country. Not every province can copy Dong Nai. However, every province can allow its own best talent to find profitable activities. A permissive and mildly supportive environment would allow the astonishingly small private sector in Vietnam to assume a more normal, and larger, role in the nation's economic and industrial future.[15] The alternatives are reliance on a weak and slow-growing state sector or dependence on a foreign sector that has cooled its interest in Vietnam and is unlikely to provide adequate employment opportunities on its own.

The recently initiated trade agreement with the US is a positive step that *allows* but does not *guarantee* a resumption of economic growth. It is a necessary, or highly useful, but not a sufficient condition for renewed export growth. If Vietnam can improve its 'brand name' among investors, it should again become an attractive place for high quality exporters to establish production. As more come, thicker supply networks will allow more local value added. Domestic investors will also begin to co-operate with the foreign exporters, and ultimately also to compete with them. However, the well-known complaints of investors, especially export-oriented investors, need to be dealt with. If foreign investors are hampered with restrictions and find they cannot make money, they are likely to find other places to invest. The frustrations of recent years explain why actual inflows of FDI are so low.[16]

One risk has to be acknowledged. Act One of the Asian Crisis is over, but it is not clear if the play is over or if this is only an intermission. Japan's economy remains fragile. China may dump products if US markets dry up. South Korea may find recovery more difficult as reform lags. The United States' economy, and its imports, could finally move into recession, though few now see a long or deep recession, if there is one. An export-oriented strategy does face risks from fluctuations in export markets. It is better than relying on isolated and small domestic markets, but it does have risks. However, Vietnam really has little choice if it wants to sustain growth. It wants foreign capital goods and technology. These have to be paid for in hard currency. Exports are needed to earn hard currencies. Raw material exports are limited. So, manufactured exports are about the only other way to attain what is wanted and needed. It also happens that manufactured exports will create many more jobs

15   The private formal sector excludes households, farmers and also co-operatives. It refers to licensed private businesses above the family level. This sector accounted for only 7.1% of GDP in 1998, and has grown only 6.6% a year from 1995 to 1998.

16   Capital goods imports by foreign firms in 1999 were US$633 million, or 2.2% of GDP. This excludes up to US$100 million of capital imports by firms operating in EPZ. The same figure for 2000 was US$852 million.

than import-substituting products and have much more potential for growth and profit. However, moving forward on manufactured exports will require allowing foreign and domestic private firms to play a larger role. It will favour the South unless there is intensified administrative reform in other parts of the country. The need for more balance in regional growth is yet another strong argument for pushing ahead with the second stage of the *Doi Moi* reforms. With better and more business-friendly administration, the poorer parts of the country could use their low-cost labour and other advantages to good advantage and attract more foreign and domestic investment.

The recent passage of the enterprise law (January 2000) created a much more secure legal base for private domestic industry. Since then, the number of new private firms (above the household level) has greatly increased. That is, 17,000 firms were added in the 14 months after the enterprise law was passed, while only about 27,000 existed at the end of 1999. Many of these may have existed before but remained statistically hidden, so it is hard to know yet how much of this is real growth and how much a mirage. Even so, it is clear that many now believe that it is safer and easier to enter into formal private activity. Growth rates of private domestic industry are higher as well. This is a positive step, in that such firms are likely to improve job creation and also to use scarce capital more carefully than either state or foreign firms. However, it is too early to tell how significant this will be for longer term growth prospects.

In summary, Vietnam has weathered the Asian Crisis, taken initial steps to allow better capital formation and private sector industrial growth and managed to increase exports at a rapid rate in a less-than-ebullient international environment. If it manages to take advantage of the trade pact with the US (ratified on 10 December 2001) by allowing and encouraging provinces to deal directly with investors, it is likely that more provinces will follow their southern neighbours and reduce red tape. While major questions remain about the banking, state enterprise and public investment sectors, the stance of many observers is cautiously optimistic. The fundamental advantages of a young, educated and enterprising people will shine through and spark sustained growth if the government moves further to facilitate economic growth rather than implementing and regulating it.

Bibliography

Acosta Santana, José (1982), *Teoría y práctica de los mecanismos de dirección en Cuba* (Havana: Editorial de Ciencias Sociales).

Agencias (2000), 'Pastrana, Chávez y Fox deciden relanzar el G–3', *El Mercurio*, (9 April).

Aguilar Trujillo, Alejandro (2000) 'Un escenario hipotético en la normalización de las relaciones económicas Cuba–Estados Unidos', *CUBA, investigación económica*, año 6, no. 1 (Jan.–March), pp. 55–81.

Alvarez, José and Peña Castellanos, Lázaro (1995), *Preliminary Study of the Sugar Industries in Cuba and Florida within the Context of the World Sugar Market*, International Working Paper IW95–6 (Gainesville: International Agricultural Trade and Development Center, Food and Resource Economics Department, Institute of Food and Agricultural Sciences, University of Florida).

Alvarez González, Elena (1995), 'Una actualización del significado económico de los escenarios sobre bloqueo', *Investigación Económica*, no.2 (Havana).

Alvarez González, Elena and Fernández Mayo, María Antonia (1992), *Dependencia externa de la economía cubana*, Working Paper (Havana: Instituto Nacional de Investigaciones Económicas).

Arellanes, Paulino Ernesto (1995), 'Cuba: crisis, anticrisis, integración e inversión extranjera', paper presented at the Seminario Internacional: América Latina y Cuba ante la Economía Mundial Contemporánea (Havana, July).

Aronson, Bernard W. and Rogers, William D. (2000), 'US–Cuban Relations in the 21st Century' (http://www.cfr.org/p/pubs/Cuba_Task.Force.htlm), uncorrected proof

Banco Central de Cuba (BCC) (1999), *Informe Económico 1998* (Havana: Banco Central de Cuba).

Banco Central de Cuba (BCC) (2000), *Proyección de la Balanza de Pagos de Cuba 1999–2001* (Havana).

Banco Central de Cuba (BCC) (2000a), *Informe Económico 1999* (Havana: Banco Central de Cuba).

Banco Nacional de Cuba (BNC) (1978), *Cuba. Economic Development and Prospects* (Havana: Banco Nacional de Cuba).

Banco Nacional de Cuba (BNC) (1981), *Highlights of Cuban Economic and Social Development 1976–80* (Havana: Banco Nacional de Cuba).

Banco Nacional de Cuba (BNC) (1996), *Informe Económico de 1995* (Havana: Banco Nacional de Cuba).

Brundenius, Claes (1983), 'Some Notes on the Development of the Cuban Labor Force 1970–80', *Cuban Studies*, vol. 13, no. 2.

Brundenius, Claes (1984), *Revolutionary Cuba: The Challenge of Economic Growth with Equity* (Boulder and London: Westview Press).

Brundenius, Claes (1987), 'Development and Prospects of Capital Goods Production in Revolutionary Cuba', in *World Development*, vol. 15, no. 1 (Jan.).

Brundenius, Claes (1999), 'Economic Restructuring and Implications for Science and Technology in Transition Economies', in C. Brundenius, B. Göransson and P. Reddy (eds.), *Reconstruction or Destruction? Science and Technology at Stake in Transition Economies* (Hyderabad: Universities Press).

Brundenius, Claes (2000), *The Role of Human Capital in Cuban Economic Development, 1959–1999* (Copenhagen: CDR Working Papers. 008).

Brundenius, Claes and Monreal, Pedro (2001), 'The Future of the Cuban Model: A Longer View', in C. Brundenius and J. Weeks, *Globalization and Third World Socialism: Cuba and Vietnam* (London: Macmillan/Palgrave).

Brus, W. (1969), 'El funcionamiento de la economía socialista' (Barcelona: Oikos).

Bulmer-Thomas, Victor (2000), 'The European Union and MERCOSUR: Prospects for a Free Trade Agreement', *Journal of Interamerican Studies and World Affairs* (Spring), pp. 1–22.

Byron, Jessica (2000), 'Square Dance Diplomacy: Cuba and CARIFO-RUM, the European Union and the United States', *European Review of Latin American and Caribbean Studies*, no. 68 (April), 'Problems of Democracy'.

Cámara de Comercio de la República de Cuba (2000), *Foreign Trade*, no. 3 (Havana).

Carranza, Julio (1997), 'Cuba: las finanzas externas y los límites del crecimiento', *Economía y Desarrollo* (July–Sept.).

Carranza Valdés, Julio, Gutiérrez Urdaneta, Luis and Monreal González, Pedro (1995), *Cuba: la reestructuración de la economía. Una propuesta para el debate* (Havana: Editorial de Ciencias Sociales).

Carranza Valdés, Julio, Gutiérrez Urdaneta, Luis and Monreal González, Pedro (1996), *Cuba: Restructuring the Economy – A Contribution to the Debate* (London: Institute of Latin American Studies).

Carranza Valdés, Julio, Gutiérrez Urdaneta, Luis and Monreal González, Pedro (1999), 'La petite et moyenne entreprise à Cuba: le point de vue de trois èconomistes cubains', *Cahiers des Amèriques latines*, vols. 31/32, pp. 103–21.

Carriazo, George (1996), 'Cuba cambios económicos', in *Economía y Desarrollo*, no. 2.

Castro Ruz, Fidel (1973), 'XX Aniversario del Ataque al Cuartel Moncada', in *Economía y Desarrollo*, no. 19.

Castro Ruz, Fidel (1975), *Informe Central al I Congreso del PCC* (Havana: Departamento de Orientación Revolucionaria).

Castro Ruz, Fidel (1978), *Informe Central al Primer Congreso del Partido Comunista de Cuba* (Havana: Editorial Pueblo y Educación).

Castro Ruz, Fidel (1987), *Por el camino correcto: compilación de textos* (Havana: Editora Política).

CEDEM (1995), *Cuba. Transición de la fecundidad. Cambio social y conducta reproductiva* (Havana: Centro de Estudios Demográficos).

Comité Estatal de Estadísticas (CEE) (1982), *Censo de población y viviendas 1981:* vol. 16 (Havana: Comité Estatal de Estadísticas).

Comité Estatal de Estadísticas (CEE) (1986), *Series cronológicas: trabajo y salario* (Havana: Comité Estatal de Estadísticas).

Comité Estatal de Estadísticas (CEE) (1989), *Anuario estadístico de Cuba 1988* (Havana: Comité Estatal de Estadísticas).

Comité Estatal de Estadísticas (CEE) (1990), *Anuario estadístico de Cuba 1989* (Havana: Comité Estatal de Estadísticas).

Centro de Estudios de Economía Cubana (1997), *La economía cubana en 1996: resultados, problemas y perspectivas* (Havana: Universidad de la Habana).

Comisión Económica para América Latina y el Caribe (CEPAL) (1986), 'La planificación y las políticas públicas en 1982–1984 y perspectivas para la segunda mitad del decenio', *Cuadernos del ILPES* 31 (Santiago de Chile).

Comisión Económica para América Latina y el Caribe (CEPAL) (1992), *El comercio de manufacturas de América Latina, evolución y estructura 1962–1989* (Santiago de Chile).

Comisión Económica para América Latina y el Caribe (CEPAL) (1997), *La economía cubana. Reformas estructurales y desempeño en los noventa* (Mexico: Cepal and Fondo de Cultura Económica).

Comisión Económica para América Latina y el Caribe (CEPAL) (2000), *La economía cubana. Reformas estructurales y desempeño en los noventa* (2nd edition) (Mexico City: Fondo de Cultura Económica).

Comisión Económica para América Latina y el Caribe (CEPAL) (2000a), *Estudio económico de América Latina y el Caribe*, Cuadro IV.2, p. 67.

Comisión Económica para América Latina y el Caribe (CEPAL) (2000b), *Balance preliminar de las economías de America Latina y el Caribe* (Santiago de Chile).

Comisión Económica para América Latina y el Caribe (CEPAL) (2001), *Panorama de la Inserción Internacional de América Latina y el Caribe*, Cuadro II.3b.

Consejo de Ministros (1998), 'Bases generales del perfeccionamiento empresarial', *Gaceta Oficial de la República de Cuba* (14 Sept.).

Crawley, Andrew (2000), 'Toward a Biregional Agenda for the Twentieth Century', *Journal of Interamerican Studies and World Affairs*, vol. 42, no. 2 (Summer), pp. 9–35.

Cuban Communist Party (1976), *Plataforma Programática del Partido Comunista de Cuba. Tesis y resolución* (Havana: Department of Revolutionary Orientation of the Cuban Communist Party Central Committee).

Dahlman, Karl (1988), ' Inversión extranjera y transferencia de tecnología', in *Comercio exterior: apertura comercial y proteccionismo; fomento industrial e inversión extranjera* (Mexico City: Colegio Nacional de Economistas. AC, México).

De Miranda, Mauricio (2000) 'Estado, mercado y reforma de la economía cubana. Alternativas de política económica', paper presented to Latin American Studies Association XXII International Congress, Miami, 16–18 March.

De Miranda, Mauricio (2000a), 'Estado, mercado y reforma de la economía cubana', in Mauricio De Miranda (ed.), *Reforma Económica y cambio social en América Latina y el Caribe. Cuatro casos de estudio: Colombia, Costa Rica, Cuba, México* (Santa Fe de Bogotá, Colombia: Tercer Mundo Editores).

De Miranda, Mauricio (2000b), 'Alternativas de política económica para la reforma de la economía cubana', paper presented to the Segundo Simposio del Proyecto de Investigación sobre Reforma Económica y

Cambio Social en América Latina y el Caribe. Cuatro Casos de Estudio: Colombia, Costa Rica, Cuba y México (Cali, Colombia).

Deere, Carmen Diana (1997), 'Reforming Cuban Agriculture', *Development and Change*, vol. 28.

Deere, Carmen Diana and Meurs, Mieke (1992), 'Markets, Markets Everywhere? Understanding the Cuban Anomaly', *World Development*, vol. 20, no. 6.

Díaz Vázquez, Julio (1998), 'Cuba: ajuste en el modelo económico', in *Enfoque sobre la reciente economía cubana* (Madrid: Agualarga Editores, S.L.).

Díaz Vázquez, Julio (1998a), *Economía Internacional*, tomo II (Havana: Editorial Félix Varela).

Díaz Vázquez, Julio (2000) (unpublished.), 'China: reforma o revolución' (Havana: Centro de Investigaciones de Economía Internacional, University of Havana).

Dore, Ronald (1990), 'Reflections on Culture and Social Change', in Gary Gereffi and Donald L. Wyman (eds.), *Manufacturing Miracles. Paths of Industrialization in Latin America and East Asia* (Princeton: Princeton University Press).

Dorticós Torrado, Osvaldo (1972), 'Análisis y perspectivas del desarrollo de la economía cubana', *Economía y Desarrollo*, no. 12.

Durán, Alejandro (1999), *El turismo en el mundo y Cuba. Evolución, impacto y tendencias*, PhD thesis, Centro de Investigaciones de la Economía Internacional, Universidad de la Habana.

Economist Intelligence Unit (EIU) (2000), *Country Risk Service* (London: EIU) (1st quarter).

Economist Intelligence Unit (EIU) (2000a), *Cuba. Country Report, 1st Quarter 2000* (London: The Economic Intelligence Unit).

Economist Intelligence Unit (EIU) (2000b), *Cuba. Country Report, May 2000* (London: The Economic Intelligence Unit).

Economic Research Service (various nos), *Sugar and Sweetener Situation and Outllook Yearbook*, SSSV21N4 (Washington, DC: U.S. Department of Agriculture).

Ellison, Christopher and Gereffi, Gary (1990), 'Explaining Strategies and Patterns of Industrial Development', in Gary Gereffi and Donald L. Wyman (eds.), *Manufacturing Miracles. Paths of Industrialization in Latin America and East Asia* (Princeton: Princeton University Press).

Escaith, Hubert (1999), 'Cuba pendant la "Période Speciale": Adjustment or Transition', in *Cahiers des Amériques Latines*, vol. 31/32, pp. 55–83.

Escaith, Hubert (2001), *Les petits économies d'Amérique latine et des Caraïbes: croissance, ouverture commerciale et relations inter-régionales*, Serie Temas de Coyuntura, no. 14 (CEPAL, March).

Escaith, Hubert and Morley, Samuel (2000), 'The Impact of Structural Reforms on Growth in Latin America and the Caribbean: An Empirical Estimation', CEPAL Serie en Macroeconomía y Desarrollo (Nov.).

Evans, Edward A. and Davis, Carlton G. (1999), *Recent Developments in the U.S. Sugar and Sweeteners Markets: Implications for CARICOM Tariff-Rate Quota Holders* (Gainesville: Food and Resource Economics Department, University of Florida).

Executive Yuan (1996), *Statistical Yearbook of the Republic of China 1996* (Taipei: Directorate-General of Budget, Accounting and Statistics).

Fabienke, Rikke (2000), 'Labor Markets and Income Distribution during Crisis and Reform', in C. Brundenius and J. Weeks, *Globalization and Third World Socialism: Cuba and Vietnam* (London: Macmillan).

Fernández, María Antonia (1999), 'Las zonas francas y la economía nacional. Cuba en este proceso', *Boletín Informativo, Economía Cubana*, no. 31 (Havana: CIEM).

Fernández de Bulnes, Carlos (1994), 'Contenido tecnológico y competitividad: elementos para la reconversión de la industria cubana', *Boletín de Información Comercial Española*, no. 2433 (Madrid).

Fernández Font, Marcelo (1995), 'Perspectivas del mercado mundial azucarero hasta el año 2000, participación de Cuba', *Revista Bimestre Cubano*, vol. LXXVIII, Epoca III. (Jan.–June), pp. 109–41.

Fernández Font, Mario (1995), 'La reestructuración tecnológica de la economía cubana en los próximos años', *Boletín Informativo de Economía Cubana*, no. 23 (Sept.–Oct., Havana).

Fernández Font, Mario (1999), 'Scientific and Technological Development in Cuba in the Context of Economic Reforms', in C. Brundenius, B. Göransson and P. Reddy (eds.), *Reconstruction or Destruction? Science and Technology at Stake in Transition Economies* (Hyderabad: Universities Press).

Ferriol Muruaga, Angela (2000), 'Apertura externa, mercado laboral y política social', *Cuba: Investigación económica* (Jan.– March).

Figueras, Miguel (1990), 'Analisis de las políticas de industrialización en Cuba en el período revolucionario y proyecciones futuras' (Havana, mimeo).

Figueras, Miguel (1994), *Aspectos estructurales de la economía cubana* (Havana: Editorial de Ciencias Sociales).

Figueras, Miguel (1998), 'Reflexiones sobre los acuerdos regionales y eventuales acuerdos multilaterales de inversión', Cuba's presentation at the Reunión de Expertos sobre Acuerdos Regionales y Multilaterales Existentes y sus Consecuencias para el Desarrollo (Geneva: UNCTAD, April).

Figueras, Miguel (2000), 'Colaboración internacional: doctrina y política cubanas', paper presented to the XXII International Congress of the Latin American Studies Association , Miami, 16–18 March.

Fry, James (1997), 'Que nos dicen las tendencias en los costos de producción sobre la conducta a largo plazo de los precios del azúcar mundial', *Temas Controvertidos del Mercado Mundial Azucarero* (Havana).

García, Adriano, Pons, Hugo, Somoza, José and Cruz, Víctor (1999), 'Bases para la elaboración de una política industrial', *Cuba: Investigación Económica*, año 5, no. 2 (Havana, April–June).

García, Mercedes (1996), *Los mercados financieros internacionales: tendencias actuales y participación de los países en desarrollo* (Havana: Centro de Investigaciones de la Economía Internacional).

García, Mercedes (1997), *El financiamiento externo actual* (Havana: Centro de Investigaciones de la Economía Internacional).

García Hernández, Adriano (1996), 'Reestructuración del sector industrial', *Cuba: Investigaciones Económicas*, no. 2.

García R., Mercedes (1999), 'La deuda externa en monedas libremente convertibles: situación actual y perspectivas' (Havana: Universidad de la Habana. Centro de Investigaciones de la Economía Internacional, Sept.).

García Valdés, Carlos M. (1988), *Economía cubana. Del trauma a la recuperación* (Havana: Editorial Pueblo y Educación).

Goering, Laurie (2001) 'Havana Office Head Report', in *Chicago Tribune* (18 March).

González, Alfredo (1993), *Economía emergente: logros, dificultades y perspectivas* (Havana: Instituto Nacional de Investigaciones Económicas).

González Cruz, Víctor y Riech Benítez, Guillermo (1998), *Diagnóstico sobre los bienes de consumo alimenticios manufacturados del MINAL* (Havana: MINAL).

González Gutiérrez, Alfredo (1998), 'Economía y sociedad: los retos del modelo económico', *Temas*, no. 11.

González Gutiérrez, Alfredo (1999), 'El nuevo modelo de análisis de las finanzas internas', *Cuba: Investigaciones Económicas*, año 5, no. 2.

González Gutiérrez, Alfredo (2000), 'Prisas y sedimentos de la economía', interview in *Juventud Rebelde* (26 Nov.).

Goskomstat. Rossiyskiy Statisticheskiy Ezhegodnik (1998), *Russian Statistical Yearbook 1998* (Moscow: State Statistical Committee of the Russian Federation).

Gunn, Gillian (1993), 'The Sociological Impact of Rising Foreign Investment', *Cuba Briefing Paper Series*, no. 1 (Jan.) (Washington, DC: Georgetown University).

Hoekman, Bernard and Karsenty, Guy (1992), 'Economic Development and International Transactions in Services', *Development Policy Review*, vol. 10, no. 3 (September).

Institute of Development Studies (IDS) (1999) *GSP Options for a Post-Lomé EU–ACP Trade Regime. Phase I Report* (June).

Instituto Brasileiro de Geografia e Estatística (IBGE) (1999), *Síntese de indicadores sociais 1998* (Rio de Janeiro: Instituto Brasileiro de Geografia e Estatística).

Instituto Cubano de Investigaciones de los Derivados de la Caña de Azúcar (ICIDCA) (2000), *Manual de los derivados de la caña de azúcar* (Havana. ICIDCA).

Instituto de Investigaciones Financieras (1995), *La reforma económica de Cuba en las circunstancias actuales* (Havana).

Instituto Nacional de Estadísticas (1992), *Censo de Población y Vivienda* (Santiago, Chile: Instituto Nacional de Estadísticas).

Integration & Trade, no. 11, vol. 4 (May–Aug. 2000).

Inter-American Development Bank (IDB) (1998), *Economic and Social Progress in Latin America. 1998–99 Report* (Washington, DC: Inter-American Development Bank).

International Labor Organization (ILO) (1999), *Yearbook of Labor Statistics 1999* (Geneva: International Labor Organization).

International Sugar Organization (1998), *Flujos de comercio azucarero en los 90: posibles escenarios para una proyección*, Comité de Evaluaciones de Mercado, Consumo y Estadisticas, MECAS (98) 15 (15 May).

International Sugar Organization (1998a), *Quarterly Market Review* (May).

IRELA (1997), *Closer European Union Links with Eastern Europe: Implications for Latin America* (Madrid).

IRELA (1999), *The Rio Summit: Toward a Strategic Partnership?* (Madrid).

IRELA (2000), *European Policy on Cuba: Perceptions and Interests of EU Member States* (Madrid, 18 April).

Junta Central de Planificación (JCP) (1975), *Censo de población y viviendas 1970* (Havana: Junta Central de Planificación).

Junta Central de Planificación (JCP) (1977), *Economía cubana 1960–1975: análisis de los principales indicadores* (Havana: Junta Central de Planificación).

Katz, Jorge (1996), 'La transformación del desarrollo industrial de América Latina', *Revista de la CEPAL*, no. 60.

Klinger Pevida, Eduardo (2000), 'El proceso de integración caribeño: el CARICOM', in *Diplomacia*, no. 84 (July–Sept.), pp. 35–55.

Kornai, János (1992), *The Socialist System. The Political Economy of Communism* (Oxford: Clarendon Press).

Krugman, Paul (1994), 'The Myth of Asia's Miracle', *Foreign Affairs* (Nov–Dec.).

LACCAR (1999) *Latin American Regional Reports, Caribbean and Central America*, RC–99–01 (London, 19 Jan.)

Lage Dávila, Carlos (1995), *Intervención en el quinto período ordinario de las sesiones de la Asamblea Nacional, documentos Poder Popular* (Havana).

Lage Dávila, Carlos (1995a), 'Intervención en el Foro Económico Mundial celebrado en Davos, Suiza', *Granma* (Jan. 28).

Lage Dávila, Carlos (1995b), 'Discurso en The Economist Conferences' (Havana: Palacio de las Convenciones, 23– 25 Oct.)

Lage Dávila, Carlos (1996), 'Conferencia de prensa del Vice-presidente del Consejo de Estado y de Ministros', *Granma* (25 July).

Lage Dávila, Carlos (1997), 'Clausura de la II Reunión Nacional del Ministerio de Economía y Planificación', *Granma* (1 April).

Lage Dávila, Carlos (1998) 'Los resultados de 1998 son positivos y confirman la tendencia a la recuperación económica. Intervención del Vicepresidente del Consejo de Estado y Secretario del Comité Ejecutivo del Consejo de Ministros en la Asamblea Nacional del Poder Popular, 21 de diciembre 1998', *Granma* (23 Dec.).

Lage Dávila, Carlos (2000), interview in *Trabajadores* (Havana, 1 Jan.).

Lage Dávila, Carlos (2000a), Discurso en la Reunión de Directores de Empresas en Proceso de Perfeccionamiento Empresarial, *Granma* (15 June).

Lage Dávila, Carlos (2001), 'Resistimos y preservamos las conquistas del socialismo', interview in *Trabajadores* (1 Jan.).

Lange, O. (1966), 'Problemas de la economía política del socialismo' (Havana: Publicaciones Económicas).

León Delgado, Francisco (1995), 'The International Reinsertion of Cuba: Emerging Scenarios', in Arch R. M. Ritter and John M. Kirk (eds.*), Cuba in the International System: Normalization and Integration* (London: Macmillan), pp. 105–30.

León, Francisco (1996), 'El desafío regional de la inserción internacional cubana', *Socialismo y participación*, no. 76 (Dec.).

León, Francisco (1998), 'ALCA–CUBA: participación o marginación', in Francisco Rojas Aravena (ed.), *Globalización, América Latina y la diplomacia de las cumbres* (Santiago de Chile: LACC & FLACSO–Chile), pp. 461–83.

León, Francisco (1999), 'Formación de recursos humanos y empleo en Cuba. Qué hacer después del período especial?', paper presented to a symposium on 'The Cuban Economy: Problems, Policies, Perspectives', Carleton University, Ottawa, 28–30 Sept.

León, Francisco (2000), 'Die staaten lateinamerikas und die wethandelsorganisation', in Wolfgang Hirsch-Weber and Detlef Nolte (2000) *Lateinamerika: okonomische, soziale und politische. Probleme im zeitalter der globalisierung* (University of Hamburg: Institut Für Iberoamerika-Kunde).

León, Francisco (2001), 'Foreign Investment and Labor Relations in Cuba Today: Challenges of an Upgrading Strategy', *Looking Ahead* (NPA, Washington, DC), Special Issue on the Current State of Foreign Investment and Workers Rights in Cuba, vol. XXII, no. 2 (Jan.), pp.11–17.

LMC International, Ltd. (1999), 'Trends in Global Sugar and Sweetener Consumption', *Sweetener Analysis* (Sept.).

Love, John (1999), 'USDA Predicts More Low Sugar Prices', *PR Newswire* (Washington, DC: US Department of Agriculture. 9 Aug.).

Machado Rodríguez, Darío L. (1993), *Nuestro propio camino. Análisis del proceso de rectificación en Cuba* (Havana: Editora Política).

Maddison, Angus (1995), *Monitoring the World Economy 1820–1992* (Paris: OECD Development Center).

Madrid-Aris, Manuel (1997), 'Growth and Technological Change in Cuba', *Cuba in Transition*, vol. 7 (Washington, DC: Association for the Study of the Cuban Economy).

Madrid-Aris, Manuel (1998), 'Investment, Human Capital and Technological Change: Evidence from Cuba and its Implications for Growth Models', *Cuba in Transition*, vol. 8 (Washington, DC: Association for the Study of the Cuban Economy).

Marquetti Nodarse, Hiram (1995), *Cuba. Desempeño del sector industrial 1990–1995* (Havana: Centro de Estudios de Economía Cubana).

Marquetti Nodarse, Hiram (1997a), 'Cuba: el desempeño del sector industrial en 1996', in CEEC, *La economía cubana en 1996. Resultados, problemas y perspectivas* (Havana: Centro de Estudios de Economía Cubana).

Marquetti Nodarse, Hiram (1997b), 'Cuba. Deuda y déficit externo. Principales restricciones del proceso de reanimación de la economía', *Economía y Desarrollo*, año II, no. 7.

Marquetti Nodarse, Hiram (1998a), 'La economía del dólar. Balance y perspectivas', *Temas*, no.11.

Marquetti Nodarse, Hiram (1998b), 'Cuba: balance y perspectivas del proceso diversificación de las exportaciones', *Semanario Negocios* (Havana, Dec.).

Marquetti, Hiram (1999), *La industria cubana en los años 90: reestructuración y adaptación al nuevo contexto internacional*, PhD thesis, Centro de Estudios de la Economía Cubana, Universidad de La Habana (July).

Marquetti Nodarse, Hiram (1999a), *Cuba: El impacto de la industria biofarmacéutica* (Havana: Centro de Estudios de Economía Cubana).

Marquetti Nodarse, Hiram (2000a), *Cuba. Los retos de la recuperación de la industria azucarera* (Havana: Centro de Estudios de la Economía Cubana).

Marquetti Nodarse, Hiram (2000b), *El sector externo de la economía cubana. Una evaluación actual* (Havana: Centro de Estudios de la Economía Cubana).

Marquetti Nodarse, Hiram and García Alvarez, Anicia (1999) 'Proceso de reanimación del sector industrial. Principales resultados y problemas', en CEEC, *Balance de la economía cubana a fines de los años noventa* (Havana: Centro de Estudios de Economía Cubana).

Marx, Carlos (1973), *El capital: crítica de la economía política* (Havana: Editorial de Ciencias Sociales).

Mesa-Lago, Carmelo (1981), *The Economy of Socialist Cuba* (Albuquerque, University of New Mexico Press).

Mesa-Lago, Carmelo (ed.) (1993), *Cuba after the Cold War* (Pittsburgh and London: University of Pittsburgh Press).

Mesa-Lago, Carmelo (1994a), 'Are Economic Reforms Propelling Cuba to the Market?' (Miami: North-South Center, University of Miami).

Mesa-Lago, Carmelo (1994b), *Breve historia económica de la Cuba socialista: políticas, resultados y perspectivas* (Madrid: Alianza Editorial).

Mesa-Lago, Carmelo (1996), '¿Recuperación económica en Cuba?' *Encuentro de la cultura cubana,* no. 3 (Winter 1996–97), pp. 54–61.

Mesa-Lago, Carmelo (1998), 'Assessing Economic and Social Performance in the Cuban Transition of the 1990s', *World Development,* vol. 26, no. 5 (May).

Mesa-Lago, Carmelo (2000), *Market, Socialist, and Mixed Economies: Comparative Policy and Performance of Chile, Cuba and Costa Rica* (Baltimore and London: The Johns Hopkins University Press).

Milanovic, Branko (1998), *Income, Inequality and Poverty during the Transition from Planned to Market Economy* (Washington, DC: The World Bank).

MINAZ (1992– 99) *Anuario Estadístico MINAZ* (Havana: MINAZ) (various nos.).

MINAZ (1993), *Documentos sobre la creación y perfeccionamiento de las Unidades Básicas de Producción Cooperativa* (Havana: MINAZ).

Ministerio de la Industria Básica (MINBAS) (2000), *Informe sobre la evolución del Ministerio de la Industria Básica* (Havana: MINBAS).

Ministerio de Economía y Planificación (MEP) (2000), *Resultados económicos de 1999 y plan económico y social año 2000* (Havana: Ministerio de Economía y Planificación).

MINVEC (1996), *Guía para el inversionista en Cuba* (Havana: Centro de Promoción de Inversiones de la Habana).

Monreal González , Pedro (1999), 'Migraciones y remesas familiares: notas e hipótesis sobre el caso de Cuba', *Lateinamerika Analysen und Berichte,* no. 23 (Verlag: Horleman), pp. 73–96.

Monreal González, Pedro (1999a), *Cuba's Economic Reforms in the 90s: Ready for One World?* (Havana: Centro de Investigaciones de la Economía Internacional (CIEI)).

Monreal González, Pedro (2000), 'Los dilemas de las trayectorias económicas de Cuba: apuntes sobre una polémica', in *Temas de la economía global: perspectivas desde Cuba* (Havana: Centro de Investigaciones de Economía Internacional (CIEI), Universidad de la Habana).

Monreal González, Pedro (2000a), 'Estrategias de inversión sectorial y reinserción internacional de la economía cubana', paper presented to Latin American Studies Association XXII International Congress, Miami, 16–18 March.

Monreal, Pedro and Carranza, Julio (2000), 'Los retos actuales del desarrollo en Cuba', *Problemas del Desarrollo. Revista Latinoamericana de Economía*, vol. 122 (July–Sept.), pp. 87–127.

OECD (1998), *Human Capital Investment. An International Comparison* (Paris: Center for Educational Research and Innovation).

Ofer, Gur (1987), 'Soviet Economic Growth: 1928–1985', *Journal of Economic Literature*, vol. XXV (Dec.).

Oficina Nacional de Estadísticas (ONE) (1998), *Anuario estadístico de Cuba 1990–1996* (Havana: Oficina Nacional de Estadísticas), Tabla XII.8, p. 253.

Oficina Nacional de Estadísticas (ONE) (1998a), *Anuario estadístico de Cuba 1996* (Havana: Oficina Nacional de Estadísticas).

Oficina Nacional de Estadísticas (ONE) (1999), *Anuario estadístico 1997* (Havana: Oficina Nacional de Estadísticas).

Oficina Nacional de Estadísticas (ONE) (1999a), *Cuba en cifras 1998* (Havana).

Oficina Nacional de Estadísticas (ONE) (1999b), *Anuario estadístico 1998* (Havana: Oficina Nacional de Estadísticas).

Oficina Nacional de Estadísticas (ONE) (2000), *Anuario estadístico de Cuba 1998* (Havana: Oficina Nacional de Estadísticas).

Oficina Nacional de Estadísticas (ONE) (2000a), *Cuba en cifras 1999* (Havana: Oficina Nacional de Estadísticas).

Oficina Nacional de Estadísticas (ONE) (2001), *Anuario estadístico de Cuba 1999* (Havana: Oficina Nacional de Estadísticas).

Oleinik, Iván (1977), *Manual de economía política del socialismo* (Havana: Editorial Ciencias Sociales).

Overlander, Michel (1997), 'Problemas con la calidad de los mercados de futuro mundiales', *Temas controvertidos del mercado mundial azucarero* (Havana).

Partido Comunista de Cuba (1976), *Plataforma Programática del Partido Comunista de Cuba* (Havana: Department of Revolutionary Orientation of the Cuban Communist Party Central Committee).

Pastor, Robert A. (1992), 'Succesion Crisis: The Boundaries of Influence', in *Whirlpool: U.S. Foreign Policy toward Latin America and the Caribbean* (Princeton: Princeton University Press).

Pastor, Manuel and Zimbalist, Andrew (1995), 'Waiting for Change: Adjustment and Reform in Cuba', *World Development*, vol. 23, no. 5.

Pearson. Ruth (1997), 'Renegotiating the Reproductive Bargain: Gender Analysis of Economic Transition in Cuba in the 1990s', *Development and Change*, vol. 28.

Peña Castellanos, Lázaro and Alvarez, José (1997), *The Processing Sector of the Sugar Industries of Cuba and Florida, International*, International Working Paper IW97–18 (Gainesville: Food and Resource Economics Department, Institute of Food and Agricultural Sciences, University of Florida).

Peña Castellanos, Lázaro and Alvarez, José (2000), *The Cuban Agroindustry and the International Sweetener Market in the 1990s: Implications for the Future*, International Working Paper IW 00–1 (Gainesville: Food and Resource Economics Department, Institute of Food and Agricultural Sciences, University of Florida).

Pérez, Humberto (1976), *Economía política del capitalismo: breve exposición de la doctrina económica de Marx* (Havana: Editorial Orbe).

Pérez, Humberto (1982), 'La Plataforma Programática y el desarrollo económico de Cuba', *Cuba Socialista*, no. 3.

Pérez, Omar Everleny (1995), 'La inversión extranjera en Cuba', in *El sector mixto en la reforma económica cubana* (Havana: Editorial Felix Varela).

Pérez, Omar Everleny (1996), *Las reformas económicas en Cuba en los 90s* (Santiago de Compostela: Universidad de Santiago de Compostela).

Pérez, Omar Everleny (1997), 'La inversión extranjera en Cuba. Peculiaridades', presentation at the XX LASA International Congress, Guadalajara.

Pérez, Omar Everleny (1998), 'Cuba's Economic Reforms: An Overview', in Jorge F Pérez López y Matías Travieso-Diaz (eds.), *Perspectives on Cuban Economic Reforms. Special Studies*, no. 30 (Center for Latin American Studies Press, Arizona State University).

Pérez, Omar Everleny and Brisuela, Roxana (1991), 'Los NIC's asiáticos: ¿modelos para el Tercer Mundo?', *Cuba Económica*, año 1, no. 2 (July–Aug.–Sept.).

Pérez Izquierdo, Victoria (2000), 'Ajuste económico e impactos sociales', *CUBA, investigación económica,* año 6, no. 1 (Jan.–March), pp. 81–124.

Pérez-López, Jorge F. (1987), *Measuring Cuban Economic Performance* (Austin: University of Texas Press).

Pérez-López, Jorge F. (1995), *Cuba's Second Economy: From Behind the Scenes to Center Stage* (New Brunswick and London: Transaction Publishers).

Pons Duarte, Hugo (1997), 'La industria de bienes de capital en Cuba: situación actual y perspectivas, en Cuba', *Cuba: Investigaciones Económicas,* año 3, no. 2.

Porter, Michael (1990), *La ventaja competitiva de las naciones* (Buenos Aires: Editorial Vergara).

Ramos, Joseph (1998), 'Una estrategia de desarrollo a partir de complejos productivos en torno a recursos naturales', *Revista de la CEPAL,* no. 66 (Dec.).

Regueiro, Lourdes M. (2000), 'América Latina: integración en los umbrales del siglo XXI', *Cuadernos de Nuestra América,* vol. XIII. no. 25 (Jan.–June), pp. 8–31.

Reinhardt, Nola (2000), 'Back to Basics in Malaysia and Thailand: The Role of Resource-Based Exports in their Export-Led Growth', *World Development,* vol. 28, no. 1, pp. 57–77.

Ritter, Archibald (1998), 'Cuba's Economic Reform Process, 1998: Paralysis and Stagnation?', Department of Economics and School of International Affairs, Carleton University, Ottawa, Canada (mimeo).

Rodríguez, Carlos Rafael (1983), *Letra con filo* (Havana: Editorial de Ciencias Sociales).

Rodríguez García, José Luis (1990), *Estrategia del desarrollo económico en Cuba* (Havana: Editorial de Ciencias Sociales).

Rodríguez García, José Luis (1994), interview in *Granma* (Havana, 22 Nov.).

Rodríguez García, José Luis (1997), 'La revitalización de la economía nacional: perspectivas de la economía cubana para 1996–1997', *The Economist Conferences,* Fourth Round Table with the Cuban government (Havana, March).

Rodríguez García, José Luis (1998), 'Informe sobre los resultados económicos de 1998 y el Plan Económico y Social para 1999', *Granma,* Havana, 23 Dec.).

Rodríguez García, José Luis (1999), interview in *Y sin embargo…Ciencia* (Havana: Editorial Abril).

Rodríguez García, José Luis (2000), interview in *El Economista de Cuba* (Jan.–Feb.).

Rodríguez García, José Luis (2000a), *Intervención en la reunión anual del Ministerio de Economía y Planificación* (Havana: Ministerio de Economía y Planificación, 16 March).

Rodríguez García, José Luis (2000b), 'Informe sobre los resultados económicos del 2000 y el Plan Económico y Social para el año 2001 en el VI período ordinario de la Asamblea Nacional del Poder Popular', *Granma*, 23 Dec.

Rodríguez García, José Luis and Carriazo, George (1987), *Erradicación de la pobreza en Cuba* (Havana: Editorial de Ciencias Sociales).

Rodríguez García, José Luis et al. (1985), *Cuba: revolución y economía 1959–1960* (Havana: Editorial de Ciencias Sociales).

Romero, Antonio (1996), *Las transformaciones económicas en Cuba* (Havana: Centro de Investigaciones de la Economía Internacional).

Romero, Antonio (2000), 'Economía cubana: transformaciones y reinserción internacional a fines del siglo XX', paper presented to Latin America Studies Association XXII International Congress, Miami, 16–18 March.

Ronnas, Per and Sjoberg, Orjan (1990), *Doi Moi – Economic Reforms and Development Policies in Vietnam* (Stockholm: SIDA).

Salas, Carola and García, Mercedes (1997), *Las finanzas externas de Cuba. Situación actual y perspectivas* (Havana: Centro de Investigaciones de Economía Internacional, Universidad de La Habana).

Seers, Dudley, Bianchi, Andreas, Jolly, Richard and Nolff, Max (1964), *Cuba. The Economic and Social Revolution* (Durham, NC: The University of North Carolina Press).

Sik, O. (1968), 'Problemas de la dirección planificada en Checoslovaquia', in *Ensayos Económicos*, Colección Estudios (Havana: Instituto del Libro).

Smith, Adrian and Pickles, John (1998), 'Introduction: Theorising Transition and Political Economy of Transformation', in John Pickles and Adrian Smith (eds.) (1998), *Theorising Transition. The Political Economy of Post-Communist Transformations* (London: Routledge), pp. 1–25.

State Statistical Bureau (SSB), *China Statistical Yearbook 1998* (Beijing: China Statistical Publishing House).

Sulroca Domínguez, Federico (1999), *Los agropaisajes cañeros y sus incidencias en los costos de producción* (Havana: Documentos ATAC– MINAZ).

Tablada Pérez, Carlos (1987), *El pensamiento económico de Ernesto Che Guevara* (Havana: Editorial de Ciencias Sociales).

Tesis y Resolución (1976), Departamento de Orientación Revolucionaria del Comité Central del Partido Comunista de Cuba, Havana.

Togores, Viviana (1996), 'Problemas del empleo en Cuba en los 90. Alternativas de solución', in L. Caramés Viéitez (ed.), *I Foro de Economía: Galicia-América Latina* (Universidad de Santiago de Compostela, Spain).

Torras, Rogelio and Ilizástegui, Ilieva (1988), 'Potencialidades de un balance intersectorial intercomplejo en las proyecciones a largo plazo en Cuba', *Economía Planificada*, year 3, no. 3 (July–Sept.).

Torres Martínez, Héctor and Sieczka, Eduardo (1993), *La opción energética azucarera: un ejemplo de política con costo social negativo para América Latina y el Caribe* (Havana: Instituto Nacional de Investigaciones Económicas, Ministerio de Economía y Planificación).

Unanue, Alberto and Martínez Carrera, Ramón (1989), 'El desbalance financiero en el desarrollo de la economía cubana', *Economía Planificada*, year 4, no. 3 (July–Sept.)

UNCTAD (1987), *Reactivación del desarrollo, el crecimiento y el comercio internacional, evaluación y políticas posibles*, Documento TD/328/add.2 (Geneva).

UNCTAD(1997), *World Investment Report* (Geneva).

UNDP (2000), *Human Development Report 2000* (New York: United Nations Development Program).

UNESCO (1998), *World Education Report 1998* (Paris: UNESCO).

UNICEF (1997), *Children and Women in Vietnam: The UNICEF Perspective* (Vietnam: UNICEF).

United Nations (1993), *The Sex and Age Distribution of the World Populations* (New York: Department of Economic and Social Development, United Nations).

US Census Bureau (1997), *Current Population Survey* (Washington, DC, March).

Vascós González, Fidel E. (1997), 'Nuevos requerimientos de la planificación socialista', *Bimestre Cubano*, no. 1.

Vera, Ignacio and Molina, Elda (1999), *Incide el NAFTA en los niveles actuales de inversión extranjera en Cuba* (Havana: Centro de Investigaciones de la Economía Internacional).

Vilariño Ruiz, Andrés and Domenech Nieves, Silvia (1986), 'El sistema de dirección y planificación de la economía en Cuba', *Historia, Actualidad y Perspectivas* (Havana: Editorial Pueblo y Educación).

Villareal, René (1990), 'The Latin American Strategy of Import Substitution: Failure or Paradigm for the Region', in Gary Gereffi and Donald L. Wyman (eds.), *Manufacturing Miracles. Paths of Industrialization in Latin America and East Asia* (Princeton: Princeton University Press).

Weber, Cynthia (1995), *Simulating Sovereignty. Intervention, the State and Symbolic Exchange* (Cambridge: Cambridge University Press).

World Bank (1999), *Vietnam Moving Forward: Achievements and Challenges in the Transport Sector,* (April), Report 18748–VN.

World Bank (2000), *Higher Education in Developing Countries. Peril and Promise* (Washington, DC: The World Bank).

Yanes, Henán (2000), 'El Gran Caribe a finales de los años 90: apuntes sobre su definición e identidad desde una perspectiva sociopolitical', *Cuadernos de Nuestra America,* vol. XIII, no. 25 (Jan.–June), pp. 134–51.

Young, Alwyn (1994), 'Lessons from the East Asian NICs: A Contrarian View', *European Economic Review Papers and Proceedings* (May).

Young, Alwyn (2000), 'Gold into Base Metals: Productivity Growthg in the PRC during the Reform Period', National Bureau of Economic Research Working Paper 7856, Aug., p. 7.

Zecchini, Salvatore (ed.) (1997), *Lessons from the Economic Transition: Central and Eastern Europe in the 1990s*, OECD (London: Kluwer Academic Publishers).

Zimbalist, Andrew and Brundenius, Claes (1989), *The Cuban Economy — Measurement and Analysis of Socialist Performance* (Baltimore and London: Johns Hopkins University Press).

Printed in the United States
5846

9 781900 039482